Growing Vegetables
With a Smile

Using printed matter as mulch
promotes earthworm literacy!

Growing Vegetables With a Smile

Nikolay Kurdyumov

Translated by Mark Havill, Ph.D.
Edited by Leonid Sharashkin, Ph.D.

DEEP SNOW PRESS
Ithaca · New York

Gardening with a Smile Series
Book 1

Growing Vegetables with a Smile
by Nikolay Kurdyumov

Translated from the Russian by Mark Havill
Edited by Leonid Sharashkin

Artist: Andrey Andreev
Cover photograph: Maya Kruchenkova

ISBN: 978-0-9842873-3-8
Library of Congress Control Number: 2011936280

Printed on 100% post-consumer recycled paper.

Published by Deep Snow Press
www.DeepSnowPress.com

Contents

Chapter 3
How to Improve Fertility Or
A Short Course in Soil Cultivation   65

Chapter 4
Beds With Varying Degrees of "Intelligence" Or
Growing Vegetables in a Very Small Space 135

Chapter 9
Fertilizing and Watering Intelligent Beds Or
How to Feed and Water Plants
Without Causing Harm   251

Chapter 10
The Benefits of Plastic Or
A Tale About How to Deceive Winter   283

Chapter 11
In Care of Our Young Or
A Tale About Seeds and Seedlings   297

The author thanks everyone who knows how to read for graciously affording me the opportunity to publish this book.

In Lieu of an Introduction

There are very few good books. I hope that with the appearance of this one, there will be even fewer.

Andrey Knyshev

What this book is about

Bring your backyard garden to the front of your mind!

As with my other books, this one is about how to create a productive and beautiful garden—not a place filled with struggle and hard work, but rather a pleasant haven to while away your time in such pursuits as creatively designing garden beds, training plants, mowing, and devising tricks to avoid work altogether. It is a place for intelligently tending plants with hopeful anticipation, pausing to admire the lush greenery of vegetables and ripening fruit, marveling at a flower unfolding its petals, escaping from the problems of everyday life, sharing barbeques with friends and family, and even such luxury as lounging around and napping in broad daylight with complete peace of mind. In other words, this book is about true *success** in the garden.

After ten years of mingling closely with gardeners at their dachas,** I have observed that our traditional system

1

of gardening is clearly going downhill. In these post-Soviet times, people are accustomed to viewing the land as a source of sustenance, but for most our dacha gardens are not places of rest but for hard work—a second "full time job." Here is the typical scenario: eager gardeners pore through books and diligently hunch over their work in the garden, but their harvests are nonetheless pitiful. Literally, "they read the book... and then get took." How can we survive in this way?! First of all, gardening should give us joy and abundance. Secondly, in these times it is as important to know how to relax and enjoy life as it is to work.

If you look around, you will notice that nature yields a plentiful harvest thanks to no effort of our own. Obviously, we simply do not understand how to work with nature in order to raise fruits and vegetables, create beauty, and maintain our health with minimal effort. It is time for us to consider: why, in fact, do we work our garden plot? What is our goal? What's the result? And mainly, who is paying, and who is profiting?

It often happens that the very asking of these questions puts everything into perspective. Suddenly, you realize that you couldn't care less about your garden and all that hard work! One person may decide to just sell off their plot and be done with it, while another may wonder if there is some other way—this is when interest begins to return. Problems with your family seem to resolve themselves, and suddenly time spent with your spouse at the dacha actually becomes pleasurable.

* *Success* is a conscious and reproducible outcome which improves the life of a person, his partner, colleagues, and the people and natural environment around him. The ability to achieve success is, in fact, what constitutes intelligence.

** *Dacha*—a summer cottage with a garden common in Russia. [trans]

About five years ago I made an earthshaking discovery: success in the garden does not simply entail growing hundreds of kilos of fruit and vegetables. Success means *creating a living garden which brings constant enjoyment*: the vegetables you need, the fruits you enjoy, and beauty, too—all without becoming stressed out and exhausted, without struggle or boring routine, with genuine pleasure. *This* is success!

This realization turned my life onto a new course. Since then I have been constantly innovating techniques and arranging my garden plot to reflect my ideal. Each year I change something for the sake of comparison. Progress towards my goal has not been quick, but it has been steady. This makes my life really quite nice. The essence of happiness is in this distinction: is my life today better and more successful—even by just a little—than yesterday?

This is the quest which I hope to share in this book—and I literally mean quest. There are not, nor can there be, ready-made, one-size-fits-all gardening instructions. I am simply offering ideas, general principles, and examples from my own and others' experience in intelligent vegetable gardening. I invite us all to do this together.

Although containing a wealth of specific details, this book is above all about how to minimize unproductive labor, thereby gaining more personal freedom in our lives. Truth be told, I am a very lazy person. I tip my hat to hard work, yet I can say with certainty that it is not the answer—we already work much harder than we ought to. The reality is that our gardening efforts are not efficient. A truly lazy person—that is, Lazy with a capital "L"—will not lift a finger until he has thoroughly considered how he might save himself from unnecessary work!

And now let me introduce myself:

Hello!

I am your humble servant, Nikolay Kurdyumov, but to my wife and friends—just Nick. My body recently celebrated its forty-ninth anniversary, but I still see myself as being more like thirty. In the early '80s, my wife Tanya and I attended Timiriazev Agricultural Academy. We took full advantage of the opportunities afforded to us as students, frequently traveling to the mountains, learning photography, and immersing ourselves deeply into theater and music, a guitar ever at our side. Before long three charming children appeared, and we became enamored with pedagogy and alternative health care. In the end, we became teachers and moved to the Cossack village of Azovskaya in the Kuban Region of Southern Russia where we have lived ever since. Our children successfully finished high school, then the university, and are now successful professionals.

In my attempt to survive the hopeless period of mass unemployment during perestroika at the end of the Soviet era, I remembered that I had once been taught to prune fruit trees. As it turned out, this skill was in high demand. Over the next few years, it became clear to me that, while scientists, gardening book authors, and agribusiness salesmen offer an amazingly beautiful ideal, the reality of our orchards and gardens is much different. I realized that our wild frenzy of hard work and obsolete cultivation methods are by no means inevitable, but are rather the direct outcome of our unquestioning faith in agricultural tradition.

Thus arose my new career as a professional gardener. Over time I grew into a fairly proficient horticulturist specializing in southern Russia, but I dreamed of becoming a master gardener in the fullest sense of the word—in the olden days of Russia there were people who could grow everything from radishes to oranges. It was at this time that I discovered that my true calling was to research and write about useful gardening practices. This is certainly no less important work.

Now my goal is to popularize intelligent gardening. I feel that it is very important that this book be clear and straightforward, so that you will understand everything exactly as I understand it myself. Or even better! Therefore:

How to read this book

A conclusion is what you arrive at when you are too tired to think anymore.

1. Read carefully. The main reason that a text may seem incomprehensible, uninteresting, or unimportant is *misunderstood words*—those occasional words which you only partially understand or incorrectly interpret. You may not even notice it, but *after skipping a word, a memory gap appears.* Then, after maybe another half a page, you suddenly realize that you no longer feel like reading, you become irritated, or you just want to go take a nap—somehow the author is "too clever" and, anyway, you never "finisht Hi Skool." These are the exact symptoms of a misunderstood word. What should you do? Go back through the text to where everything was still easy to understand and clear. Find the unintelligible word and figure out its meaning. Then things will fall into place.

I will attempt to clarify in footnotes all suspect words which you may not know, or those to which I have attached my own specific meaning. Be sure to read these footnotes, so that we will be speaking the same language. If you do not find a specific term in the footnotes, do not hesitate to dive into a dictionary!

2. Be observant. Whenever you notice something in someone's garden which you read about in this book, consider how it was done, and what worked out well. You will not be able to try out everything in your own garden, but you can learn a lot from other people's experiences—this is far more valuable than book learning.

3. Experiment. If you want to find out more about something which intrigues you in this book, test it out yourself on a small plot, even on just 10 square feet (1 m^2). Your own experience is the most valuable of all!

4. Don't hurry. Give yourself time to learn. And don't be discouraged if things do not work out right away. Even Mittleider's gardening practices which he meticulously recorded—step by step, minute by minute—require several years to master; fortunately, the time spent learning is highly enjoyable!

5. Please don't take everything I say literally, and don't base your opinion on a single chapter. Also, don't accept anything on faith—I only offer ideas for your consideration. Each of us has his own unique gardening conditions. What works well in Moscow (Zone 4) may not be suitable for Krasnodar in the south (Zone 6). If something works out for one person, it may not work out for you if you just blindly imitate it. However, you are always welcome to figure out how to do it your own way!

Chapter 1

A Brief Course in Garden Successology

or

What Constitutes Freedom?

Ultimately, a person is left face-to-face with himself in the struggle for survival against himself.

Andrey Knyshev

What is success? Success is when you yourself—without some random stroke of blind luck—can gain or produce exactly what you desire. We enjoy life insofar as we feel ourselves to be the primary *cause* of our success.

We live in a world in which everything alive helps everything else to live. By helping your environment, you help yourself as well. Others, in helping you, improve their own lives—may God grant that you have more such people around you! But no one can help you if you do not want to help yourself. Success is an individual affair. It is always personal, based on your own decisions and actions. Nothing can happen in your life without your personal participation. You are the source of your own success. Also, you can't count on anyone but yourself to help your friends and family, your country, humanity, Nature, or even the entire Universe! Therefore, if in some way you are able to make life better by helping yourself and others, this, indeed, is personal success.

True success always pertains to an actual person. A "team" cannot achieve success. The success of a group is the sum of the substantive successes of each person. *Together means everyone*; otherwise, there is no "together."

Life is prosperous—such is its nature. This is precisely what parasites depend on. You may twist, undermine, or suppress the will to live, but it cannot be exterminated. Therefore, success of every kind, like a malicious virus, keeps popping up everywhere. Our culture advances due to the efforts of individuals who are the authors of success. People may have done something in a certain way for thousands of years, convinced that to do it otherwise would be impossible, and then suddenly some crackpot questions things, performs some experiments, racks his brain, and voila!—he figures out how to do it significantly better. There are millions of examples of this. I enjoy collecting these success stories. A part of my collection can be viewed at www.kurdyumov.ru. When looked at with a thoughtful and easy-going attitude, life becomes simple and successful. If we can only get out of the way!

For example, many people have learned how to maintain perfect health without the help of medicine, sometimes even contrary to its recommendations. Authors Boris and Lena Nikitin taught themselves how to give birth to and raise healthy, precocious children. Imagine how many sacred medical canons they must have had to reject over the years! It is the same in education. Nina Berger, with her Doctorate in Music, decided to work with "tone deaf" children. Within a year they were confidently playing music and sight reading in any key. An American educator Hellene Hiner invented a method for learning music naturally, and her students effortlessly read music and perform from the age of four. The educator Anatoly Stukov discovered that musical instruction sometimes actually hinders technical skill, and his students brilliantly perform advanced pieces without having to go through the trouble of lengthy rehearsals. Their methods are very different from those of ordinary music teachers. Similarly, the educator and writer Vadim Levin created a system for introducing art to elementary school children. Within three years the children had developed their artistic taste to a high level, could interpret art creatively, and were producing fine art themselves. Many creative educators have taught other subjects just as successfully.

Such outstanding success has also been achieved in agriculture. Igor Mikhailov of St. Petersburg set up a mini-farm where caged rabbits are raised in perfect health. They develop twice as quickly, and their fur has the luster of sable—yet he only tends the cages once a week. The beekeeper Valery Shcherbak of Krasnodar annually harvests from each hive up to 485 pounds (220 kg) of honey, several pounds of pollen, and two new nucleus colonies.

As far back as the 19th century, the agronomist Ivan Ovsinsky developed a system of no-tillage farming which promoted buildup of organic matter in the soil and yielded maximum harvests without excessive expense. Similar agricultural practices were later successfully employed by Edward Faulkner, Terenty Semenovich Maltsev, and Fedor Trofimovich Morgun, and are now popular throughout the world. The famous Japanese farmer Masanobu Fukuoka abandoned technology and chemicals altogether, creating a system of natural farming in which all you do is sow and harvest.

A hundred years ago, the German gardener Nicolas Gaucher figured out how to train trees into almost any form, controlling the development of fruiting organs and quality of fruit. Musos Z. Guliev raises potatoes from individual eyes and obtains seven to eight times the normal harvest. Ivan Zamiatkin from Siberia harvests up to four pounds of potatoes per square foot (20 kg/m^2) without any fertilizers or chemicals at all. And the multi-purpose hoe designed by Vladimir Fokin (see Chapter 3) is simpler than a regular hoe and much quicker and easier to work with. It performs twenty gardening tasks, replacing nearly all other gardening tools!

Examples of this kind of success can be found everywhere. I have no doubt that many ingenious practices have been invented ten times over since ancient times. Yet we keep stumbling blindly along towards false goals. Why don't we apply successful methods to our lives? Why don't we think things through more carefully? Why are common everyday routines more acceptable than success? The reason is all in our minds.

Success means independence and courage. Usually we prefer to depend on others, so that we can pass off our failures onto our spouse or colleagues, or blame them on the "injustices of the world." Success always requires change, but we do not like to change. When we hear the phrase "change for the better," we generally only hear the first word and not what follows. Success is always a clear choice, but we are accustomed to someone else making that choice for us. We must take responsibility to achieve success, but we do not like to bear responsibility alone. Finally, success means being different from everyone else. Initially, a successful person is often misunderstood and will be met with incomprehension, rejection, worry, disapproval, and antipathy—it's terrible! It is so much easier to simply share everyday joys and sorrows with the rest of us. Only a strong, self-sufficient person can be true to his own success. But how many such people are there among us?

Imagine somebody finally manages to successfully improve something. Eureka! However, he often falls into a trap: he tries to make his success the property of the entire world, striving for universal recognition, but in the end he suffers complete failure. The truth of the matter is that genuine success is never advantageous to the powers-that-be because it liberates people and makes them independent. If people become successful and free, why would they pay for the services of small-minded leaders and shortsighted politicians?

It is better to focus on our own personal success—our only true source of happiness. The science of success is probably the most practical knowledge of life. Businessmen can try and make their profit, marketing to us mountains of useless junk, but whether their gain becomes *your* pain depends on no one but *you*!

Getting to know success, or general principles for becoming successful

Anyone can do good to others. But to do something good for oneself—this truly requires courage!

This section is for those who love to dig down to the very root of things.

Overall, success consists of three main components:

a) *the intention to achieve something*;

b) *a precise vision of the desired result**—that is, a clear understanding of exactly what you want to achieve; and

c) a certain *nonattachment to accepted norms* and opinions, sometimes even to accepted values.

Intention—this is when you have made the decision to do something, and actually do it.

Do not confuse it with desire. Desire is an emotion, not supported by any kind of decision. Often there is desire, but no intention at all. It is as if we want to have something, but without our direct participation; we want others to get it for us. We fill ourselves with fairy tales! For instance, I have always had the desire to be thinner, but to run three miles each morning!? Obviously, there is no intention.

My vegetable harvests are far from record-breaking. This means that I do not have the intention to achieve record harvests. But I do have a definite intention to reduce the size of my vegetable garden and the amount of work I put into it while bringing in an equal harvest—and this has indeed happened.

Strong people stubbornly work towards their goals, refusing to recognize obstacles in their path. Weaker people simply "desire"—that is, they dream. In youth, we are full of both desires and intentions, but as adults we often lose this capacity. So we create masses of problems, hardships, and hazards in order to force ourselves to want to achieve something—to be able to say: "I did it!"

How do you allow yourself to desire and achieve without getting all stressed out? Very simply, it's all in the advertising. Take time to be curious, to look at and want something new and different. For example, would you like to grow the pumpkin variety Big Moon? No? Obviously, you have never seen it—bright orange, up to 3 feet (1 m) in diameter, and

---

* *Result*—here: that which you want to obtain, the goal of intelligent action and its immediate outcome; also, that which is suitable for marketing, what people will pay for. A result either exists or does not exist. A "bad result" is really just the lack of a result.

straw!) and be healthy and undamaged (Take measures!); they should ripen around the middle of July (Build a plastic cold frame!), with bright color (Remove that sickly peach tree so it doesn't block the sun!); they should weigh at least 500 pounds (Research special gardening techniques for this particular variety!); and they should require very little watering (Dig a hole and fill it with 20 cubic feet, or 0.5 m³, of nutrient-rich compost covered by a thick mulch of straw!); and so on. This is what is called know-how.*

The law: the more detailed a result is visualized, the better chance you have of achieving it. Conversely, if a result is not visualized in detail, you won't be able to develop the know-how to achieve it. Even simpler: *it is impossible to achieve something when you do not even know what it is that you want to achieve*! Actually, it is possible, but you will end up with junk. In fact, this is exactly what we usually do, blindly following what is generally accepted or recommended by experts!

---

* *Know-how*—literally: I know how to repeat a good result, and I can even improve on it.

It would seem that those universally revered saints, Faith and Hope, are by no means natives of our city of Happiness. They have one and the same prescription for everyone—promises. They are nowhere near success! Catching sight of Knowledge and Intention, Faith and Hope hide their eyes and flee to the other side of the street, because they know that their work is to delude and comfort us. They do not serve us, but rather the person who thought up what we should believe in, what we should hope for!

Independence, or belief in yourself, is the third aspect of success.

Success is not what others praise you for. Rather, it is what actually improves your life. "Always be your own advisor, hold fast to your own intentions, and make your own decisions" (L. Ron Hubbard).

The one thing which can rob you of your success is the opinion of others. If these people are in the majority, their opinions are called the "moral code." It is not easy to stand up against them. Therefore, sadly, most of our convictions turn out to be other people's opinions. From earliest childhood they teach us to be obedient rather than to analyze our own experiences, to blindly believe rather than to base our convictions on our own results. We are accustomed to giving up our success to someone else, often to someone we do not even know. This can be taken to the absurd: month after month, year after year we do something we are absolutely convinced of, yet we attain the exact opposite results. Somehow we manage not to notice this and believe that we are not to blame! We do not realize that family relations, their health and talents, our own character, behavior, and emotions, the condition of our bodies, our surroundings, customers, finances, mood—all these are actually the result the dirt and want only to kick back at their dachas—plants are completely alien beings to them. We will call them romantics. The second type are eager to water and hoe day and night—their family needs fruits and vegetables! They often tend to suffer from overwork, which they effectively invoke with proud contempt while grumbling at friends and family prone to romanticism. We will call them realists, or more exactly—workaholics. Workaholism in our culture is an extremely infectious disease, easily transmitted by contact, association, and over meals. Russian popular scientific literature about gardening, written by PhD's at various research institutes, is especially infectious. For this reason, romantics are now in the minority. They are mainly husbands and children; women are much more susceptible to workaholism in the garden. Incidentally, workaholism drastically diminishes feminine attraction and allure every bit as much as ostentatious, manicured idleness. This is definitely worth taking into account by both genders when spending time in their garden.

Here is a very typical Russian scene: the wife is a workaholic, the husband a militant romantic. He feels like having a beer, but she tosses him a shovel! It seems that there is no compromise. The garden is transformed into a battleground: instead of cucumbers, seeds of dissent sprout up in the garden beds. She has Female Gardener Syndrome (FGS), and he—Husband of Female Gardener Syndrome (HFGS). This often goes on for years and in time gives rise to serious family discord. As an experienced garden psychotherapist, I can state with certainty that the main reason for these maladies is a lack of proper understanding of the purpose of the garden itself. The romantic compulsively spurns the garden while the workaholic is compulsively attached to it. To help alleviate this common scene, let me offer you my understanding of how you might make better sense of your garden.

Above all, the garden is our cohabitant. We live in a relationship of symbiosis with our plants—that is, in natural cohabitation. We and our garden are symbionts, close friends, and partners. But a partnership should increase the freedom and well-being of both partners, and it certainly must be reciprocal and equitable.

First of all, partners should be carefully and thoughtfully chosen. Do you really need these potatoes? Or would it be easier to get by with store-bought ones? A meadow of wild grasses is an excellent partner, but for some reason it is often ignored. A forest makes an ideal partner, but few gardeners ever grow one. And what about all the various strains and species of vegetables? Do you plant any and all kinds? Or only those which you know how to grow well? And how much? An optimal amount? Or too much, so that you have to give many away? Or even dump the surplus onto the compost pile? And so on and on (there will be an entire chapter about this).

Secondly, partnership entails good communication and mutual understanding. After researching communication with plants for many years, the Moldovan Academician Sergey Maslobrod demonstrated that plants and microbes react to our mental commands. Whether we like it or not, every living being responds to our thoughts! So what are we telling them, my dear workaholics?

In order to understand plants, it is necessary to communicate with them. Do you have enough time and energy for this with so much weeding, watering, and spraying to do? Imagine cultivating relationships with friends according to advice given in a book: you read something, say it to them, but do not bother listening to their answer—you are too busy reading further in the manual about what to say world and human existence. The principles of intelligent agriculture are expressed by permaculturists with amazing simplicity and clarity. They make so much sense that it behooves us to consider them in earnest.

First of all, let's elucidate the essence of a living ecosystem. We have been indoctrinated into believing that the struggle for survival is constantly taking place in natural communities. But this is just the point of view of scientists fixated on struggle. As it turns out, struggle does not exist in nature at all! Actually, the basis of any ecosystem is cohabitation, mutual feeding, and mutual adaptation of its members—that is, *cooperation.* "In the language of botany, which even Darwin readily utilized, the word 'struggle' does not mean annihilation of other similar creatures, but only self-defense, the victory of life over the adverse forces of nature" (Kliment Timiriazev, 1891).

In 1978, the Australian Bill Mollison realized that we human beings can cohabitate with plants and animals in the same way it happens in the natural world. "Permaculture is first and foremost a design system. The aim is to use the *power of the human brain*, applied to design, to replace human brawn or fossil fuel energy" (Patrick Whitefield). I would add saving time, cash, and trouble. To utilize our own intelligence to bring ease into our lives is definitely worth learning. How accustomed we have become in the past hundred years to living according to other people's concepts!

The principles of permaculture are extremely thought-provoking. Judge for yourself:

1. Work is what you have to do because you have not arranged things so that it will be done by itself. Or even partially by itself. For example, mulch* from plant residues preserves moisture, feeds soil creatures, supplies available nutrients to roots, and structures the soil. Or drip irrigation: water percolates on its own directly onto the feeding roots and, if required, provides supplemental fertilization, too. Or covering the soil with cardboard and old rags—weeds will not grow. Or setting up a chicken coop under mulberry trees and acacias—for half the summer feed will rain down on the heads of the chickens. Or installing solar pumps and hot water heaters, water wheels and turbines, and other equipment which work without consuming fossil fuels. Or incorporating basic principles to plan garden improvements and plantings. Or intelligently arranging beds and gardening zones for a twofold decrease in labor. The world-famous Austrian Sepp Holzer transformed a hundred acres (40 ha) of mountainous terrain into a productive forest farm. Now his only work is to create new garden terrain. Harvests of vegetables, fruit, and grain, as well as hundreds of pounds of fish and mushrooms, are produced on their own without his direct participation at all.

2. Waste products are what you have not yet figured out how to utilize to your own benefit. Weeds, sawdust, excrement, kitchen wastes, paper, wood chips—in fact, any organic matter which decomposes—all can become compost or, better still, nutritious feed for worms and microbes right in the garden bed itself. Old rags, mats, cardboard, plywood, particle board, and other sheet material can be used as mulch for bushes and young trees, for pathways, and for spaces between rows. Containers and plastic bottles can be used for watering, as traps for insects, cloches, and for

---

* *Mulch*—everything which covers the surface of the soil, as in nature. To most Russians both the word and the gardening practice itself are virtually unknown.

germinating seedlings. Even glass and scrap metal come in handy as concrete filler. In fact, only synthetic materials have to be burned—and we could probably even think up some use for them!

3. Any requirement can be satisfied by many different sources. For example, watering: you can get water from precipitation or collect it in containers, or you can conserve it under mulch or by dense planting; additionally, soil well-textured by roots and worms absorbs and accumulates moisture from the air—four times more than plowed soil without such a structure. Feeding plants: manure, humus, compost, or plant residues. Chicken feed: berries and seed-bearing trees, sorghum and corn, insects and slugs in the orchard (fenced off from the vegetables), or forage grasses. Heat sources: decomposing organic matter, the sun, or electricity. Sources of electrical energy: running water, sun, or wind. And so on—the list is endless.

4. Any plant, animal, or garden implement can be put to multiple uses. Of course, as much as possible. Plants yield food, compost, medicine, and cooking herbs, attract bees to make honey, deter pests, and fix nitrogen (legumes). They can even improve soil structure with their roots. For example, weeds which are cut down before they go to flower improve soil as powerful green manures* at no expense. Trees can give fruit, attract bees for honey, provide firewood, and serve as plant supports or as ornamentals. Animals give

---

* *Green manures*—plant growth which structures and feeds the soil. Virtually any plants which are grown for this reason. Their main purpose is to provide soils with fresh organic matter. As in nature, green manures are most effective on the surface as a mulch.

food and manure, and birds can clear the garden of pests. An elevated swimming pool can serve for bathing, irrigation, water storage, and as a feature in your landscape design. There are also general-purpose tools. For example, the Fokin hoe performs a multitude of functions, transforming into almost any garden implement. This list is also endless.

5. Intelligent arrangement, zoning, and division of the garden plot can greatly relieve work. "Vegetables best serve you when they are visible right outside the kitchen window." Indeed, the farther plants are from us, the less our interest in them. The garden should be situated alongside the house and near a water source while those plants which do not require frequent attention—trees and shrubs—are planted in the back. The same applies to a garden bed: the plants which need daily contact are placed up front.

I discovered zoning through practice. This is the foundation of intelligent gardening. Each section of cultivated ground should be sharply delineated and surrounded by a border. The remaining ground can then be allowed to overgrow with wild grasses, forming a natural turf, or be mulched over with various materials. The cultivated area suddenly becomes very small, but the harvest keeps increasing! Labor and watering are significantly reduced, and the plot is pleasing to the eye. I grow grass in the paths between beds, and I am now contemplating how I might shrink the cultivated area even more. This topic will be covered in its own chapter later on.

So let's get to work! Not physical work, God forbid, but mental. The intelligent garden needs your brains more than your muscles!

This page is intentionally left blank.
See? It's all about *intention*!

Chapter 2

A Tale About How Love of Hard Work Destroyed Soil Fertility

There are few grains of truth in the bottomless bins of the Motherland!

Two of my books are devoted entirely to the topic of restoring fertility: *Classics in Soil Fertility* and *Growing with your Garden*. The first reviews the ideas of the most famous proponents of no-till farming: Ivan Ovsinsky, Edward Faulkner, Terenty Maltsev, Masanobu Fukuoka, and Harry Allen, as well as the fundamentals of classical Russian agriculture as presented in articles by Williams, Kostychev, Timiriazev, and Dokuchaev. The second book relates the real-life experiences of farmers and gardeners, demonstrating how to achieve abundant harvests at one third the cost while restoring soil fertility in the process. This chapter is primarily about the unparalleled work of Ivan Evgenievich Ovsinsky.

Nothing is new under the sun: what we consider "new" is often either what has been thoroughly, even conscientiously, forgotten from the past, or knowledge—both Russian and foreign—which has been deliberately kept hidden from us. How did it happen that our modern-day system of agriculture, with all its mechanization and chemicals, invariably symbolizing the progress and triumph of science,

33

has in a mere hundred years surreptitiously and completely destroyed most of the fertile soils of the world, including the famous Black Earth soils of Russia? Their restoration is not even an issue of discussion! Meanwhile, nature, having eluded "improvement" by science, steadfastly continues to *create fertility*. Natural soils never become exhausted, although they produce much more than we do in our very best fields, without any supplemental labor or introduction of substances or energy from the outside.

Isn't it time we seriously considered this? If we did everything right, then the fertility of our soils would consistently increase in our gardens and farms, and our plants would delight us with their vigor and yields without any added fertilizer or pesticides.

Following the advice of erudite books on horticulture, virtually every farmer and gardener plows and digs the earth twice a year. We dutifully cultivate our entire plot, never noticing that vegetables occupy only a third—or at most half—of the garden. The remainder is painstakingly worked, and then repeatedly hoed in a constant battle against weeds, which leads to overheating, compaction, and drying of the soil, so that you have to water even more and muck through the mud in rainy weather. Yet plants, despite all our senseless and even harmful tactics, continue to be weakened and diseased. Now, folks, let's be honest. This is a pretty ridiculous way to manifest our love for work! We should be asking: what are we doing wrong—so completely wrong—that not only hard work but our stubborn *addiction* to hard work has not been eliminated by horticultural progress in the modern era?!

Actually, the answer to this question was found a hundred years ago. Intelligent agriculture was developed in detail and successfully applied in practice, and not only in Russia.

The Russian agronomist Ivan Evgenievich Ovsinsky developed a no-till system of agriculture which completely solved the problem of drought (it turns out that even this problem has been artificially created!) while increasing harvests many times over. Then in the 1920s, the Academician Vasily Robertovich Williams developed his "agrobiological doctrine" for restoring fertility to soils. He demonstrated that plants cannot properly assimilate nutrients in unstructured* soils (which are continuously plowed or dug), and that soil structure is primarily created by plant roots and worms. As far back as the nineteenth century, Pavel Andreevich Kostychev had already developed theories about the accumulation of humus in soils, showing that humus is produced from plant residues by microorganisms in the presence of a stable crumb structure. The list of intelligent farming experts goes on. It is astounding how their recommendations have been completely ignored by agricultural science, and especially by modern farming practices. As a result, even our gardens have fallen into a very pitiable state.

For this reason, I offer you "A Brief Historical Sketch of Intelligent Soil Science and Agriculture"—a freestyle presentation of the principal ideas of the authors mentioned above with commentary.

---

* *Structure*—here: not simply the physical condition, but a natural, optimal, and long-term (permanent) soil formation which provides for the life of plants, animals, and microbes, ensuring self-regeneration of fertility. In other words, the normal condition of natural soils.

A very brief history of agriculture

Enough repeating old mistakes! It's time to make new ones.

Categorical statements—in particular, scientific ones—are prone to extremes and constant fluctuation. We tend to think rather primitively: if something is false, then the opposite must be true. Simply stated, science advances as a battle between two hostile schools of thought. The truth always lies beyond both of them, but its adherents are persistently ignored. This absurdity can be very profitable for some, and even has a basis in philosophy. Take, for example, "the law of negation of negation." Or this which I found in an old textbook on logic: "Given two statements, one is true, the other is not—there is no other possible variant." What a pearl of wisdom that is! One would think that we believe our inability to think is universal law!

Scientific agriculture arose at the beginning of the nineteenth century. Having observed that soil with more humus is more fertile, the German agronomist Albrecht Thaer proposed the humus* theory of fertility. European scientists subsequently agreed that plants are nourished by humus. Then in 1840 another German, Justus von Liebig, published his work *Organic Chemistry and Its Application to Agriculture*, in which he proposed the mineral basis of plant nutrition.

---

* *Humus*—"dregs and scraps"—more exactly, "leftovers from the feast" after microbes and fungi have decomposed the organic matter of plant residues which accumulate in the soil. The final product of microbial decomposition, which contains very little energy or available organic substances.

Spurred on by a research competition announced by the Academy of Sciences in Göttingen, scientists demonstrated that plants could be grown in sand, gravel, or even just plain water with applications of potassium, phosphorus, nitrogen, and magnesium salts.* The humus theory was crushed; the mineral theory triumphed! The experiments of Dr. Louis Grandeau confirmed the connection between soluble salts and yield, and he declared: "the supply of potassium and phosphorus in the soil constitutes the very question of life of agriculture itself." Actually, the supply of these nutrients in soil is immense, but at that time they were considered to be insoluble, so it was the soluble salts which were proclaimed the primary nutrients for roots. The idol of mineral nutrients arose, and chemical fertilizers started to be applied on a vast scale. They were imported from countries as far away as Chile and the United States, produced in new factories which sprang up all over the world. And things only got worse. Liebig discovered that potassium and phosphorus predominate in the subsoil. Believing that roots grow principally in the topsoil, farmers began to plow deeper to invert the soil layers. The farm equipment industry flourished. Fixated on

---

* *Potassium*—an essential nutrient responsible for general regulation of life processes, development of fruit-bearing organs, immunity, and tolerance to adverse conditions in the outer environment.

Phosphorus—an essential nutrient which influences flowering and fruiting.

Nitrogen—an essential nutrient found in all proteins. A surplus of nitrogen causes "obesity"—excessive growth of plant mass, bloatedness, and weakness of tissues with a decrease in resistance to disease and cold. It is such rank, swollen vegetables which are so appealing to the eyes of modern-day farmers.

Magnesium—an essential nutrient found in chlorophyll, the basis for photosynthesis.

separate pieces of the problem, science pushed us onto a false and destructive path which we still tread today.

It soon became clear that mineral fertilizers often produce no effect at all. Dr. Grandeau conducted extensive research and proposed his organic mineral theory. He found that productivity is determined by the *proportion of minerals to humus*. The vital role of microbes came to light: bacteria can accumulate nitrogen, sulphur, and other nutrients and convert them into available forms. Liebig fell out of favor, and humus again occupied the place of honor. But what about the highly-developed farm equipment industry and billion dollar chemical fertilizer business? "Literate" farmers, instead of utilizing organic matter as mulch, tried plowing animal and green manures even deeper, mixing them into the soil. Without air, the manure would not decompose for years. There was no nitrification,* nutrients were unavailable to roots, and yields did not offset expenses. Farmers attempted to remedy this by applying even more chemical fertilizers! This is when crop farming became a very expensive pastime.

In Russia after the 1917 Revolution, research in plant nutrition was carried out by two principal schools of thought. One was led by the soil scientist and agronomist Academician Vasily Williams, and the other by the agro-chemist Academician Dmitry Prianishnikov. They vehemently disagreed. Williams was demonstrating that plants can absorb nutrients only in well-structured soil, interpenetrated by roots of grasses and permeated with air and microbes. He proposed a grass rotation** system of farming, in which structure

---

* *Nitrification*—the conversion of the nitrogen in organic matter into simple nitrates easily absorbed by roots. In the soil this is performed by nitrobacteria.

and fertility of soils are periodically restored by means of perennial grasses. The agrochemists ignored structure and microbes, advocating copious and balanced chemical fertilization of soils. Williams often repeated bitterly: "I am not against fertilizers; I just want to feed the plants, not the soil!"

Grass rotation was recognized by the Soviet government, but it never really caught on, since it demanded a deep knowledge and understanding of the nature of plants. Agronomists had to adapt it to local conditions, developing individual farming techniques according to their specific

** *Grass rotation* system of farming—a complex agronomy which brings together four basic farming practices: wind protection and snow retention utilizing hedgerows; grass rotations (the field is left under perennial grasses for three out of eight years); wise cultivation of the soil; and rational fertilization of plants.

situation, and in times of rigid State control this was nearly impossible. On the plus side, we outstripped the entire world in production of mineral fertilizers! The result: soils were destroyed over vast areas, and for the most part farming became unprofitable. In our gardens we still dig, cultivate, and fertilize—"feeding the soil" and ignoring the plants. Meanwhile, manufacturers of farm equipment, chemicals, and fertilizers continue to amass huge profits. Apparently, science cares very little about making crop cultivation affordable or assuring reliably high yields!

So let's look at the true basis of soil life and plant nutrition.

The "new" system of farming of Ivan Ovsinsky

If we wished to destroy farming by concocting a system which impedes the absorption of nutrients from the soil, we would not have to look very far for it: all we would need to do is quote the advice of adherents of deep plowing, who have settled the question of inactive nutrients in the soil in a most meticulous manner.

Ivan Ovsinsky

My dear gardeners! Looking realistically first at a natural ecosystem and then at our plowed fields, let's make this fact absolutely clear: *we are not the ones producing fertility in our soils.* With all our cultivation, hoeing, irrigation, and fertilization, we in fact deplete fertility.

Soil fertility is produced by living organisms. They have been doing this successfully for millions of years. Actually,

soil is their output. Fertile soil is a "living sponge," a community of thousands of living organisms, constantly rebuilding and adapting their homes so that they can thrive and proliferate. These soil creatures know genetically that plants are the source of their sustenance and prosperity, so it is in their interest to meticulously care for them.

The primary producers of fertile soils are the plants themselves. They interpenetrate the soil with millions of roots, creating billions of pores and channels which form a conductive, breathing structure. These channels are filled with the organic remnants of roots—nourishment for worms, insects, and microbes. On the surface, dead plants cover the soil with a layer of organic matter which also serves as nourishment for microbes, insects, and other living creatures. Under this cover, the soil is always moist and at optimal temperatures, and as morning dawns copious amounts of soil moisture precipitate onto its underside, launching the biochemical processes heralding the new day.

After the roots, earthworms are the principal soil archi-
tects. They penetrate the soil with miles of channels, converting organic matter from plants into a well-balanced
bacterial and humic concentrate—biohumus. Rootlets of
plants actively seek out these clumps of biohumus and glee-
fully "bite" into them, interpenetrating them completely.

But the main warehousers, breadwinners, and biochem-
ists of soils are the microbes and fungi. Some are responsible
for making minerals available—they convert phosphorus
and potassium into soluble forms. Others fix large quantities of nitrogen from the atmosphere into the soil. And still
others live among the roots, providing nutrition and protection. Microbes and roots are intimate partners. Consider the
fact that, in order to attract and feed necessary microbes,
plants release through their roots one third of all the organic matter they produce! Furthermore, microbes generate
huge amounts of biologically active substances—vitamins,
stimulants, enzymes, phytoncides,* and antibiotics. But
their principal output is carbon dioxide gas, containing the
most important nutrient, carbon, which constitutes about
half of plant mass. Most of the carbon absorbed by the roots
is in the form of carbon dioxide in solution.

Due to a stable structure undisturbed for centuries and
a cover of mulch from organic residues, natural soil provides for itself everything it requires. It actively "breathes,"
exchanging gasses with the atmosphere (Photograph 32).
It absorbs two times more moisture from the air than it receives from precipitation! Mulch maintains soil moisture
and temperature at a consistent level. Under these conditions bacteria thrive and "breathe." Carbon dioxide gas

---

* *Phytoncide*—various bacteria-killing substances synthesized by
plants. [trans]

penetrates the lower strata of the soil, where it is converted into carbonic acid which dissolves minerals—potassium, phosphorus, sulphur, calcium, and magnesium. Nutrient solutions are drawn upwards through the capillaries of a structured soil, as well as along plant roots. Aggressively decomposed by microbes and fungi, organic mulch lavishly feeds surface roots.

Deep plowing (or digging) destroys this elaborate and precisely organized soil structure. Plows demolish the channels and ruin the top layer of mulch. "Civilized agronomists" remove straw and plant residues from the field, causing the living soil ecosystem to wither and die due to lack of nutrients and energy. Roots lose their microbial partners which provide them with nourishment. Carbon dioxide gas is not produced, minerals are not dissolved, and carbon is catastrophically lacking.

Plowed soil loses its ability to breathe and absorb water from the atmosphere. After rains it compacts—all the air is squeezed out of it. Anaerobic bacteria* proliferate, robbing oxygen from molecules, and nutrients are converted into unavailable forms. Even with cultivation and fertilization, soil dries up quickly and plants starve. An unstructured soil conducts very little water, and even lavish watering is mostly lost into the atmosphere. Heavy rains run off in torrents, carrying with them the fertile topsoil. Plants, deprived of their natural environment and microbial partners, slip into emergency survival mode—this is exactly what you see on heavily cropped fields. Plants are weakened, exhausted by all the "attention" given to them. And the farmer is, too!

* *Anaerobic* organisms are those which live in an airless environment. *Aerobic* bacteria breathe oxygen in the air.

We must understand that fertility of soils is not a parameter, not just potential, and not a stockpile of nutrients. *Fertility is a living, dynamic process. Essentially, it is feeding and ingesting—a rich and sumptuous banquet!—the purpose of which is to return carbon to plants. Fertility is the carbon cycle itself. Vegetative organic matter fuels it, and microbes and fungi are its engines.* This is the essence of fertility. Applying manure, digging the garden plot three times in the spring, daily cultivation, hourly watering and fertilizing, applying the latest stimulators, observing the lunar calendar, horoscopes and dream books, warming the soil in your hands, against your breast, or even in your mouth—these efforts kill fertility. Only Nature Herself can produce fertility.

Ovsinsky published his work in 1899. His small booklet, which had been consigned to oblivion, was recently discovered and published in the magazine *Intelligent Farming* by the Academician Yuri Ivanovich Slashchinin, founder of the association "Folk Wisdom." I later edited it and included it in my book *Classics in Soil Fertility*. Following is a brief summary of the principal chapters of this work.

The dynamic self-identity of plants

> *Plants are extremely sensitive to the torment which people inflict on them, and they "retaliate" for this by giving flowers and fruit.*
>
> Ivan Ovsinsky

In textbooks we are taught that good conditions are all that plants require for proper growth. This seems to be a universal assumption. However, all too often we provide the "correct" conditions, yet plants do not want to bear fruit.

Cereal crops give huge quantities of straw but little grain, cucumbers and tomatoes on nutrient rich organic soils are all "stems and leaves," grapes grow a tangle of fruitless vines, and trees suffer from gigantism at the expense of fruit production. Alternatively, root crops, onions, and lettuce often "bolt," going to seed when this is not desired.

Ovsinsky tried to get to the bottom of this "paradox." Relating to plants with genuine respect, he acknowledged them as living beings endowed with self-awareness, sensitivity, and a "dynamic self-identity." Indeed, plants do consistently decide for themselves how to behave in order to survive better. Ovsinsky's approach to plants is a model of genuine partnership.

> Above all, you must determine exactly where a conflict between the self-identity of plants and the goals of the farmer may occur.

> Under favorable conditions plants do not attempt to produce flowers, fruit, and seeds. Fruit formation exhausts a plant's strength and can even cause it to die off. Therefore, healthy plants growing in favorable conditions primarily strive for development of vegetative (i.e., body) mass. On the other hand, plants located in a poor environment, or those whose existence is threatened by some external danger, produce seeds, in the hope that they may be reborn into better living conditions.

> This is well demonstrated by flowers and trees. By removing flowers, you strengthen the development of shoots and branches. Also, removing spent blossoms at the proper time will significantly prolong flowering. Conversely, if you allow plants to set seeds, they will soon stop blooming and "go on vacation." Transplants which are particularly bad off will

hardly grow at all, yet become covered with fruit-buds and flowers as if saying: "Oh, well, life didn't turn out so good this time. If only I can manage to produce a few offspring before I wither and die."

Suffering and dissatisfied with their situation, flowers bloom and produce fruit and seeds. It is not that Nature smiles at us with Her flowers—this smile is more like a painful grimace.

Consequently, farmers should employ well-known practices which compel plants to flower and give fruit; otherwise, even the very best cultivation and fertilization will be for naught. Conversely, gardeners should strive to raise plants not cultivated for fruit or seeds in the most favorable conditions possible.

Under good conditions plants build up vegetative mass, but when feeling threatened, they wisely produce a multitude

of fruit. All we have to do is sensibly utilize this understanding. This does not mean that "you should create poor conditions!" Rather you must compel plants to "retaliate" under circumstances which are "too good." On our plowed fields, we create conditions where plants have no strength left to "retaliate," while in greenhouses the Japanese receive up to 220 pounds (100 kg) of tomatoes per plant. Now that's what I call "retaliation"!

What nourishes plants

Under normal conditions soil is composed of vast quantities of nutrients. Yet an enormous amount of money is continually spent on chemical fertilizers, and a whole literature on soil fertilization has been born.

Ivan Ovsinsky

Normal soil is packed with nutrients. It is true that a large part of these nutrients is in an unavailable, insoluble, or unoxidized* state—i.e., in the form of rocks and minerals. But in nature all these are somehow eventually dissolved! Consequently, it is possible to create an agricultural system which converts unavailable nutrients into available ones. It is precisely such a system which Ovsinsky developed.

In nature plants utilize various sources for nutrients.

* *Unoxidized state*—not combined with oxygen—that is, in a reduced form. Conversely, oxygen compounds are oxidized states of substances. It is these forms which are assimilated by plants. Combustion is the oxidation of organic matter accompanied by the generation of energy. We breathe in order to oxidize what we eat—i.e., to "combust"—and to utilize the energy produced by this process to live.

The atmosphere with its precipitation and dust particles is fairly close to soil in composition. Natural soil receives *nitrogen, hydrogen, and oxygen* from atmospheric water vapor, and *carbon* from carbon dioxide gas. These elements make up 93% of plant mass. For this reason, plants can receive principal nutrients—the basis of their organic matter—directly from the air. The atmosphere also conveys nitrates* to the soil, as well as ammonia, methane, hydrogen sulfide, iodine, phosphorus, minerals, and organic particles. The composition of these particles is so rich that they can wholly sustain life in lichens, many mosses and ferns, orchids, bromeliads, and other plants which live without soil.

The mineral foundation of soil—sand, clay, and mineral substances in subsoil contain all the key elements: potassium, phosphorus, calcium, magnesium, chlorine, and sulphur; as well as the trace minerals: boron, iodine, zinc, aluminum, silicon, iron, manganese, cobalt, molybdenum, and essentially Mendeleev's entire periodic table. There are literally hundreds, even thousands of times more of these elements in the soil than what is removed each year with the harvest.

Mineral deposits lack only nitrogen, but in a structured soil even this element is in large supply. Following are the analytical data of experiments conducted by several leading scholars of that time—Dehérain, Schlössing, Grandeau, Kolesov, and Wollny.

For a normal harvest, required **nitrogen** levels are about 130 pounds per acre (15 g/m²). Dew and precipitation

---

* *Nitrates*—nitric acid salts, a form of available nitrogen. Further on: *ammonia* is a compound of hydrogen and nitrogen; *methane* is a basic hydrocarbon, a flammable gas; and *hydrogen sulfide*—hydrogen combined with sulphur—is a flammable gas which smells like rotten eggs. All these supply nutrients to plants.

provide approximately 18 pounds per acre (2 g/m^2). On an unstructured soil that is all there is, but on a structured soil covered with a mulch of rotting compost, there are many additional sources of nitrogen as well.

1. The layer of rotting compost cools down more quickly, causing twice as much dew to precipitate out of the air—not a whole lot, you say? 2. Mulched soil is always damp, and a moist loam fixes twenty times more nitrogen than when dry. 3. What is not taught in agriculture textbooks is that during the day underground dew precipitates out in pores and channels of a structured soil—twice as much water in a year as normal precipitation provides—and with it up to 50 pounds per acre (6 g/m^2) of nitrogen. This is already enough! 4. With an abundance of microorganisms and ample moisture beneath the mulch, active bonding of atmospheric nitrogen by microbes and vigorous nitrification take place, producing up to 1,300 pounds per acre (150 g/m^2) of nitrogen. And only 130 pounds per acre (15 g/m^2) are needed!

Plowed, unstructured soil almost entirely lacks these additional sources of nitrogen, and so we apply saltpeter* and urea,** causing plants to become bloated and diseased. And then to add insult to injury, we pour poisons all over them. Hail to the production of chemical fertilizers!

Potassium is required at about 90 pounds per acre (10 g/m^2). Soils may contain anywhere from 270 to 1,700 pounds per acre (30–190 g/m^2) of this nutrient. Our steppe soils are some of the richest.

Phosphorus is required at around 45 pounds per acre (5 g/m^2). Natural soils usually contain 2,700–7,100 pounds per acre (300–800 g/m^2) of phosphates, but they do not readily dissolve in the flask for analysis. Who says that everything should be available in the soil immediately?

Calcium should occur at 220 pounds per acre (25 g/m^2). Its natural supply in soils is approximately 1,800–18,000 pounds per acre (200–2,000 g/m^2).

There are many other elements in soil as well. They become soluble through the action of acids—above all, by carbonic and humic acids. These acids are produced by microorganisms from organic matter in the presence of adequate moisture and air.

Evidently, they [the adherents of plowing] feel that nature does not know how to properly allocate nutrients in soil, providing an abundance of some elements but forgetting about others, or supplying them in an unavailable

---

* *Saltpeter*—industrial name for any salt of nitric acid (i.e., nitrate).

** *Urea*, or carbamide—the most concentrated of nitrogen fertilizers, containing 46% nitrogen. In a dilute solution, it is easily assimilated by plants.

form. And so the intervention of professors and fertilizer manufacturers is made indispensable. They forget that in virgin steppes and forests, where man has not destroyed the soil by plowing, nature produces without mineral fertilizers an abundance of plant life, such as no devotee of plowing could ever create with a whole wagonload of fertilizers. And even if fertilizers were provided to a farmer free of charge, and if they actually did benefit plants, adherents of plowing would still be impotent in the battle against drought. Likewise, during frequent rains plowed soil becomes so saturated that it can destroy crops completely.

Four conditions for fertility

> *If nutrients occurred naturally in a form available to plants, then achieving abundant harvests would be an easy task. You would just have to scatter seeds onto the earth in order to receive the harvest you desire.*
>
> Ivan Ovsinsky

Actually, the task of achieving an abundant harvest was not difficult for Ovsinsky. He learned how to create conditions which maximize the production of available soil nutrients and their uptake by plants. These are:

1. Constant and adequate *moisture*.
2. A system of *air pockets and channels* connected to the atmosphere.
3. Conditions which ensure that during summer the *soil is consistently cooler than the air*.
4. An abundance of *carbonic and humic acids*.

We will examine why these conditions are required, and how best to achieve them.

1. Moisture

Ovsinsky: a) never plowed deeper than 2 inches (5 cm), and b) constantly kept this upper layer in a loosened condition. The results were astonishing. "In Bessarabia and in the southern districts of the Podolsk Province, where drought often causes horrendous damage, the weather was never a problem for me, my field work was never cut short, and my soil was constantly moist enough to be molded into balls."

Mulch—an unconsolidated mass of crop residues on the surface—reliably protects the soil from the sun while in normal farming constant cultivation causes the soil to dry out. The reason for this is that beneath Ovsinsky's mulch was undisturbed, monolithic, solid ground. Penetrated by millions of channels, it maintained both *capillarity** and good *thermal conductivity*. These conditions promoted *underground condensation*—daytime precipitation of dew onto the cool walls of the soil spaces, all the way down to the deepest strata of the subsoil. And during the nighttime, dew precipitated out onto the cooled-off organic mulch covering the surface. His intelligent soil accumulated water both day and night.

The mechanism of underground condensation is simple: the hotter the air temperature, the more water vapor it can hold. This vapor condenses onto a cool surface, causing droplets to precipitate out. The soil "mists over," like a

---

* *Capillarity* (from the Latin word *capillus*, "hair")—the presence in soils of tiny fissures and channels, along which water can percolate down or even rise up, since the forces of adhesion of water to the walls (wetting) are much greater than the weight of the water itself. This is how water moves up along a wick.

cold glass in hot weather. On a summer day at a depth of 14 inches (35 cm), it may be 22°F (12°C) cooler than at the surface. This ensures condensation. A structured soil is continually breathing—it draws in air through the "pulsation" of the root mass, movements of small creatures, and the temperature fluctuations of the soil itself. As it penetrates deeper, the warm air releases more and more of its moisture. A cubic foot of air may contain up to one tenth of an ounce (100 g/m³) of water and release half of this into the soil.

"When cultivation is done wisely, so much water settles into the soil that even during intense drought mud may be found beneath the dry, fine upper layer. On the very hottest days, this daily settling of dew is like 'rain' occurring right under our feet—again, only in conjunction with wise soil cultivation."

During the night this process is reversed: the upper "blanket" of mulch quickly cools, and warmer air rises up from the

depths of the soil. On reaching the cooled-off mulch, dew precipitates out, and water is again provided for the plants. In this way, natural soil accumulates huge quantities of water. In the shade of forests, so much of it is collected under litter that it can form creeks and even rivers!

Photobacteria may also play an important role in underground condensation. These bacteria live deep in the soil, utilizing infrared radiation for photosynthesis. V. P. Tsigikalo, a researcher in the Orel Region, determined that, if there is sufficient organic matter in the soil, photobacteria will absorb much of the heat, significantly lowering soil temperatures. Similarly, the research of Teruo Higa, the developer of EM technology, demonstrates that greater numbers of photobacteria in the soil increase the ability of roots to absorb moisture.

Microorganisms flourish in a damp environment, which promotes vigorous fixation of nitrogen as well as its conversion into available nitrates. Also, in moist conditions microbes consuming organic matter excrete a mass of enzymes, forming a kind of "nutrient soup"—food for themselves as well as for plants. And as they feed, they "exhale" a flood of carbon dioxide gas. In this way, roots are provided with a sumptuous feast of both food and drink.

2. The capillary layer

Imagine seeds lying on an even, compact layer of soil *which has maintained its structure and capillarity.* This upper layer is covered over with a loose "blanket" of mulch. Under these conditions, moisture is constantly being drawn upward from deep in the soil, rising along the capillaries. The compacted surface layer under the mulch is always moist—perfect conditions for good germination. Sensing the water below, the young rootlets cling to this porous layer, vigorously growing downward along the ready-made channels. Drought will not threaten such plants.

Air channels. All forms of nutrients available to plants are oxygen compounds. Humic acids in conjunction with oxygen dissolve phosphates and other minerals ten times faster than carbonic acid. Nitrogen fixers, nitrifying agents, and the various soil creatures are aerobic—they all breathe oxygen. The disintegration of organic matter and its conversion into soluble forms of nutrients is also an aerobic process.

Thirty years after Ovsinsky, Vasily Williams wrote about "the antagonism between water and nutrients in an unstructured soil." After a rain, plowed soil quickly settles and compacts, and anaerobic bacteria immediately start converting soil compounds into unavailable forms. When the soil finally does dry up through capillary action, suffusing it with oxygen, then the required moisture is lacking! And again the plants starve.

Root channels interpenetrate the entire soil mass, similar to blood capillaries in muscles. Just like blood, water and air are transported along these channels, vigorously activating aerobic processes—that is, if the soil is structured and covered in mulch.

The channels also play another important role. The rootlets of young plants, not encountering any resistance as they grow along them, quickly and easily penetrate the subsoil to a depth of up to 13 feet (4 m) where they "link up" with the water table and gain access to various sources of minerals. Our carefully tended and plowed topsoil is poor in nutrients compared to the volume available to them in the depths! This is why green manure* is the most effective method for producing a vigorous soil structure.

3. Soil temperature

A loose, rotting mulch: a) is rapidly warmed by the sun; b) quickly cools down at night; and c) is a poor heat conductor. In other words, a layer of mulch acts as a "blanket." During the day, it is cool underneath, which allows for precipitation of daytime dew into the soil; and at night it shelters the soil from the cold, causing water vapor to condense as it rises upwards.

But this is not all. Nitrifying microbes live under the mulch on the surface of the soil. In the spring the darker humus layer warms up quickly, activating nitrification, which supplies plants with nitrogen at the beginning of the growing season. Additionally, under its protection lower soil layers are warmed more slowly, and so better absorb the moisture in warm air penetrating downwards. In order to support this process, Ovsinsky harrowed his fields in late autumn. He explained that, when fields are deeply plowed before winter, and the "furrow slice" is allowed to freeze solid, spring nitrification is hindered. And it is in the spring and beginning of summer that nitrogen is especially needed by plants.

4. Carbon dioxide gas

Ovsinsky left most plant residues on the field, dug into the upper two inches of soil. He never plowed them deeply into the ground. In the presence of air, organic matter quickly decomposed, releasing large quantities of carbon dioxide gas.

Carbon dioxide is a most valuable commodity. Plants use it for synthesizing organic matter through the process of photosynthesis. They also need it to dissolve minerals—the

---

* *Green manure*—plants grown to improve the soil, often overwintered for snow retention, and then cultivated into the surface layer of the soil.

more, the better. On the downside, it suppresses nitrification, since nitrifying agents breathe oxygen!

In plowed soils this contradiction cannot be resolved, but in natural soils there is no contradiction at all. Rotting mulch produces a hundred times more carbon dioxide gas than a cleared field. But carbon dioxide gas is: a) heavier than air, and b) a hundred times more soluble in water than either nitrogen or oxygen! Since a natural soil is interpenetrated by a myriad of tiny channels saturated with dew, nearly all of the carbon dioxide gas dissolves into soil water, transforming it into carbonic acid. Some of the carbon dioxide gas also moves downwards through the channels into the subsoil, where it diligently dissolves minerals. Most of the carbonic acid is absorbed by the roots, and free carbon dioxide gas released into the atmosphere is assimilated by leaves. This is why there is always enough oxygen on the soil surface under the mulch to allow rapid nitrification to proceed unimpeded.

Principles of sowing and Ovsinsky's farm equipment

These farming implements should be displayed in museums side by side with the tarred pickets of ancient peoples, yet we willingly pay out our hard-earned cash to buy them.

Ivan Ovsinsky about plows

One hundred years ago, Ovsinsky was using farming tools which performed the same functions as modern-day disks and cultivators. He berated German implements, very popular at the time throughout the world, preferring English ones, although even these he altered for his own purposes. He only used a shallow-tilling plow (nowadays disks do this work), a horse-drawn subsurface cultivator to cut off weeds near the surface, harrows, and a cultivator with V-shaped sweeps.

Ovsinsky never plowed deeper than 2 inches (5 cm). This was extremely important! First, because it formed a layer of loose mulch on the surface of the soil; and second, weed seeds were not worked deeper into the soil—on the surface they quickly germinated and after 3–4 years were completely eradicated. He cut weeds down with a subsurface cultivator, which also loosened the mulch. The cultivator was adjusted so that the sweeps, as they cut through the soil, left behind a smooth, even surface—ready for planting and mulching. He improved the seed-furrow opener, so that seeds would fall onto the bed evenly—not in clumps, but one by one—at the appropriate density. In certain rare situations he used a roller.

Ovsinsky referred to any and all other farming implements as "harmful toys" and a complete waste of money.

He sowed his fields in strips 12 inches (30 cm) wide with the same distance between them. Two rows of beets, three rows of beans, or six rows of wheat could be planted in each strip. Most importantly, the surface under the mulch—the seedbed—had to be perfectly smooth. It was always moist there, and all seeds sprouted at the same time, even when there was no rain. This never happens with plowing, even less so with digging—seeds at various depths and in various degrees of contact with the soil sprout unevenly.

Germinating seeds cling securely to the capillary surface, which allows the farmer to harrow seedlings three times at 2– 3 day intervals: Ovsinsky always let seedlings recover after harrowing. The day after a rain, he would harrow again in order to

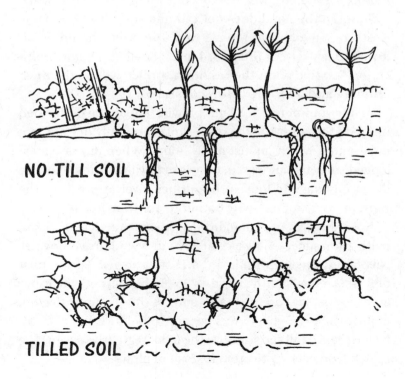

NO-TILL SOIL

TILLED SOIL

loosen the mulch. In this way, he maintained the soil's ability to accumulate moisture, and seedlings quickly gained strength.

The mulch must always be kept loose. This was his basic procedure for tending young plants. Before they began shad-ing the soil, Ovsinsky would make two or three passes with his subsurface cultivator. He cultivated after the harvest as well—on weedy fields with a light plow, on less-weedy fields with a cultivator, and on weed-free fields with a harrow. The final harrowing was done just before the onset of winter. This enabled plant nutrients to be produced in the soil through fall and winter for the following year.

Williams often proclaimed this fundamental law for cultivating the soil: *soil should be cultivated only at optimal moisture levels.* Not wet, not dry, but when it is "ripe"—when a clump in the hand does not crumble, nor dirty the palm. Kostychev wrote that after a rain, the crust should be allowed to dry out for 5/8 to 3/4 inch (1.5–2 cm) before cultivation—at this point the resulting surface will be the most crumbly, and moisture below conserved.

In late summer or fall, light plowing should be performed immediately after the harvest—soils can easily dry out in a day—and if windy, in just a few hours. When dry or water-logged soils are cultivated, they lose fertility. Think about it: do you manage to loosen the surface layer at precisely the right moment? If not, why bother to cultivate at all?

Nowadays, many thoughtful farmers practice wise soil cultivation successfully (see articles at www.kurdyumov.ru). Nikolay Andreevich Kulinsky, a Distinguished Agronomist of Russia, consistently harvests 75–80 bushels of wheat per acre (5–5.5 t/ha) on the loamy soils of the Vladimir Region, applying only 35–45 pounds per acre (40–50 kg/ha) of fertilizer. He leaves all the straw on the field, regularly loosens the mulch, and uses cultivators instead of plows.

Anatoly Ivanovich Shugurov, director of the "Pugachevs-koe" farmstead located on the steppes outside of Penza, does not even use a cultivator and consistently harvests 45–52 bushels per acre (3–3.5 t/ha) of wheat. This may not seem like much, but total production costs are only $.40 per bushel ($15 per ton) of grain, and fuel consumption 4.4 gallons per acre (41 l/ha). The key point is not maximum yield, but rather an inexpensive and healthy harvest.

After four years of practicing "organic mulching," the head of the agro-company "Topaz," Sergey Nikolaevich Svitenko, doubled his yields, harvesting 160 bushels per acre (10 t/ha) of corn and 3,600 pounds per acre (4 t/ha) of sunflower seeds. He utilizes an ordinary piece of farm equipment—a mulcher-shredder—to produce organic mulch. After the corn harvest, it spreads an even layer of finely chopped stalks onto the surface, up to 27,000 pounds of dry organic matter per acre (30 t/ha)—even better than manure!

The fact is that *we can increase harvests, decrease expenses, and improve soil fertility all at the same time.*

Ovsinsky's yields were five, sometimes ten times larger than average for his time. In an extended drought, when neighboring fields were scorched, he always received a harvest. After developing intelligent farming, Ovsinsky was full of optimism:

The old system of soil cultivation impedes the supply of nutrients to plants. Cultivation methods and fertilizer recipes have been obsolete for quite some time [this was in 1899!], but advocates of the old system, even as they damage the earth with their cultivation, try to mask their folly with applications of fertilizers and lime. They are like a physician who passes out poison with one hand and the antidote with the other, while arguing all the while that the entire procedure helps his patient.

Shallow cultivation, less than two inches, promotes mineralization* in the soil—particularly when using a subsurface cultivator. This is the mysterious factor which protects farmers from the dreadful specter of drought. Now I await this bane of farmers calmly and even with a certain satisfaction. Plants in our fields dependably sprout and grow, even without rain, and nitrification and cooling of gasses are robust. Good weather makes our fieldwork—otherwise hindered by rain—even easier.

The bottom line is that for over a hundred years we have had (and still have) at our disposal a sensible system which everyone can use for establishing an intelligent vegetable garden. So the question arises: "Why isn't this system practiced universally?! Why do we still dig and plow to our own detriment?"

Why we dig?

Teach your children well,
And things will go to hell!
                    Efim Samovarshchikov

Someone is always lying in wait to profit off of any and every problem.
However, success is not profitable for them, since by definition it is the absence of problems, which means there is no need to accept their offers of "salvation and succor." If you do not fear the problems they helped create, then you will have no need to purchase their solutions. The farmer who

---

* *Mineralization*—the decay of soil organic matter into simple compounds; the disintegration and dissolution of minerals.

masters the processes of Nature Herself is free and independent; he cannot be exploited. Natural farming is not profitable for agribusinesses and, as we know, our governments became subjugated to corporations a long time ago.

How has the American agro-industry conquered nearly the entire world so quickly, even nations of the Far East where traditional farming practices are the exact opposite? It is very simple: the powers-that-be survive on high volume of trade, and chemicals, fertilizers, and farm equipment represent billions of dollars in sales.

We live in a society which cashes in on problems. In a way, it is just plain ridiculous: they are constantly creating new problems to frighten us, while subsequently offering solutions for our rescue—and we obediently open up our wallets. It does not take a genius to realize that nearly all major problems have been artificially manufactured. In order to save us, the medical industry needs really cool diseases. To feed their families, the military must have wars—and wars happen for this very reason. How many criminals are rehabilitated into

good citizens because of police? The press needs scandals and conflicts, inflating them in every possible way, and if they can't find an angle, they just make something up.

It is always cheaper to create new science than to lose power and volume of production. Not so long ago, we survived perfectly well without worrying about the natural odors of our bodies—even dandruff was not a sin. It will not surprise me in the least if in the future our grandchildren are horrified by people who don't meticulously remove every hair on their bodies!

Without bothering to think first, we run around like caged hamsters on a wheel. The "resolution" of one problem only creates another, and we keep paying, and paying, and paying... "After polishing off a hamburger, potato chips, and some ice cream (!), don't forget the Dirol for Kids chewing gum!"—and Mezym for digestion, Galstena for the liver, and Bittner Balsam for its "healing properties." Then we can continue poisoning ourselves with more potato chips followed by more medicine. "The Center for Healthy Hair" is now all the rage, but what will come next: "The Center for Fragrant Armpits," or "The Center for Medicinal Vodka"? Our hearts are touched by how much these advertisers seem to care for us, so we no longer see through this new "science" being peddled by profiteers.

It has always been profitable in our vast country for the powers-that-be to pay for quantity rather than quality—rewarding obedient service on the job instead of results accomplished; sick leave certificates rather than promotion of health; "faith in science" over success; and trust in benevolent leaders instead of "dynamic self-identity." No wonder we are bogged down by so many problems. We just keep digging our gardens, complaining all the while about the climate, and how hard life is. By our faith shall we be rewarded! Amen.

Chapter 3

How to Improve Fertility

or

A Short Course in Soil Cultivation

Sooner or later, all my reasoning ripens on well-prepared soil!

Generally speaking, you can grow vegetables with a nutrient solution in whatever medium you like—in sand or perlite,* clay pellets or crushed stone—this is called hydroponics. Or small peat blocks can be packed into a pipe or trough which a nutrient solution flows through—small-scale hydroponics. You can even grow plants in the air, periodically misting their roots with nutrients—aeroponics. These methods are very expensive, troublesome, and unhealthy. It is not safe to eat these vegetables, and you would not want to anyway; they are all but tasteless.

Good-tasting, healthful vegetables grow on living soil—preferably in permanent raised beds (colder regions) or in trenches (hot, dry regions) filled with humus-rich soil and compost and covered with a layer of plant residues. Crops

---

* *Perlite*—a mineral, white when milled, elastic, and light-weight; it absorbs water at thirty times its own weight. Good for rooting cuttings and for loosening soil. Unfortunately, it is in short supply.

grown in such an environment are inexpensive, prolific, extremely delicious, and, most importantly, you do not have to work very hard to grow them. This is precisely how I garden.

Ideas about how gardeners can create rich, fertile soil while remaining independent of the agro-industrial complex have been developed and applied for over a hundred years. All of them are based on one simple rule: *return to the soil as much or more organic matter than you remove from it.* This keeps it alive and fertile—and such soil will give back to you even more. These methods are called by various names: organic, regenerative, sustainable, and, in Russia, natural farming. They all are combinations of various schools of thought with a common core idea: "Learn from nature."

In the early part of the 20th century in Germany, the biodynamic system of agriculture was developed based on spiritual awareness of natural processes. Practitioners of biodynamics believe that plants, animals, mankind, and the Universe are part of a single, unified whole. Their approach to farming strives to achieve maximum harmony of all factors influencing plants. They have especially mastered the art of compost and humus, learning to increase the vigor of plants, animals, and humans within a closed cycle of exchange of biological waste products. However, the very depth of their understanding of the dynamic processes of nature is sometimes unattainable to the layperson.

In the 1950s, due to governmental soil conservation policies and the publications of such revolutionaries as Faulkner and Rodale, *organic* farming rapidly spread throughout the United States and Canada. The Rodale Institute researched and developed methods which allow greater accumulation and utilization of natural forces—sun, water, air, and soil creatures, as well as the properties of plants themselves—importing minimal quantities of outside energy, chemicals, fertilizers, and irrigation water.

The 1970s saw the emergence of *permaculture* in Australia. Towards the end of the 1960s in France—and subsequently in the United States based on the work of Alan Chadwick and popularized by a book by John Jeavons—*biointensive mini-farming* was developed. At the heart of this system are permanent organic beds and mulch.

Doctor Jacob Mittleider should also be mentioned. He developed a very sensible layout for gardens—narrow beds. These are now used by "intelligent gardeners" throughout Russia.

In recent decades it has become irrefutably clear that healthy plants can only be grown in a sustainable ecosystem. Research in agroecology has pressed forward. For over half a century, the European association "Bioland" has been researching natural living systems in soils and the ecological causes for epidemics of pests and disease. Farmers achieve healthy plants and good harvests by establishing diverse and sustainable ecosystems on their fields.

Effective microorganisms (EM) technology has been developed in Japan over the past several decades and is now spreading throughout the world. By cultivating beneficial microbes, organic matter is decomposed more efficiently, the environment is cleaned up, soil fertility increases, and pathogenic microflora are suppressed. Techniques for processing manure with earthworms are also extensively used.

In Russia natural farming is being developed by numerous farmers and scientists, each adapting techniques to their unique conditions and devising their own agricultural practices. Their methods are described in my book *Meeting Pests with a Smile.*

By observing plants carefully, you too can create your own personal intelligent gardening system. To aid you in this task, following are the fundamental principles of regenerative farming as I understand them.

Forms of organic matter

We shall not waste our mournful toil!
It all goes back to feed the soil.

Folklore

Variant: *As you gobble down that delicious sandwich, remember: you are now working for the benefit of the soil!*

Organic matter consists of anything that is dead: dead leaves and stalks of plants as well as the bodies and wastes of insects and animals—that is, everything that can decay and break down into compost and humus.* Of course, organic matter is not separate from the biomass of decomposing microbes, whose volume is no less than that of the organic matter itself!

Plowing, cultivation, fertilizers, pesticides, and all such expensive farming practices have already managed to destroy two thirds of the fertile soils of this planet, so why do they continue to be utilized to this day? Because agronomy, it seems, does not understand the primary benefit of soil organic matter. It is not its nutrients, nor its nitrogen, nor

---

* *Compost* is a partially decomposed mix of various organic materials. *Humus* is the stable, fully decomposed outcome of the composting process.

its friability and water-holding capacity, not even its protection of soils from erosion.* All these are bonus effects "free of charge." The most important benefit of organic matter is its *energy*.

Organic matter is the fuel, the food. Energy from the sun, stored up by plants over the course of the growing season, is subsequently passed on to soil creatures. These creatures feed and multiply, decomposing organic matter back into carbon dioxide gas and water. In this way, carbon is returned to plants, so that in the future they can synthesize new organic matter. Thanks to this soil life, plants receive back their carbon and all the other nutrients they require.

Last year's organic residue becomes this year's biomass. This is called the *carbon cycle*, the dominant cycle of our planet—without it there could be no life. For hundreds of millions of years, the exact same carbon has manifested as leaves, fruit, and seeds; it has fed all living things, from microbes to humans, always cycling back to plants. All of us organic matter eaters are actually consuming the sun's energy which was originally stored by plants. All carbon incorporated into the bodies of plants and animals—including our own bodies—invariably and wholly returns to the soil. This is how our biosphere operates.

Remove organic matter from the fields, and the cycle of life is broken. Where there is no energy or carbon, there is no fertility. So people are forced to use chemical substitutes, consuming huge amounts of fuel and electricity in the process—and entire new scientific disciplines are created. Having starved the entire microbial workforce in the soil, farmers are forced to do the work themselves, wasting money

* *Erosion*—loss of soil exposed by plowing, and subsequently washed away by rain or blown off by wind.

and sacrificing their health and well-being. But all of these efforts are in vain: chemical fertilizers lack that essential ingredient—carbon. I consider such farming as the greatest folly of human civilization.

Organic gardeners have long known about the importance of organic matter. A garden is different from a field; a small plot can be completely covered with compost and will yield an excellent harvest. It is for this reason that gardeners rarely contemplate the energy of soils. For them organic matter is above all fertilizer, soil loosener, and source of humus, which they apply in the form of compost.

Compost is the most well-known and popular organic fertilizer. Let's consider it from the viewpoint of an ordinary gardener.

Compost

A kind person makes a richer compost.

Well-prepared compost is truly "gold" in the garden. It makes plants incredibly strong and protects them from disease. I consistently see this in my own garden: volunteer plants which sprout up in the compost pile invariably outstrip my planted vegetables, and they are twice as vigorous. In Europe and the United States, entire institutes are dedicated to researching compost, and scientists are always uncovering more and more benefits.

In the early 1920s, practitioners of biodynamic farming in Germany researched compost in great depth. Believing in cosmic influences and the "intelligence of molecules," they considered compost the quintessence of these influences. Their experiments were both thorough and beautiful. They learned to consciously influence the composting process by applying infusions of herbs and minerals. They also established quality distinctions between various types of compost, demonstrating that an animal's feed determines the traits of its manure, and thus the compost and eventual harvest. They truly raised the "art of composting" to perfection.

Organic gardeners consider compost the underlying basis for prosperity. Their appreciation can even border on reverence. They view compost as alive, and for good reason: rotting manure is life in the truest sense of the word. It is a complex community of microorganisms, insects, and earthworms, which together diligently transform organic matter into the best possible environment for roots. They are our invaluable helpers. Look into a microscope, and you will see how industriously they exert themselves. What is good for them is also good for plants, and this means that it is good for us, too.

These soil creatures are our symbiotic partners—like cows and turkeys, cats and dogs—but incomparably more important. We can survive without cows, but without microbes? Impossible! Organic gardeners have learned how to interact with them for our mutual benefit—for some preparation of compost can well-nigh be a religious rite!

Microorganisms require three conditions to proliferate: *food, moisture,* and (for most) *oxygen.* Generally, food and moisture are not issues. Providing oxygen, however, is more problematical, but it affects both the microbial composition of the compost and the rate of decomposition. In compost factories, where air is forcibly pumped into piles which are stirred constantly, compost can be finished in two days. For the rest of us, though, there is no need to hurry. The quality of compost is more important—poor compost does not help and may even harm plants.

So, let's get down to making good compost.

What can be composted?

We will begin with what should never be put into the pile—grease, fat, bones, and all synthetics including plastic. Dairy products, meat, and fish scraps are bad because they attract our animal brethren, especially rats, and can permeate an area with unpleasant smells. It is better to bury these in the ground; they rot faster this way and pose no problem.

All organic matter can be divided into two categories: "green" (rich in nitrogen—i.e., protein) and "brown" (poor in nitrogen, but rich in carbon—i.e., fiber*). These materials behave differently in the pile and have diverse roles.

Green matter rots quickly with conspicuous heating and often with an unpleasant odor. It is the "reactor" of the pile. Microbes which break down fiber cannot work without the nitrogen it provides. In general, green matter is the primary source for nitrogenous nutrients.

Brown matter breaks down slowly at cooler temperatures, primarily due to fungi. In both the pile and the soil, it ensures porosity, allowing for retention of air and moisture—this is what loosens soils. It also enriches compost with minerals, especially calcium and silicon. Cellulose decomposition depends on nitrogen—sawdust saturated with urea rots much quicker. However, this does not mean, as sometimes believed, that sawdust mulch depletes the soil of nitrogen! Partially rotted straw and sawdust are a source of sugars for nitrogen-fixing bacteria which feed on carbohydrates.

---

* *Fiber*, or *cellulose*—a polysaccharide, or "starch which has been stitched tightly together" found in the cell walls of plants. It imparts rigidity and helps create structure. Woody tissue is cellulose "stitched" by a similar polymer—lignin.

Under mulch, active nitrogen fixation is constantly taking place.

Let's look at these materials more closely.

GREEN: manure, feces, bird droppings, kitchen scraps, fruit wastes, legume hay, green leaves, mowed and partially dried grass, the leafy tops of root crops, green corn stalks, weeds—in fact, all green matter.

Manure mixed with straw or sawdust is best for compost. Litter from under livestock with an 80% straw content is excellent. The best quality in composition is horse manure— the nitrogen and cellulose in it are nearly balanced, and it can be added to beds almost fresh. The hardest of all to work with is pig manure. It is very acidic, watery, and nitrogenous. In order to make good compost from pig manure, you should layer it with dry straw, sawdust, or seed hulls, add a little lime—3.5 to 4 pounds of lime powder per cubic yard (2–2.5 kg/m³), and let it compost until it no longer smells of manure.

Human feces, a fertilizing product from our own life processes, is a most valuable manure. In Ovsinsky's time, it was respectfully referred to as "human gold." "The nutrient value of human gold is 8–10 times greater than manure. It is principally used where agriculture is so intense that it requires a highly concentrated fertilizer" (People's Encyclopedia, 1912). Nowadays we are warned about parasitic worms,* but this is actually farfetched. Who ever said that parasitic worms can only live in human fecal matter? They can live in any droppings or manure. Our much beloved dogs and cats are virtual walking parasitic worm factories. Soil, too, is not

---

* *Parasitic worms*—parasitic intestinal worms. Generally, they pass through their various phases of metamorphosis in diverse habitats.

sterile, and vectors of disease can be found in it as well, but this doesn't stop us from enjoying fresh garden vegetables. We don't eat them right out of the ground—we wash them, peel them, and cook them.

My outhouse is a biotoilet to which I add peat and bioactivators.* We also have an indoor biotoilet, "Mr. Little," which uses bioactivators as well. Once a week, I empty out the contents into a hole dug under a tree or in a trench along a garden bed, sprinkling it with dirt and covering it all over with grass. The contents of the outhouse accumulate all summer, and so are already partially composted when removed. In the fall, I spread it over garden beds, under bushes, or let it fully decompose in the compost pile, again covering with grass or seed hulls. My plants are very grateful! And there are no toxic waste products.

Bird droppings, too, are a very concentrated fertilizer. It is best to infuse them in water to make a tea. Or, if you have extra to spare, you can throw some in the compost pile—blending it well with any kind of brown matter. Pigeon droppings contain the most nutrients. City dwellers in Russia sometimes collect them by the bagful out of attics.

Kitchen and fruit wastes should be thinly spread and interspersed with brown matter just like manure. Otherwise, they will compact and turn sour.

Hay—that is, any grass that has been mown and dried—is excellent, but it must be moistened and layered with dirt or compost, or else it will dry out on top and turn sour below.

---

* *Bioactivators*—bacterial preparations which speed up decomposition of organic matter in biotoilets and compost piles—for example, preparations of the Belgian company Agrostar. They contain living microbes and a range of enzymes.

Grass, **green leaves**, and other vegetation should be allowed to wilt first before blending with brown matter. Fresh greens in the pile compact, squeezing out all of the air. Under such conditions they cannot decompose, but instead "burn," which causes them to sour and turn into "silage." Such compost should be turned more often than usual.

BROWN: *dry leaves, straw, shredded and dried stalks and reeds, dried plant residues, chaff,* rice hulls, dried and shredded corncobs, shredded paper and cardboard, sawdust and fine woodchips, shredded brush, and bark.* An excellent material is the spent substrate which remains after cultivating oyster mushrooms.

Brown matter is the primary component of compost. A compost pile should contain 70–80% of it. If there is not enough green matter, brown matter will still compost without it. If you dampen the pile with a solution of urea (carbamide) at the rate of 1.5–2 ounces per cubic foot (1.5–2 kg/m³), decomposition will take place much faster. However, if you do have sufficient green matter, simply build a "layer cake": two thirds brown, one third green.

An excellent base material for compost consists of branches of trees and brush shredded together with leaves. Shredded weeds, tops of root crops, and all manner of green plants can be added as well. The greens provide sufficient nitrogen, and the pile quickly begins "combusting"—i.e., heating up. You only have to add water and a little soil for successful composting. Incidentally, I use this compost for mulching. You will never find a better mulch.

---

* *Chaff*—the outer hulls, shells, or seed husks which are removed in the process of threshing grain.

How do you compost it all?

First off, do not dig a compost pit. Water will accumulate in it; it is very difficult to turn the pile and to remove compost; and decomposition is anaerobic—there is very little air in an underground pit. Digging a pit only makes sense for people who live in hot, dry conditions with sandy soils.

A compost bin has three walls up to a meter high made from any type of material. To ensure an adequate air supply, the floor should be soft and porous without standing water—this is good for worms. An earthen floor is the simplest, with straw or sawdust spread over the bottom. If the floor is solid—for instance, concrete—it is easier to clean out the compost. The straw covering over concrete should be thicker, up to 8 inches (20 cm).

The minimum volume for a pile is about 35 cubic feet (1 m^3); otherwise, it will dry out too quickly. For the same reason, it is better built in the shade. If a pile is located in an exposed area, it should be covered—in the winter and spring with plastic (organic matter decomposes better

under warm conditions), and in the summer with any kind of non-transparent "cloak" to protect it from drying out or overheating. If a pile is left uncovered, nutrients will wash out with the rain.

Composting can be done *cold* which is slower, or *hot* which is faster. Honestly speaking, nowadays I just try to lay whatever organic matter I can directly beneath the plants, where it will eventually become compost to enrich the soil. However, at the beginning of summer grass clippings and weeds start stacking up—and it is not good to immediately spread fecal matter directly onto the garden either—so I usually have to build a pile at some point during the summer.

It goes without saying that I practice cold composting since it is less work.

Cold composting is for lazy people. You just keep stacking various materials onto the pile—grass, manure, fecal matter, and kitchen wastes—and cover it all over with straw, hay, husks, shells, or sawdust. *It is essential that you sprinkle a couple shovelfuls of dirt on top of each layer*—composting will progress more quickly, and in the end the humus will be well-rotted and stabilized. Add weeds when they are still

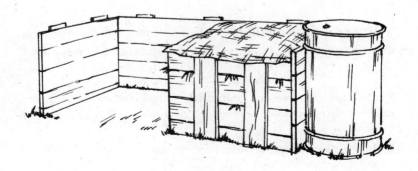

young, before they go to seed; otherwise, you will have to weed beds more often than usual.

In the fall, I remove the upper, uncomposted layer of the pile and use it to cover overwintering garlic, lilies, dahlias, or any bed containing fresh organic matter. Then I spread the remaining nearly-finished compost onto unplanted beds, again covering it over with some material. Adherents of digging should not put tops of diseased plants into the pile: tomatoes "burned" by late blight* or cucumbers by peronospora.** Disease spores are dangerous only in the air. If you dig your beds, you keep bringing the infection up to the surface. I do not dig beds, but instead cover the surface with new compost and mulch. This keeps the spores deep in the soil. I never give any special attention to diseased plants— you can't protect them from everything. There are no root rots in my garden, nor is it likely that they would be found in compost.

If I manage to turn the pile once during the summer, by fall the compost will be nearly ready. Usually I do this in the middle or end of May, just in time for the cats to destroy mole cricket nests. If you turn a pile twice, the compost will be ready even sooner. And if you turn it every week, it will ripen in a month or two, but then this would actually be hot composting.

Hot composting: In order to not overexert themselves, organic gardeners have contrived all sorts of composting

---

* *Late blight* (*Phytophthora infestans*)—fungal disease of the nightshade family (Solanaceae)—see chapter "Meeting pests with a smile."

** *Peronospora*—fungal disease, false powdery mildew—see chapter "Meeting pests with a smile."

devices. For instance, some fasten an axle onto a large steel barrel with an opening on the side. Like a cement mixer, they simply rotate it, and they are done. Others use an ordinary 50-gallon (200-liter) steel barrel which they roll along the ground. The barrel has a removable lid, and air holes are punched into the butt-end. Liquids cannot be used in this kind of composter, only materials with normal moisture content.

But the simplest way is to use a pitchfork. The hot compost pile is built up on one half of the bin, and then periodically turned from side to side. New material is not added to the pile; the compost is brought to maturity as a whole. It should be moistened as needed.

Compost will turn dark, almost black, when it is ready. Its consistency will be more or less homogenous, crumbly, with a pleasant smell like forest litter.

In summary:

The Laws of composting

1) Mix together both green and brown matter at a proportion of 1:3 to 1:4. If there is not enough green, you can add some kind of nitrogen fertilizer.
2) Do not make the pile higher than 25–38 inches (60–70 cm), or the lower layer may become compacted.
3) Alternate various materials frequently: the looser and more aerated the pile, the less turning it will require.
4) Cover the pile to keep moisture in and to protect it from overheating.
5) The more thoroughly the contents are mixed, the better the process works. And the finer the components, the quicker they will decompose.
6) Always add a little finished humus and dirt to inoculate the pile.

7) Allow grass to wither before layering it with brown matter. Moisten dry grass.

8) Do *not* put grease, bones, synthetics, sticks, or thorny branches into the pile. Bury "meat and dairy" directly into the ground.

Of course, only a dedicated professional could fully observe all these rules. Personally, I do not worry much about them. I simply gather together everything I can find, stack it up in layers, and turn the pile once or twice during the summer, keeping it covered the whole time with grass or plastic. This results in a perfectly adequate compost replete with nutrients.

How to use organic matter wisely: composting the natural way

Organic gardeners are the first to dispense with organic chemistry!

Important: you never really have to make a compost pile at all. In nature compost is created *all by itself.* In this process, soil receives everything it needs from organic matter—its energy, nutrients, bioactivity, heat, structure, and the full reproductive cycle of microbes, worms, and insects. Yet we prefer to see a "beautiful garden" out our window, so we relegate all this to the compost pile.

Let's be honest here: with all its inherent value, humus is actually fully decomposed organic matter. Only a quarter of the mass of the source materials remains, so the soil receives only a quarter of the original carbon, having lost the other three fourths to the atmosphere. And only a fifth of the energy and nutrients remain for the microbes and worms. The rest have already been consumed—not in the garden bed but in the compost pile, with no benefit to the soil. We separate the natural process of fertility from the garden, instead of allowing it to play out right in the beds.

All plant residues and kitchen waste can be strewn directly onto the garden. This technique is known in Russia by the name "Finnish garden beds." One of my readers in Kuban (Zone 6), Tanya Zorina, used this method for four years to transform her sun-baked clay soil into a moist, nutrient-rich "fluff" full of humus. Working patiently, persistently, and thoughtfully, she achieved true success.

Tanya's half-acre (0.2-ha) garden plot is located next to an open field and surrounded by abandoned garden plots overgrown with tall weeds. The conditions are extremely harsh: there is no electricity, water must be pumped by hand from a well, and it is located far from the town where she lives. To be honest, I would not own such a dacha. But Tanya was serious and set to work with organic matter and mulch.

Her kitchen wastes and weeds as well as those of her neighbors, plus all the leaves she could find, forest litter from a nearby windbreak, cardboard and shredded paper from her workplace, pigeon droppings from her loft, three haystacks of straw in autumn—all this she hauled to her dacha garden. She never arrived there empty-handed.

Tanya planned her permanent beds to be one meter wide by ten meters long. Some of them were lined with boards, others were not, but never again would these beds be "touched by human feet," only by hands. Over time she covered the half-meter wide walkways with cardboard and straw or sawdust.

Her main preparation of the soil occurs in the winter. After the harvest, Tanya plants a green manure crop—peas, mustard, rape, wheat, or rye. In the late fall, she cuts it down with a Fokin hoe* or, if plants are still young and green, she simply covers them with a layer of organic mulch. Then she spreads a 1–2-inch (2–4-cm) layer of kitchen wastes over the bed. Weeds are placed on top of that, and everything is covered with a layer of straw or sawdust no less than 4–6 inches (10–15 cm) high. Under this "blanket," the microbes continue working all winter. Sometimes she sprinkles small amounts of rotted manure or bird droppings onto the straw for better decomposition. If there is no rain or snow for at least two weeks, Tanya will moisten the mulch with at least 3–4 watering cans per bed. This is vital for quick decomposition.

In the spring, any uncomposted stalks or straw are raked onto the pathways, so the beds will quickly warm up. When seedlings begin emerging, the beds are covered with a thick mulch. She waters very rarely.

Now Tanya can even plant potatoes with her bare hands— the soil is so friable that no metal tools are required. She never digs the beds, preserving the structure created by roots and countless worms. When neighboring gardens suffer drought, Tanya remains calm—it is always moist under her mulch and cardboard. Crop rotation—rotating plantings between beds—eliminates any threat of exhausting the soil or build-up of disease, so her plants stay healthy.

The garden "feeds" Tanya in another way as well: she sells her strawberries, surplus vegetables, and ornamental plants. Her goal—to grow an abundant harvest yet not have to slave over the garden all summer long—has become a reality. Now she feels that her garden is a part of herself, and she always knows exactly what to do.

* *Fokin hoe*—see section "The Fokin multipurpose hoe" later in this chapter.

Some of Siberia's prominent gardeners also have dispensed with compost piles: Ivan Zamiatkin, Alexander Kuznetsov, Oleg Telepov, Andrey Isakov, and many others. They quickly and efficiently improve soil by means of weeds and green manure crops. Their main principle is that *soil should never be bare and exposed for even a single day*. It should always be covered with mulch or growing plants.

In their gardening systems, weeds are a potent green manure crop provided "free of charge." They are left purposefully in the garden to produce a maximum of biomass, and cut down before flowering and setting seeds. The powerful roots of weeds are excellent at loosening the soil, and the greens are rich in nutrients.

After cutting them down, both tall weeds and grasses serve as a fertilizing mulch and a means for eliminating other weeds. They are piled directly on top of the weeds which have been stamped down in the rows as well as in pathways between beds of potatoes, cabbages, tomatoes, or root crops. By the middle of summer, the smothered weeds die back from lack of sunlight. Weeds growing nearby are likewise stamped down, the pile is moved onto them, and a green manure is sown on the newly cleared area. In this way, the weed piles continuously feed and protect the soil. Also, the pathways between the beds are not left bare but constantly covered by a layer of rotting vegetation.

In the early spring after the snow has melted, the beds are sown with cold-resistant green manures: phacelias,* rye, or vetch. Within 1–1½ months, they will produce a fair amount of biomass. These greens are cut down with a Fokin hoe before seeding the beds. Some of the phacelias can be left for

---

* *Phacelias*—early, cold-resistant plants, excellent green manures and very strong nectar bearers.

another week since they are an excellent cover for newly transplanted tomatoes, peppers, and cucumbers.

Just before the final harvest in the fall, the beds are sown again with green manure: annual lupine, oats, rape, oilseed radish, or winter cress. Sunflowers, amaranth, or various vigorous grasses—corn, sorghum, foxtail millet, or Japanese millet—provide even more organic matter. A tall stand will grow up before the frost, freezing in the winter, which helps to retain snow. In the spring, it is cut down and used as mulch.

In this way, an intelligent garden does not need compost piles. Everything is always covered over with plant residues or lush greenery buzzing with bees. This feeds a mass of beneficial insects, utilizes every ray of sunlight, and yields a superb harvest: up to 3 pounds of potatoes per square foot (15 kg/m^2), or 20-pound (10-kg) heads of cabbage—all without chemical fertilizers, and without compost piles.

Even manure can become wiser!

I've got first class shit! I don't trade in crap!

Fresh manure, mixed with brown matter and made less acidic with lime or ash, is excellent to spread around the trunks of weak trees and berry brambles. It can be applied in a ring 4–6 inches (10–15 cm) thick. This mulch does a good job of rehabilitating weak young saplings. Manure is also exceptional for piling around current and gooseberry bushes, between rows of strawberries, and especially in raspberry rows—these brambles cannot bear dried-out soil and love an abundance of organic matter. With the addition of lime, manure is good as the bottom layer of a bed planted in cabbages or cucumbers. This is exactly how our grand-fathers grew early cucumbers in greenhouses: manure underneath, covered with an 8-inch (20-cm) layer of soil mixed with more rotted manure. As it decomposes, the manure heats up the soil; warmth in the soil is much more important than the air temperature.

Infused in 20 parts water, manure is particularly good as a tea for liquid feeding. Soak bird droppings, which are more concentrated, in 40 parts water.

Partially-rotted manure or unfinished compost can be used in the same way as fresh manure: under bushes and transplants, or infused in water. I often spread it over garden beds in the fall as well. In preparation for winter, I cover it with chaff, hulls, straw, or plastic—by springtime the manure will have completely seasoned. Plastic is superior for preserving nutrients because, when covered with organic materials, much of the nutrient content is lost from winter rain and snow.

Manure is the most popular fertilizer, but also the most troublesome to apply.

Currently in Russia, more than 300 million tons of manure are produced each year. Only 10% of it ends up where it should—on fields. The rest, at best, piles up on farms, forming huge "mountain ranges," and at worst pollutes soil and water. This is especially catastrophic in the vicinity of huge hog factories—and not only in Russia. In fact, only the most affluent countries can afford to pay to remove manure to fields.

The problem is that manure is the most labor-intensive of fertilizers—heavy, slimy, repulsive, and unsafe, containing ammonia, hydrogen sulfide, disease-carrying microbes, and parasitic worms. It is cost-prohibitive to haul it more than 2–3 miles (3–5 km), yet 20–30 tons of manure per acre

(50–80 t/ha) should be applied and dug into the soil to be effective. Working with it is extremely troublesome. If it is not plowed in immediately, it loses nearly all its nitrogen. Piled up, it loses half its nutrient value in just three months. But the main issue is weeds. In a ton of manure there can be up to 12 million seeds! "I would curse manure, but it is the most available fertilizer there is," says Nikolay Andreevich Kulinsky, whose fields are so "smart" that people come to visit them from all over the world.

It is also important to note that manure usually comes from animal feed grown on huge industrial farms that use massive amounts of expensive chemicals.

How utterly absurd is it that we pour chemicals onto the earth in order to generate organic wastes! True, chemical fertilizers are more fool-proof and easier to work with, but who is keeping us from inventing organic fertilizers with these same qualities and convenience? This task was first addressed in the mid-'70s by scientists in Stockholm, who developed organic fertilizer granules (OFG). In essence, they are biologically enriched, dry, granulated manure which has been processed by microbes in a controlled environment. In Holland, Denmark, and Sweden, factories are producing OFG through anaerobic processing of manure. Similar technology has also been adopted in Germany (Delaplant) and the United States (Harmony).

OFG are a combination of everything positive about both organic and chemical fertilizers. The dry granules the size of beans are easy to transport, unload, apply, and work into the soil. They have no odor or disease pathogens, and are consistent in nutrient composition. The recommended application is only 2,650 pounds per acre (3 t/ha), or one bucket per 300 square feet, yet they contains all the positives of organic matter: cellulose and protein, nutrients, biologically active

substances (BAS), and a balanced complex of beneficial microorganisms. Like compost, they are long-acting, raise humus content, increase fertility, and markedly purify the soil of pathogens. The main negative is that production costs are very high—a ton of OFG can consume up to 1,800 pounds (800 kg) of fuel!

At the end of the 1980s, Perestroika put the brakes on two remarkable projects in Russia. Irina Alexandrovna Arkhipchenko, a professor of Agricultural Microbiology at the All-Russian Scientific Research Institute, developed her own form of OFG, utilizing a simpler, aerobic-anaerobic method of processing. Granules were produced less expensively with a higher nutrient content. Arkhipchenko's procedure is versatile—any kind of manure or droppings can be transformed into OFG. The most researched product is Bamil (biomass of active sludge microorganisms)—OFG derived from the waste products of factory hog farms. It is highly efficient in the field and is nearly as effective as Omug (granulated organic microbial fertilizer) and Poudrette (OFG produced from cattle manure and bird droppings).

Around that same time, technology was being researched in Bashkiria to produce organo-mineral granules (OMG) from any kind of manure. Its developer, Doctor of Industrial Science Oleg Vladimirovich Tarkhanov, worked out a unique, low-cost process to produce a ton of OMG while expending only 220 pounds (100 kg) of fuel and 100 kW of electricity. A ton costs $130-$140—five time cheaper than analogous European products. Also, the efficacy of the Bashkir OMG is extremely high. A single application of 1,800 pounds per acre (2 t/ha) increased yields by 550–700 pounds per acre (600–800 kg/ha)—four years in a row.

As it turns out, you can improve just about anything— even manure! We now have rational methods *to return all manure to the fields*. Why they have not been sought out and utilized by the whole world remains a riddle to me.

Compost tea

Infusions of organic matter are excellent liquid fertilizers. Besides providing nutrients, they contain multitudes of living microbes, stimulators, and bioactive substances. They have been used in traditional Russian agriculture for ages. Manure, compost, or fecal matter is covered with water and allowed to steep for 2–3 weeks with occasional stirring. Ashes, plants, and grasses can be added as well. For example, you can fill a 50-gallon (200-liter) barrel with 2 pounds (1 kg) of ashes, a couple buckets of compost or greens, and a bucket of manure or fecal matter (or a half-bucket of bird droppings). The resulting tea, diluted down another two-three times, can be poured directly onto plantings.

Lately, various kinds of liquid compound fertilizers have been appearing on the market. All of them are dark, murky liquids—cocktails based on extracts made from peat, compost, or worm castings. On the whole, they are more beneficial than individual fertilizers or stimulators. This is as you would expect: the closer in composition a compound is to living compost, the more reliable its effect.

You can prepare a highly complex "punch" in barrels by adding yeast, lactic acid bacteria, or hay bacillus. This will be covered in a later chapter on feeding plants.

Earthworm essentials

A rooster dreamed about a worm,
"Oh, boy! Now there's a great snack!"
"What a nightmare!" thought the little worm,
And rolled over onto its back.

Recently, I was researching vermiculture—raising earthworms—and the production of biohumus for a Russian company. Reading so many paeans in scientific literature to worms is impressive, but seeing with your own eyes how millions of these practical little creatures transform manure into soil's most valuable organic substance is simply extraordinary. Worms deserve a good book all to themselves! Here is a summary of my principal discoveries.

First of all, we are definitely blind. Like Krylov's pig under the oak tree,* we do not recognize who our real friends are, simply because we do not care to observe and reflect on what we see. We domesticate all imaginable and unimaginable

animals, but the most important of them—the earthworm—
we hardly notice! The world is now beginning to understand
them properly. The common earthworm turns out to be a
veritable mother lode of blessings.

We have learned in textbooks that worms consume organic matter and loosen soil with their burrowing. They also
enrich it with nutrients and microbes, left behind in their
castings. We may think: "So what? Modern farming practices
do exactly the same thing!" But look at the final outcomes:
agrotechnology *destroys* soil fertility while worms *create* it.
Earthworms are the basis and primary attribute of fertility.
In fact, it is the very presence of worms which is now considered the primary strategic indicator of soil potential. If
worms are present, the soil is alive. If they are absent, it is
already too late to even speak of fertility!

Three types of worms work in the soil: on the surface are
the red composters, in the topsoil the pink tillers, and in the
subsoil the large colorless burrowers. Together they create
ideal soil conditions for plants. Above all, they construct the
soil's architecture. The composters penetrate the surface organic matter with their burrows, mixing and dissipating it
under the mulch. Their castings become food for the tillers.
These dig vertical passageways—ducts for water and air to
pass into the soil, and feeding channels for young rootlets.
The remains of roots and the castings of the tillers become
food for the burrowers. They complete the overall system
of channels with their horizontal burrows at depths of half
a meter or more. The entire network can increase the volume of soil air by 25%! These channels are the trachea and

---

* In this fable, a pig chews on an oak tree's roots, unable to understand the connection between the oak and the acorns which sustain
the pig's life. [trans]

bronchi, the arteries and veins of the soil. Is there any type of farming equipment in existence which is capable of producing an equally impressive result?

Scientists have long known the benefit of compost—its crumbly texture, water holding capacity, humus, microbes, and biologically active substances—but worm casts* upstage everything. In a literal sense, casts are highly concentrated "kernels" of fertility. Science has yet to discover a more complex system of microbes, organic matter, and mineral constituents combined so ingeniously and effectively together.

Worm casts are held together by fungal mycelia and endure in the soil for a long time. They contain high concentrations of nutrients and biologically active substances as well as an abundance of microflora. Concentrations of beneficial microbes are hundreds of times higher in worm casts than in the surrounding soil. Especially numerous are nitrogen fixers, nitrifiers, and microbes which serve the root zone. Worm casts literally radiate a favorable microbial environment. For tiny roots, casts are a veritable gift—powerful stimulators to vigorous development. One cast furnishes the nutrients and microbial population for many inches of root growth.

It is a shame not to utilize the biochemical uniqueness of worm casts. Back in 1990, the Russian scientist Igor Nikolaevich Titov discovered how to make a special alkaline extract from biohumus. It exerted a powerful, multidimensional, stimulatory effect on various plantings. This preparation was given the name Humisol and is currently produced by several companies. Working at GreenPeak, Titov later

---

* *Worm casts*—bits of worm excrement. They have a special name because of their unique qualities and special role in soil formation.

produced Humistar—an improved preparation enriched with complex nutrients and trace minerals.

I know many people who successfully raise worms. However, you should understand that there is no point in hunting down "thoroughbred" worms—for example, California Reds. It has been shown that in good conditions with an abundance of food any red worms will triple their productivity—both in appetite and rate of procreation. So it really does not matter! Even the purest-bred worms, if they experience stress and poor living conditions, will lose their "high-cultured attributes."

The most essential thing is good "wormiculture." As with plants and aquarium fish, you need to understand them, to know how to create proper conditions for them. For instance, it is important to realize that worms cannot tolerate temperatures over 95°F (35°C) or an excess of water—i.e., soil drips when squeezed. Also, if their usual food is abruptly changed, worms will stop reproducing, and only the next generation, accustomed to the new diet, will gradually again gain momentum. Finally, ammonia and hydrogen sulfide are deadly poisons to worms, so manure provided for them should be partially rotted.

Worms are very ingenious, and there are many subtleties to their behavior which will greatly facilitate your working with them. Quite a lot of literature has been written about this. In my book *Greenhouse Gardening with a Smile*, my personal experiences with worms are described in great detail.

The benefits of worms are not limited to their work in the soil. After all, worms are biologically unique in nature. They can regenerate their bodies, restoring living tissue. Medical researchers have discovered amazing active substances in them. Numerous studies conducted in the United States, China, and India have demonstrated that "worm preparations" can efficiently rejuvenate tissue and impede the progress of many diseases, even cancer. This has made worms a subject of active research for many medical researchers and cosmetologists.

But our overall theme here is organic matter. In order for worms and microbes to produce fertility, they require massive amounts of organic plant matter. I can already hear you exclaim: "You know, organic matter is not always so easy to come by!" But I can say quite honestly that, in fact, it is hardly in short supply! Organic matter is everywhere, all around you—wherever you look on any wasteland or abandoned field. But it is mostly left unused. As soon as you begin to need it, you will notice it everywhere. I do!

Mulch and other coverings for garden beds

All you need is... mulch!

Variant: *Everyone knows that nature is divine. But few realize the divinity of rotting straw!*

In nature, mulch is the layer of loose organic matter which covers the soil—or more simply, a covering of any material. Where we live in Southern Russia (Zone 6), it is definitely necessary—it helps maintain stable temperatures and moisture levels in the soil. Without mulch, we either have to hoe every day, or plants fry in the sweltering sun. When it is hot, most gardeners rush out to water their garden, but pouring water onto bare soil is a Sisyphean task: a bucket poured out onto a square yard saturates the soil at most 1–2 inches (3–4 cm)—

and this water can completely evaporate in half a day in the sun! This is what compelled me to research mulch.

Mulch can consist of soil, organic materials, plastic, or cloth. We will examine each of these in turn.

MULCH FROM SOIL consists of a layer of tiny clods which we produce through constant chopping, cultivating, and loosening of the soil after irrigation or rain. It does, in fact, conserve moisture but is very tricky: it only conserves moisture until the next rain soaks through it, and it only works if you are very addicted to hard work. It is not unlike suggesting that paper be used for roofing material, arguing that a good home owner should completely reroof his house after every rain or strong wind! In the same way, we splash water out of a hose onto the soil which quickly creates a hard crust on the surface, so then we can again reach for our favorite hoe. Furthermore, constantly loosening the soil disperses spores of potato blight, peronospora, and other fungi, all of which overwinter in the soil.

MULCH FROM ORGANIC MATTER. This section is a collection of my own experiences, recent research by American organic gardeners, and the results of prewar experiments by Russian vegetable farmers.

Straw is one of the most available mulching materials. It is spread over beds around plant seedlings in a 4- to 6-inch-thick layer (10–15 cm) after the soil warms up in the spring; in a month or two it will settle down to 2–2.5 inches (4–6 cm). This is the ideal thickness for mulch, producing maximum beneficial effect.

Straw is light-colored which reflects the sun well, cooling the soil. It also retains moisture and is an excellent weed suppressant. It is nearly impossible for weeds to penetrate through a layer of flattened straw. Placed between rows of strawberries, it prevents the berries from rotting. After all, in English they are called *straw-berries*. Mulch also protects tomatoes from rotting when in contact with the soil. Potatoes piled high with straw grow one-and-a-half times better and have fewer beetles since it is difficult for them to reach the surface. Fall-planted onions and garlic, perennials, and root crops left in the soil "sleep" peacefully under straw. A straw mulch is a long-lasting "blanket" for covering the garden "bed."

Hay is less enduring and does not smother weeds nearly as well. However, it is richer in nutrients and quickly forms a healthy layer of humus. Unfortunately, it can be full of seeds. Therefore, I do not put it on beds. On the other hand, it is great for choking out grasses in new beds, and for spreading around the trunks of trees and bushes. Its other merits are the same as straw.

Sawdust, wood chips, and wood shavings do an excellent job of blocking off heat and preserving moisture. They are different than straw and hay in that weeds easily grow right through them. Even under a thick layer, only annuals are successfully smothered; perennials can work their way up to the surface.

When finally consumed by fungus, sawdust forms a nutrient-rich layer of humus. In the Altai Region of Siberia, the agronomist Alexander Kuznetsov has covered his entire fruit tree nursery with sawdust for many years, and his saplings flourish together with the fungi. As it turns out, fungi living beneath a layer of sawdust form a mycorrhizal* association with roots of cultivated plants. You can even learn to cultivate mycorrhizal fungi, such as common stinkhorn mushroom (*Phallus impudicus*)!

I recommend that only weathered sawdust—that which has lain around for a couple months and turned dark—be spread over a bed planted in vegetables: fresh sawdust can be very chemically aggressive. American experiments have shown, however, that woody mulches do not deprive the soil of nitrogen. Woodchips are best spread between rows and on pathways since they decompose very slowly.

Bran siftings, chaff, and rice hulls are residues from the dehulling of grain with similar qualities to sawdust, but richer in nutrients. They are an ideal material which you can dig directly into the soil.

Grass clippings are rich in nutrients, provide nitrogen to the soil, and are excellent at conserving moisture. Spread them in a fairly thick layer; as they dry they will significantly decrease in volume. Once compacted, grass clippings

---

* *Mycorrhiza*—literally *"fungus root"*—is a symbiosis between fungi and roots. The mycelia of many kinds of fungi penetrate small rootlets. In exchange for sugars from roots, fungi supply roots with water and minerals. It has been suggested that it is fungi which provide soil cohesion and information exchange between all the plants of an ecosystem.

quickly "ignite" and become moldy. Therefore, it is better to let them wilt first before spreading. The same can be said about green leaves.

Dried leaves are an excellent mulch which weeds cannot penetrate. They are a good autumn material for covering the soil through winter.

Shredded paper is similar to woodchips, but it decomposes very quickly. An inch-thick layer (3 cm) of shredded paper smothers weeds completely and conserves moisture. Printers ink* may contain poisonous substances and heavy metals, so it is best not to get carried away with newspapers and magazines in the garden. As for cardboard boxes, use as many as you like!

All the above materials are light-colored and reflect the sun well. They should be spread around heat-loving plants (tomatoes, cucumbers, peppers, eggplants) later in the spring, after the soil has warmed up. Cabbages, peas, and potatoes can be covered earlier, immediately after planting. It is good to mulch over the first mat of young weeds, since under a thick mulch they will graciously perish.

Following are examples of dark, warm "blankets."

Compost and humus make very healthful mulches for plants. Saprophytic** microbes in compost excrete copious amounts of protective antibiotics. A 1- to 2-inch layer (3–5 cm) spread onto beds is plenty. Such a layer obstructs spores which are released from the soil in the spring, and its microbes suppress pathogenic fungi. Knowing that compost quickly settles and is subsequently dispersed by worms,

---

* *Printers ink*—most magazines and newspapers printed in developed countries now use non-toxic inks and are deemed safe to use as mulch. [trans]

I spread it more thickly, up to 4 inches (10 cm). If you cover a trampled down mat of young weeds with compost, most of them will die, although some new shoots may manage to grow through. You can also sow and transplant directly into compost. In order to prolong and strengthen the effect of compost, I cover it with a layer of sawdust or grass (Photograph 3).

Peat moss from the surface of bogs is light-colored, but deeper down it is dark, almost black. Surface peat is acidic and very poor in nutrients, best used to loosen soils. Darker peats are a good source of humates.[***] Peat moss is even more friable than rotted compost and compacts less, but it contains almost no nutrients. It is best mixed with nutrient rich organic matter.

Sunflower seed shells do not smother weeds at all but preserve moisture fairly well. They have two drawbacks: first, they are black, which may cause overheating of the soil. Second, fresh shells are chemically aggressive and may suppress young seedlings. Therefore, I apply them in the fall, or use spent shells from oyster mushroom[****] cultivation. I spread them directly onto vegetable and flower beds, or add them to the compost pile.

Bark, needles, and clay pellet residues are less available yet valuable all the same. Both bark and needles require two

[**] *Saprophytes*—organisms which feed on dead organic matter. All microbes and fungi which decompose plant residues are saprophytic.

[***] *Humates*—fundamental substances in humus, humic acid salts. They have a stimulatory effect. Many fertilizers based on humates are currently on the market.

[****] *Oyster mushroom*—an edible mushroom, saprophytic, which feeds on dead cellulose. Where we live in the south, it is often cultivated on sunflower seed shells.

months of aging to release volatile chemical compounds. Afterwards, they make an excellent mulch and soil loosener. Clay pellet residues do not suppress weeds or feed the soil, but they preserve moisture well. In the fall, it is easy to incorporate them into the ground, greatly increasing water-holding capacity and loosening soil.

Dark mulches warm up well, and it is better to spread them in the fall. In the spring, you can sow directly into the mulch in a furrow made with a small hoe. Seeds will sprout up well.

MULCH FROM MAN-MADE MATERIALS. As far back as the 1920s, Michurin wrote that Americans were successfully covering plantations "with paperboard saturated in tar" (i.e., tar paper, asphalt felt). After his article, Soviet farmers began using this practice as well. Similar materials were widely tested and utilized on a large scale on many of our farms. In textbooks of the 1930s and 1940s, mulch was a well-accepted practice which produced substantial benefits. Although the war interfered with research and development along these lines, it was subsequently renewed with the appearance of plastic sheeting.

Now plastic sheeting and other nonwoven synthetic materials are commonly used for mulching. All of them completely block weeds and conserve water well, but do not feed the soil. If fertility is not augmented with applications of organic matter, the soil soon becomes exhausted.

Paper and cardboard are flimsy, but they will rot. Packing board is a good way to smother weeds and conserve moisture. Cardboard works well for covering pathways and areas where pumpkins and melons will spread, as well as for plots to be cleared of weeds. Both potato beds and paths between rows can be covered completely. Transplants should be planted through small crosses cut into it with a knife. Be sure to heel in the edge of the cardboard; otherwise, weeds grow through the holes, and the soil dries out quickly. Newspapers should be overlapped, in 3- or 4-sheet layers; kraft paper (brown paper bags) in 2-sheet layers. Humus binds heavy metals found in printers ink, but nevertheless you should avoid using newspapers more than 2–3 times* on a particular bed.

Sackcloth and textiles suppress full-grown weeds excellently—I often use them for this. However, young weeds, especially grasses, easily poke through them. Woven fabrics "breathe," allowing the passage of air and water, and often even light. Therefore, the soil underneath can quickly dry out. On the other hand, you can water directly through the material, and a stream of water will not wash away or compact the soil—a big plus.

Black plastic mulch. The first reaction of Russian gardeners to black plastic is usually: "But it can't breathe! The roots will suffocate!" Remember, though, that soil only breathes when it has a way of breathing—i.e., a structure of pores and channels. If structure exists, the soil will actively breathe through those same holes which the plants grow out of. If there is no structure, the soil suffocates no matter what, even if you cultivate it every day. In my experience, even under "non-breathing" plastic, soil structure improves, because the plastic conserves moisture so well. During cool times of the day, condensation will precipitate onto the underside of the plastic, draining down into the soil. This is a big plus! But plastic does not decompose into humus—a big minus. This means that you should use

* Again, the magazines and newspapers printed in developed countries are now deemed safe to use as mulch. [trans]

plastic only on soils which have an abundance of organic matter.

People also fear that black plastic will become severely overheated in the sun. Yes, that is true. However, it is the plastic itself which heats up, not the soil. Black plastic does not create a greenhouse effect,* inasmuch as it does not allow light to pass through it.

Polyethylene plastic is the cheapest but also the least durable—it breaks apart in a year or two. Gardeners sometimes cover plastic to protect it from the sun, spreading straw, sawdust, or grass on top of it. Fortunately, very long-lasting plastics have recently appeared even on the Russian market—for instance, the plastic Svetlitsa from the Petersburg company Shar. The cost is higher than polyethylene, but due to their improved strength and durability, they prove to be two or three times less expensive in the end.

Tar paper—now somewhat out-of-date, it is nevertheless still sold for covering flat roofs. It lasts on beds for 3–4 years. No noxious fumes are given off, since tar is a natural substance. You lay it down with the sanded side facing upwards. It works very well with strawberries. The main problem with tar paper is its stiffness. You have to be very careful while working with it, or it will tear.

Plastic is widely utilized as a non-reusable material for mulching industrial-scale plantings of vegetables, melons, squash, and strawberries. Changing it every year is fairly

---

* *Greenhouse effect*—radiant sunlight passes through clear plastic (or glass) and heats up the soil. The warm soil then begins to radiate heat—infrared rays—which are reflected back by the clear plastic. The plastic becomes a "trap" for these infrared rays. The air is heated by the soil, and this warm air cannot escape to the outside, causing overheating. The smaller the volume and better sealed the greenhouse, the greater the greenhouse effect.

expensive and troublesome, so mostly it is used for strawberries. Plantings remain for three years. Weeding is not necessary, and watering is minimal—only during severe drought.
Water is poured right on top, and it drains through the plant
holes, where it is evenly distributed under the mulch. Berries
will not rot—they stay dry and clean—and runners cannot
take root. Strawberries only have to be harvested, pruned,
and fertilized—that's it! But the following subtleties should
be taken into consideration (see illustration).

After preparing a bed and covering it with a layer of fresh
compost, roll out plastic (or tar paper) onto the surface, carefully heeling in the edges. If the mulch is not sealed, the soil
beneath will dry out quickly. Next, gently press down where
the rows will be located—water will accumulate there. I repeat: do not tear out the plant hole. Large holes will make
all your hard work be for naught—the soil will dry out, and
weeds will grow through the holes. Cut a cross with a knife,
the smaller the better. Poke through each hole with a stick,

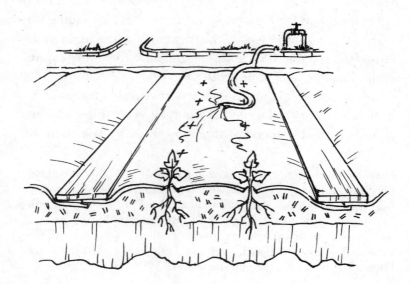

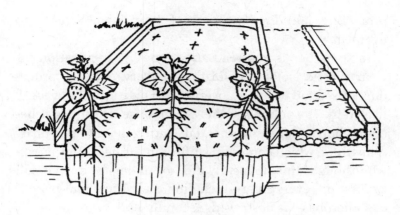

and with this same stick carefully push in the plant. Cover the roots in the hole with sand or friable soil, and lightly tamp it down. It never hurts to spread another handful of earth around each plant. Weeds should not even suspect that there is light above them to grow towards, although all the same they do sometimes manage to "nose their way out" into the light.

If a planting is large, first level and fertilize the entire area. Next, completely cover it over with plastic (or tar paper) overlapped at the edges, and lay boards along the joints. Only walk on top of the boards. You must never walk on the mulch! This is a general rule for any mulch.

Transparent coverings. *Clear plastic* produces a strong greenhouse effect and therefore is not suitable as a summer mulch. On the other hand, it serves well for covering composting beds during cold times of the year, from autumn through spring. Compost continues rotting all winter long, and nutrients will not be washed away by rains. You can also use clear plastic to cover compost and manure piles—they will rot more quickly and retain their nutrient value better. In the summer, plastic should only be used as a roof for rain protection; laid directly on top of the pile will cause it to overheat.

In some books you read about another application for clear plastic: solar sterilization—a very peculiar procedure! A section of soil is covered with plastic and the edges heeled in. The volume of the "greenhouse" is tiny, so it becomes horrendously overheated. During the summer, nearly anything which comes up withers in the heat. The person who thought this up clearly did not understand what soil is. First off, everything—including the worms and beneficial microbes—is destroyed. Secondly, early-season weeds, despite the intense heat, still manage to go to seed. So why do it at all?

Intelligent uses for transparent coverings like cold frames and cloches will be discussed later.

Nonwoven synthetic materials such as Spunbond are nearly as transparent, but they "breathe." Furthermore, they reflect a lot of sunlight, providing partial shading. On warm days, the ground will not overheat underneath them—a huge plus! But the soil dries out rather quickly—this is a minus. Sprinkler irrigation will percolate through them but should only be used on immature plants since sprinkling exacerbates fungal diseases. This means that these materials are utilized mainly for covering newly-planted crops and transplants, for spring or fall greens and radishes, and for protecting strawberries from frost. Stretched over a frame, they protect cucumbers and tomatoes from morning dew, and eggplants from the Colorado beetle. For more serious applications, these coverings are too flimsy and short-lived to be warranted.

Mulch to suppress weeds and clear new ground

There are no bad plants. There are only farmers who don't know how to use them.

Permaculturists and organic gardeners often utilize the following intelligent method for establishing new beds.

In May, trample down the lush young meadow grasses, smashing them flat. They will be a veritable gift to worms. If the soil is poor, scatter some manure or bird droppings, or even mineral fertilizer, on top of the grass. Then spread paper over the top of this: a 2- or 3-sheet layer of newspapers, brown paper bags, or used packaging—whatever is available. You can even lay down packing board. Next spread a thick layer (4–5 inches or 10–12 cm) of nutrient-rich organic matter directly over this paper mulch—e.g., partially-rotted

STRAW

MANURE

CARDBOARD

WEEDS

SOIL

manure or unfinished compost. There will be time for this to finish decomposing later. This "layer cake" is topped off with "whipped cream": straw, leaves, and grasses in a 2-inch (5–6-cm) layer (Photograph 4). The cardboard (or paper) blocks out all new weeds. The compost layer preserves moisture, provides nutrients, and decomposes the cardboard (or paper) beneath. The top layer of straw protects the compost from the sun and the seedlings from birds.

In the first year, you should not sow small seeds in the new bed; rather, seedlings of larger plants are transplanted—squash, pumpkins, melons, tomatoes, peppers, eggplants, as well as potatoes and yams—in the following manner: pull apart the straw and make a small depression in the organic matter. Then pierce the paper on the bottom with a trowel; the roots themselves will find a path downward. Next, set the transplant or tuber into the depression and fill in soil around it; this protects the plant from the fresh organic matter before it fully decomposes. Water well and pile straw "up to their ears." If it rains during the summer, no more watering will be required. By the next year, the mulch will have settled and turned to compost, the soil will be well-structured, and after gathering an abundant harvest, you will be left with a weed-free organic bed. Afterwards, you only have to apply more compost each year and sow whatever you like.

We make new beds even more simply. First, we set frames made of boards or logs right on top of meadow grasses—3 feet (1 m) wide by 16 feet (5 m) long. Next, we spread a couple wheelbarrows of manure directly onto the grass, followed by a layer of paper or cardboard, some compost or more manure, and topped off with straw. That first year, we plant squash, potatoes, and tomatoes.

Or you can create a new bed in this way: after enclosing the bed in a frame, dig several large holes directly through the grasses, fill them with organic matter, and plant toma-toes in them. The young transplants start growing, but the grasses shoot up three times faster. After these grasses have yielded a good "harvest," but before they overrun the trans-plants, knock them down, covering them first with paper, and then with a thick layer of mown grass, humus, seed hulls, or whatever is available. If you keep adding more grass and greens all summer long, there will be very little weeding to do. Water thoroughly once a week.

Kitchen wastes as well as grasses and weeds can be added to the bed all summer long. Worms will proliferate in mas-sive quantities, transforming everything into humus. In this way, it is possible to significantly raise the fertility of a bed in just a couple years. What you have is called a "Finnish bed." If the Finns of the North can mulch soil in this way, then certainly, with our sun and dry conditions, God would will that we can, too!

Siberian gardeners make this even simpler: they cover vir-gin meadowland with a very thick layer of cut weeds, adding more and more through the summer. The following spring a good, reasonably fertile soil is ready for planting potatoes, which are hilled up using those same weeds and straw. Then they sow a green manure crop, followed by a planting of phacelia in the early spring. Next they sow vegetables, fol-lowed by another green manure crop. And likewise for all subsequent years. The soil improves before their eyes, and the harvests keep increasing.

The very best mulch is natural and organic. It is compact enough to smother weeds, yet loose enough to breathe. It also protects plants from disease, provides massive amounts of nutrients, and propagates the soil creatures. In conclusion, do not allow plant residues to rot away on wastelands or in compost factories, but rather in your very own garden!

The most natural soil amendment

*Come spring, a dense stand of sunflowers will
quickly comb out the dust from the shaggy thatch
of your thoughts!*

Life on our planet is based on plants. Only they know
how to produce organic matter from air and sunlight.
Plants were the first to emerge onto the land. They essentially created the animals; they manufactured the soil.
Even the atmosphere which we breathe was produced by
plants.

From the time it first sprouts, a plant is constantly per-
forming the prodigious task of improving soil; after all, the
soil is its home and will be the home of its offspring. As its
roots develop, the plant creates soil structure, leaving organic matter in channels for microbes and worms. It shades
the soil, conserving moisture. It consolidates the soil, preventing water and wind erosion. And after dying, it leaves a
tiny bit of humus on the soil surface—bequeathing its entire
body to its descendants!

One can say without exaggeration that the life of a plant is
unselfish service to future plants, which means, in fact, to all
life. How well we have allowed ourselves to be brainwashed,
forgetting this truth and not utilizing it in our gardens!

We have been taught that bare, weed-free soil is the way to
go. But in reality—especially in hot areas—bare soil means
death. It is compaction, desiccation, lack of structure, and,
ultimately, complete loss of fertility. One of the command-
ments of intelligent farming is: be afraid of uncovered
ground! Do not leave the earth without mulch or plant cover
for even a single day. *Use every possible means to structure
and fertilize the soil with the assistance of plants.*

There is plenty of time to do this in early spring and in the fall—in the tropics throughout the entire year. And we have truly remarkable plants at our disposal to help us: cereal grains and corn, amaranth, sunflowers, rape and mustard, annual lupines, and vetch. And weeds, too—they improve the soil better than anything else! In the spring, you need only to mow down their lush, green carpet at the proper time.

The inventor of the multipurpose hoe, Vladimir Fokin, always utilized everything available to him: "If you have some leftover seeds, ones you don't need or which are out-of-date, don't throw them away but, instead, sow them densely over cleared ground." Root crops are truly a luxury: "Sow root crops in July and August, and leave the roots with their tops in the ground through the winter. When everything

rots down, the soil creatures will receive an abundance of food!" Also, many substandard seeds—factory rejects—are left over after grading sugar beet seeds. They are very cheap, and their viability of 50–60% is perfectly fine for a green manure crop. An August sowing of sugar beets is an outstanding cover crop!

Green manures—these are plants or combination of plants grown for the purpose of structuring the soil, enriching it with nitrogen and organic matter, and raising minerals from the subsoil to the surface. Traditionally, they are plowed in. However, Edward Faulkner demonstrated why they should, in fact, not be plowed. Dug deeply into the soil, greens take a long time to break down. Furthermore, the buried plant layer can form an artificial barrier—subsoil moisture cannot rise from below, and it is difficult for roots to penetrate downward. These soils also dry up very quickly. In the meantime, the plow has completely nullified the structural effect of roots, and a mulch of humus has not been left to cover the surface. Everything is backwards!

It would be much wiser to dig in the young green manure to a depth of only 1 inch (2–3 cm) with a cultivator, Fokin hoe, or razor hoe (more about this later), intermixing it with mulch or simply leaving it on the surface. Under these conditions it rots quickly, releasing nutrients and eventually converting into humus. An even more intelligent technique is to trample down the green manure and pile it high with straw or grass. But it is very important to do this at the proper time—never allow green manure to go to seed.

If a bed is being prepared for root crops or greens, the soil should be temporarily cleared for sowing. In this case, it is much easier to work with young, lush annual green manures. For instance, thickly sown sunflowers are easy to cut down before they reach knee-height, or rape before it starts flowering. But if you are planting potatoes or bushy vegetables, you just push down the green manure and cover it over with a thick layer of organic matter.

Powerful plants like corn or sorghum have very tough stems, so it is better to leave them until spring—they will be killed off by the frost. Perennials like alfalfa are suitable only for orchards and perennial sods. If you try to cut them down with a hoe, you will sweat your guts out!

Weeds, of course, can always be pulled up by the roots—it is sometimes difficult to swing a hoe in a dense bed. Leave them lying on the bed, and you will truly be blessed. They too are organic matter and are useful to you; they just grew "without your permission"!

Following is a description of how Russian vegetable gardeners use green manure in their beds.

On beds designated for heat-loving plants, green manures are sown on warm days during early planting windows in February and March. We sow seeds densely and work them in with a rake. A verdant carpet soon covers the bed. Before plants begin to coarsen as they mature, we cut them down, leaving them right there on the bed. If we have some rotted compost available, we spread some on top. Then we transplant seedlings directly into the wilting tops of the green manure.

After harvesting early crops—potatoes, onions, carrots, and garlic—we always try to sow a second planting. In the south, we can plant carrots, beets, cucumbers, endive, squash, radishes, daikon, and greens in the beginning of July, or at the end of August—potatoes, lettuce, radishes, mustard, and other greens. If for some reason we do not plant a second crop, we sow a green manure immediately after the harvest. The beds grow a luxuriant green before the advent of cold weather when they freeze. At that point, we broadcast a new batch of seeds directly among the dying green manure, loosening the soil between rows with a Fokin hoe. In the spring, these seeds sprout up by themselves.

A brief digression about the grass rotation system of Vasily Williams

Alas, history never teaches us anything. It's time for it to turn in its resignation!

Which plants are suitable to plant as green manure in a large field? First and foremost, perennial legumes: alfalfa, lupine, sainfoin, clover, and goat's rue (*Galega officinalis*). Legumes are richer in nitrogen than other forage—symbiotic nitrogen-fixing bacteria live among their roots. And legume roots can penetrate downward for more than four meters. Also, they give two cuttings of hay during the summer, which compensate for the extra cost of planting them.

The originator of the grass rotation system of farming in Russia, Vasily Robertovich Williams, demonstrated that legumes vigorously create a crumb structure in soils interlaced with innumerable natural channels. For three out of eight years, fields are planted in a mix of legumes and grasses which are harvested as forage. Afterwards, the soil will store significantly more water, humus levels will be raised, and the efficiency of fertilizers and yields greatly increased.

Williams cites interesting data to support this. He started with the premise that plants can assimilate nutrients only when there is *optimal* moisture in the soil.

Moisture in a plowed (unstructured) soil constantly fluctuates from oversupply to acute shortage; as a result, plants feed normally only about half the time. This means that both watering and feeding plants are only about 50% efficient. The probability of average rainfall is also around 50%. So it turns out that labor productivity on such fields is no greater than 25%. This further implies that all the various sectors which serve agriculture are losing a comparable proportion of their production. Four times more fuel is consumed than necessary, and half the production of the farm equipment and agrochemical industries goes to waste. Consequently, agricultural processors receive raw materials at two or three times their real cost. In the end, we must conclude that Russian citizens are paying three times as much as they should for food products and other essential necessities!

"These factors have not all been fully researched, but imagine what such research might reveal!" argued Williams in numerous articles. He strongly believed that this did not

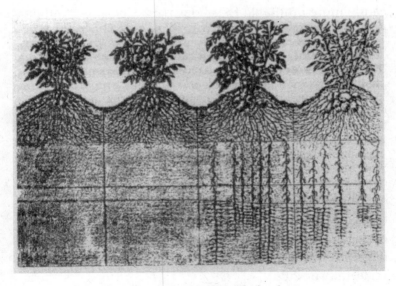

To the right: potatoes planted after lupine.

need to be the case. Actually, this Titan of scientific thought had a bit of titanic naïveté as well! Just imagine: everyone labors twice as much as they have to, and purchases products for twice as much as they should cost. The Soviet government could only dream of this! And so the free and prosperous collective farmers of those times were declared "enemies of the people."

Have things really changed that much today? Picture the farmer who knows how to increase the fertility of his fields to double the harvest at half the cost. Is he free and happy? Quite the opposite. More likely he arouses suspicions and attacks by the various offices which regulate "proper farming methods." They seek out such farmers not to learn from them but to impose fines on them.

A review of history confirms that *no government has ever promoted true restoration of natural fertility*. High fertility of soils is not profitable for the powers-that-be! It is significantly more profitable to sell farmers expensive products, fuel, equipment, and chemicals. This is how it has always been, and this is how it still is. I do not know of a single country which is seriously concerned about its soils and cutting costs of the harvest.

In 1939, Williams passed away, and his grass rotation system disappeared from view. Soviet science became based on the agronomy of Prianishnikov, and before long we were outstripping all other countries in the production of chemical fertilizers. Yet harvests continued to fall. And they still continue to fall while production costs increase throughout the world, despite all the advancements in agricultural science. And so they will fall until science, contrary to business interests, begins teaching agronomists to restore the natural fertility of soils.

But to return to cover crops: despite their value on farms, perennial legumes are of little use to gardeners—their woody stems are difficult to cut down, and many will grow up again from the roots. They are worth using for soil improvement in one way only: trample down a summer stand, pile it high with a thick layer of organic matter, and leave everything to rot until spring. There is no better method for preparing new garden plots.

For established beds, grains (wheat, rye, oats, barley) and crucifers (rape, Chinese radish, white mustard) are more appropriate. They are cold-tolerant, germinate quickly, and loosen the upper layer of soil. In the spring, you can sow vegetables right between rows of winter-killed plants.

It is a wholly different matter, however, if you want to quickly grow a large biomass for mulch. This calls for corn, sugar cane, millet, and broom and sweet sorghum. These are the so-called C_4 plants with enhanced photosynthesis. Their tripled biomass contains large amounts of sugars as well. A dense stand of 500 square feet (50 m^2) cut down in the middle of summer will mulch an entire garden.

A windbreak* of sunflowers and tall grains sown around the perimeter of the garden brings great benefit in the south. Windbreaks protect gardens from dry winds and heat, creating a mild microclimate. Cucumbers, which generally love shading, climb up the stout stalks with great relish (Photograph 21).

---

* *Windbreak*—a row or strip of several rows of tall plants sown to protect primary crops from sun and wind. In Russia, windbreak plantings of grains together with corn have been tested under various conditions. Harvests were nearly doubled. Windbreaks did not catch on, however, since "it is not as easy to harvest the field."

Any vegetable seeds you might otherwise throw away are also suitable for green manure. And be sure to consider weeds carefully before deciding to pull them up. For instance, garden purslane is edible, especially tasty when marinated. There is no need to remove the plant when young; just let it keep growing. You will be amazed at how much organic matter you'll get! And then there is common chickweed (*Stellaria media*). In the spring, it is good fresh in salads. Do not cut it down until it starts flowering; it is a good ground cover and helps conserve moisture. Actually, you do not have to cut it down at all—it will die on its own if covered with compost or seed hulls. In general, green manure is a creative endeavor.

"The farmer's primary task is to produce soil. We must give back more than we take from it. The earth itself will calculate the interest—no insignificant amount—for each person according to his service" (Vladimir Fokin).

Following are the fundamental **rules for using green manure**:

1. It is not worth growing perennial and thick-rooted plants unless you have a specific need to.
2. You should not let green manure crops grow too long. The more vigorous the plants, the earlier you should cut them down.
3. Sow green manures densely.
4. Try to broadcast seeds before harvesting or before spring cultivation so as not to spend extra time on planting.

The key point about soil exhaustion

Tractor tires are a surefire way to tire out soil!

From time immemorial, crop rotation has been utilized in raising vegetables and field crops. Essentially, this means that the same plants are not grown for several years in a row on the same plot (which otherwise causes pathogens to accumulate and harvests to decrease).

Most often this is due to the accumulation of disease. Also, soils become depleted of nutrients—the same or similar crops extract the very same nutrients from the soil. Furthermore, it has been suggested that roots of crops excrete certain toxins which cause soils to become toxic as they build up. But what are the real reasons for soil exhaustion?

A well-reasoned answer to this question can be found in a book by the brilliant Austrian viticulturist and scientist Lenz Moser. When confronted with soil exhaustion in his vineyard, he decided to set up hundreds of field experiments, from which he concluded that the main reason plants become weak over time is that specific substances—inhibitors—impede the growth of their roots. And it is the roots themselves which release these inhibitors; evidently, it is their way of inducing themselves to grow away from the original plant. And so plants develop properly only when new roots are continually leaving the "danger zone," thereupon opening up fresh areas of soil to grow in. This same mechanism allows seedlings located farther from the "mother plant" to survive better, and in this way they take over an area more quickly.

His experiments revealed that inhibitors are found in both roots and stems, and plants will react only to their own unique inhibitor—others do not bother them. Grape compost is toxic specifically to grapes, and wheat compost inhibits only wheat. If you wash "exhausted" soil with water, inhibitors are transferred into the solution. If you then water healthy plants on fertile soil with this solution, they grow feeble before your very eyes. It is important to understand that inhibitors suppress growth *even in the presence of abundant nutrients, moisture, and various protective measures.*

Clay binds these substances well, and so exhaustion rarely occurs on a moist loam, whereas on light soils it is very evident. Organic matter and microbes also play an important role, and green manure has proven to be particularly effective. After two years of growing a luxuriant cover crop and cultivating it in, Moser managed to wholly restore his soil from exhaustion.

The conclusion for us is obvious: by growing green manures and annually replenishing beds with compost, we can avoid soil exhaustion completely. However, compost in this case must live up to its name: "composed of various ingredients."

Another obvious conclusion is that you should never plant an apple tree into a hole where an apple tree grew previously, nor a new plum tree into a hole from a plum tree. Also, you should always try to grow a diverse variety of plants on beds. If you are not using either organic matter or green manure, you must rotate plants every year; otherwise, harvests will in time succumb to disease.

But now, if you don't mind, it is time to take a look at intelligent garden tools.

Not by hoe alone!

Something is always needed for something.
Wisdom

This section will illustrate that anything can always get better. Not without reason did Ovsinsky compare most brand-name farm equipment to the pitched stakes of ancient peoples. Not in vain did Williams point out the exact conditions and best types of equipment for intelligent cultivation, considering all the rest as harmful to soil and complete wastes of money. And not by accident did Vladimir Vasilievich Fokin find a way to garden after a severe heart attack limited his activity. He invented a multipurpose hoe which does nearly all gardening tasks except, perhaps, watering. If we only set ourselves the goal of improving our labor efficiency, every one of us can do the same.

A razor of a cultivator

The vegetable garden was shaved clean.
The gardener was slightly drunk.

The world has long used weeders similar to Fokin's multipurpose hoe, but in Russian post-war agriculture they became a rarity—gardeners are more accustomed to ordinary hoes and shovels. So we have to reinvent these tools using whatever materials are available. An acquaintance of mine, a flower grower named Valentin Levichkin, first showed a "razor" hoe to me. I made one—and have since thanked him many times over.

It is common to find old-fashioned "hand cultivators" purchased in the 1980s lying around unused in sheds. They are still sold today (Photograph 33). This is a simple tool mounted on a long handle with toothed wheels in front followed by a flat, sharpened stirrup having a slight free play of movement. The goal of this cultivator is noble: roll the tool along the ground and cut off weeds at their base. However, in practice it is a bit more complicated—weeds are constantly wrapping around the wheels which become caked with dirt. The stirrup part, however, is truly remarkable. The steel is of good quality, the free play is optimal, angles are correct, and the blade is sharp. Cut off the wheels (at the red mark on the

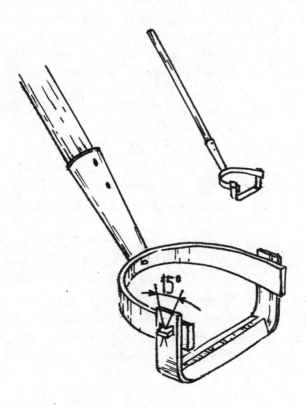

photograph), and you get an amazing, weed-cutting "razor" with very wide possibilities.

The razor is not hacked downward, like a regular hoe, but rather dragged along the surface of the ground. It is easier to pull it towards yourself, but with a little practice you can move it in both directions, carefully working the blade down into the soil about 0.5–1 inch (1–3 cm). This undercuts the weeds—even fairly mature ones—creating a loose, mulched layer on top of the soil. The razor is twice as efficient as an ordinary hoe, and if the space between rows is the same width, then three times. One pass, and the inter-row space is done.

It is very important to sharpen the edge on a regular basis. When dull, it operates incomparably worse, requiring twice as much effort.

Of course, if you have to cut down mature, coarse grasses, you will work up a good sweat and often have to shake out clogged grass. But the razor is not meant for tall weeds. In fact, you use it so that there will not be any tall weeds in the first place. Tall grasses are better removed with that "ax on a handle" which we call a hoe.

Here is another idea: instead of toothed wheels, you could attach ordinary wheels, like from a child's stroller. Then the razor would undercut weeds as it easily rolls forward and backward.

Since the first edition of this book, ten years have passed, and now similar implements can be found on the market. For instance, in Novosibirsk they make the cultivator-weeder Strizh. It is a nice little tool. Without doubt, its greatest asset is its self-sharpening blade. However, its handle is attached from above, directly onto the stirrup, and this greatly decreases the ease of working with it—although who knows what one can get used to in time!

The Fokin multipurpose hoe

He weeded peacefully, unhurriedly, and steadi-
ly—like a Colorado beetle.

Leaving the hospital and realizing that he could never take a shovel in hand again, Fokin did not despair. On the contrary, he invented the multipurpose hoe, which made it much easier for him to do his work. He patented it, arranged to have it manufactured, and wrote a detailed instruction booklet. For many years he cultivated a large vegetable garden with it.

You will notice that it is that same razor hoe described above but with one side removed (Photograph 34). The effect of this change is that, while the razor performs two functions, the multipurpose hoe performs twenty! It is a very clever little tool. The angles of all the bends are oblique, calibrated to the perfect degree. It is made of high-quality

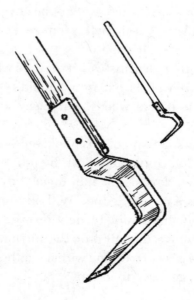

tool steel of optimal thickness, so it is lightweight, yet you can still pluck out mature weeds with confidence. It can be mounted on the handle in four different positions, depending on the operation. It takes just two minutes to change positions, and the efficiency of the new operation increases immediately. The entire booklet is dedicated to the multipurpose hoe, giving detailed instructions on various operations and how to use it. This is a truly intelligent tool—you must learn to work with it.

With the multipurpose hoe it is easy to loosen soil, to form beds, to make furrows and cover them over, to pull up and cut off weeds, and to poke out planting holes. You can cut plants down, hill them up, rake out grasses and stems, or cut off raspberry brambles and strawberry runners. You can chop or scrape with it, blend soil together, mix cement, etc. But a single fact speaks best to the efficacy of this implement: after his illness, Fokin and his wife were able to cultivate nearly half a hectare by themselves, always reaping an excellent harvest.

Over the last several years, the multipurpose hoe has spread throughout Russia. Along with many other interesting gardening tools, it is now manufactured by the company Sudogodsky Ploskorez—a factory in the city of Sudogda in the Vladimir Region.

Intelligent "hoes" of our ancestors

Let's invent something from olden times!

The drawing depicts a cultivator known as the Planet weeding harrow from *The Encyclopedia of Russian Agriculture* (F. Devrien Publications, 1902–1909).

This encyclopedia shows a wide variety of cultivators—hand-held and horse-drawn, one-, two-, and three-row. At the time, they could be found on every farm in Russia. All row crops were cultivated with them: potatoes, cabbages, tomatoes, peppers, eggplants, beets, and carrots. They were ten times more productive than hoes. As can be seen in the photograph, cultivation was by no means man's work. This immediately brings to mind very different images of fields

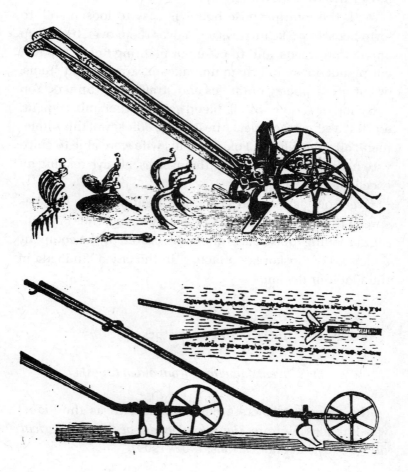

on Soviet State farms. A typical scene would show a bevy of old grannies, in groups or alone, working with their "square hoes" among the verdant greenery—by day on State farms, and after hours in their own vegetable gardens. They could be seen hacking away everywhere. As it turns out, compared to standard Soviet practices, the encyclopedia from a hundred years ago is incredibly "progressive"!

I believe that, if you tried hard enough, you could still find these tools somewhere. I encountered a similar unit manufactured in Ukraine in the 1960s in a client's garden. He praised it to the skies and was very surprised when I told him that it was not a modern invention. I realized then that I had to write about this.

Planet cultivators and similar tools rapidly disappeared after the war at the end of the 1940s. At that time, our nation started building tractors on a large scale, and no one cared about efficient hand labor anymore. How quickly we condemn intelligent tools to oblivion!

But in the end the Planet did produce offspring.

Cultivators of our times

Refusing to plow deeply does not mean you are shallow.

Modern-day hand cultivators, manufactured domesti-
cally by a few small companies, are essentially downgraded
Planets. They are highly streamlined and lighter weight, but
lack many valuable qualities of the original. Nevertheless,
they are much better than hoes. We are so used to "hacking"
with hoes that no one seems to care about these cultivators
anymore. I have tried to spark the interest of small equipment manufacturers, but so far to no avail, and they are very
hard to find for sale.

Occasionally, I encounter these machines at dachas.
Their owners all have the same look: they have been liber-
ated from the garden. Especially women: "I just wheel it
around for an hour or so, and everything is weeded—then

I go relax!" Elderly people accustomed to their cultivator would not part with it for anything.

It is very important to adjust the cultivator so that it does not dig down too deeply; it will then cut almost effortlessly. All you have to do is periodically lubricate the wheel and sharpen the blade.

Do-it-yourselfers customarily make the most successful new designs of personal tools. For example, Sergey Koliada of Krasnodar engineered a remarkable cultivator—light, mobile, easy-to-use, and optimally ergonomic. It is the best design I have seen (Photograph 35). Once you hold one, you will never want to give it back, but they are not that easy to make. Hopefully, the photograph will help you fabricate something even better.

Well, if you must dig, then...

Train hard, fight easy!

Alexander Suvorov

The various garden techniques mentioned above gradually improve the soil, but it takes time. Heavy clays, especially, progress very slowly. But what if you want to increase fertility quickly and substantially, and the amount of available organic matter is limited? In this case, **double digging** is necessary. This is a practice utilized in biointensive minifarming (see John Jeavons).

The heavy work is done only once but yields an immediate effect. The idea is to radically improve the soil layer up to 20–25 inches (50–60 cm)—to make soil crumbly and porous with better water and heat retention, and to blend it with compost and fresh organic matter. We only use this technique for certain beds because it is very labor intensive.

To begin, the necessary materials are assembled together near the future bed: compost, loose organic matter, and sand for a heavy loam, or clay and crushed stone for sandy soils. It is vital that soil be brought to optimal composition. The crushed stone is used to improve heat retention. You must dig when the soil is at the perfect moisture level; otherwise, you will not create proper structure. It is best to use a square trench shovel.

First off, we delineate the bed and mark one end by digging out a shovel-wide trench. The dirt from this strip is thrown to the side—it will not be needed until the end. We now have a crosswise trench one shovel deep and wide (see illustration).

This trench marks the beginning of our work. We pour a bucket of compost and a bucket of sand (for sandy soil a

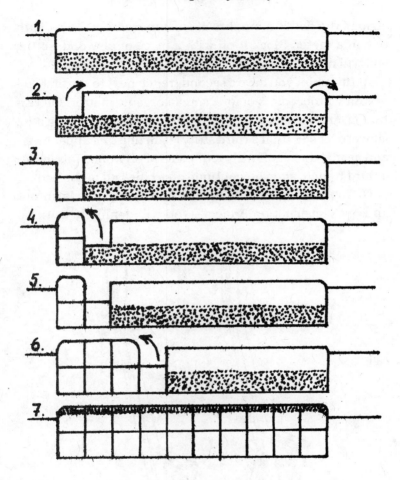

bucket of clay and crushed stone) along with a handful of some kind of compound fertilizer into the bottom. Spread everything into an even layer and dig it into the bottom of the trench a little at a time, mixing all the supplements with the soil and working them in as deeply as possible. The bottom layer is now done. Then shovel the next upper strip of soil (see illustration) onto it, again mixing in a bucket of organic matter, soil texturizer, and fertilizer. Now the first strip of the bed is a mixture of soil and compost to a depth of half a meter. Block it off with a piece of plywood, so the soil will not cave in.

At this point you have a second trench next to the first. Everything proceeds as before: spread organic matter, soil texturizer, and fertilizer onto the bottom of the trench; dig it in; shovel over soil from a third strip, fertilizing this upper layer; and again block it off with your piece of plywood. This leaves a third trench, and you continue on to the end of the bed.

Of course, double digging a bed in heavy clay is an out and out construction project—you will definitely work up

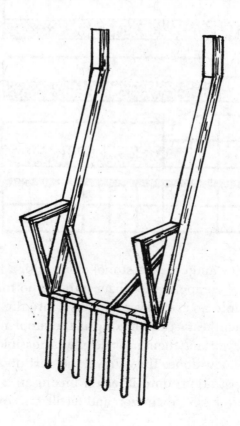

a sweat! But vegetables grown even in the first year will yield a bounteous harvest. In subsequent years, you simply loosen the upper layer of soil, adding more organic matter on top.

In order to loosen soil deeply in these beds without turning the soil over, you can use a *U-shaped garden broadfork* (or, as Fedor S. Leontiev calls it, "a wide-tine digger"). This tool breaks apart and shifts the soil, infusing it with air. Its tines extend down about 18 inches (45 cm), and the width of the area cultivated is around 28 inches (70 cm). However, a broadfork only works well in loose, organic soils. For denser soils, it is best to shorten the tines by half. It is especially good for loosening up beds which are the same width as the broadfork.

A brief summary of sensible agriculture

Let us advance civilization one garden at a time!

Gardeners of the world! I propose that we understand and acknowledge the following:

Soil is not just a mixture of chemicals and earth produced by our plows and cultivators. Soil is an elaborate and stable cohabitation of roots, plants, insects, worms, and microorganisms. These adapt themselves to the soil layer, so as to live and endure into eternity. They have already been doing this for millions of years, although we have just barely begun to understand how!

On 100 square feet of fertile ground, there are more than 6 pounds of fungi and microbes (3 kg/m^2). Often their life on this earth lasts from only thirty minutes to several hours. If there is food, they propagate at torrential speeds, constantly expelling the byproducts of their brief existence into the soil: digestive enzymes, vitamins, growth stimulators, antibiotics, and nutrients. Plants give sustenance to essential microbes and fungi, providing for them nearly half their organic matter. In exchange for this, microbes and fungi support and nourish the growing roots.

"From one pound of iron, a person can make a pound of nails. However, from a pound of seeds, nature, without any added labor or expense, can create a hundred pounds of produce," remarks Yuri Slashchinin. As he points out, Karl Marx, that sly fellow, composed his famous work *Capital* to prove that surplus value originates in labor, but it was only at the end of his four tomes on the subject that he finally admitted that the original source of absolute surplus value is nature—that is, the photosynthesis of plants. This is an obvious fact. The entire world economy is determined by a single factor: the fertility of our soils.

Solar energy use can be measured in terms of useful plant mass per hectare or square meter—not the harvest of a single planting, but the total for the entire year. Our agriculture still has not learned to fully utilize the sun! Ancient cultures measured the harvest in *selves*. A *self* was how much more you harvested than you sowed. Judging by the records of ancient Egypt and Sumeria, their grain harvests achieved 300 selves. Our best is about 30 selves.

Modern agricultural practices, chemical fertilizers, pesticides, and technology are an attempt to surround ourselves with costly prostheses and crutches, not bothering to use our own eyes, hands, and feet. Instead of utilizing our intelligence, the sun, and the natural vigor of plants, we pay huge sums of money to purchase fertilizers, chemicals, and fuel. I am convinced that we can correct this situation, beginning with our own garden plots!

Here is the gist of my advice to intelligent farmers. You might call it a **"Code of Intelligent Gardening."**

1. *Do not dig the soil without a definite need.* For loosening and creating structure, use organic wastes, mulch, compost, and green manures.
2. *Do not till the soil deeper than 2 inches (5 cm).* Deep tilling ruins soil structure. Create a friable upper layer, which produces the proper conditions for underground condensation.
3. *As with your favorite pet, feed and coddle the creatures of the soil.* Give back to the soil more organic matter than you take from it. Create compost directly on beds. Utilize everything that will rot. Raise anything that will grow.
4. *Never leave soil exposed.* Sow green manures! Time succession plantings, so that when one crop is harvested, a second is already emerging.
5. I personally would add: *consider things seven times over before believing recommendations urging you to expend more labor or money.* Everything you need is in nature. It is just that often we do not know how to utilize it!
6. *Do not hurry!* Organic matter is not like a shot of medicine, but a way of life on earth. Soil which has been ravished for decades will not be repaired in a year. It needs time to remake itself. Help it do this!

Switching to organic gardening practices is fascinating and rewarding—but certainly not easy. When organic matter and mulch are spread all at once onto bare soil, you might at first encounter various "misfortunes." Slugs and sowbugs may suddenly proliferate; mole crickets may appear; or mice multiply. *THIS IS NATURAL—after all, you have radically altered the ecosystem.* New food always generates an outburst of new mouths. But there is no need to panic. Following quickly on their heels will come predators and beneficial microbes, and after a few years everything will return to balance. The faster the predators multiply, the sooner it all bounces back. In the first two or three years of change, you must be vigilant. If your harvest is threatened, go ahead and suppress those hordes of pests as you can, but try not to harm the helpers.

* * *

The following chapter is for "lazy people." If you do not need a whole lot of vegetables, the area of ground you will have to cultivate can be measured in square feet.

Chapter 4

Beds With Varying Degrees Of "Intelligence"

or

Growing Vegetables in a Very Small Space

Small beds are the mother of invention!

Growing vegetables in very small spaces is my ideal and a favorite theme of my books. It can be rewarding and extremely interesting, but by no means is it quick or easy. I invite like-minded gardeners to share their experiences!

In the West, vegetables—especially greens and lettuce—are cultivated on small farms about the size of our typical rural lots—0.5 to 1.5 acres (0.2–0.5 ha). The most sophisticated farms in the United States can earn up to $1.40 per square foot. The return on an organic farm may pay as high as $50 per hour. In contrast, I have calculated that the average vegetable grower in Russia earns only 10–20¢ per hour—the fare to ride a city bus. Is this because we so rarely bother to think for ourselves, relying only on information from books... or on luck?

Our southern soils are mostly loams, almost always plowed to death, and completely lacking in structure. They only produce at their full potential when moisture levels are optimal, which is very difficult to achieve in our hot climate. Local villagers can raise a decent crop of vegetables only

135

by constantly watering and cultivating. Unfortunately, this does not work for the typical home gardener at his dacha. My plot is like a "dacha garden": the soil is a heavy, alkaline loam—hard as rock in the summer and like potter's clay in rainy weather. When we first moved onto this land, my shovel blade would stick fast in the gley* layer. In order to cultivate such land, you must relinquish your freedom entirely—if you get distracted for even a moment, it will bake hard in the sun, or become thoroughly drenched in a downpour. I have no desire to be a slave to my land! Therefore, I utilize organic matter.

Organic matter unleashes the full potential of plants, saving my time and labor. It gives structure and vitality to clay soils, and humus, nutrients, and stability to sandy soils. Only on fertile, compost-rich beds with drip irrigation can the true attributes of modern vegetable cultivars and hybrids be achieved and appreciated, since they are usually developed under such conditions.

When we never seem to have enough time and energy for everything which needs to be done, it is important for us to realize that what is ineffectual is, in fact, detrimental. Effort spent without return is very harmful to you. You have both wasted your time and missed out on the benefits and joy of success; you will never get them back. From the viewpoint of organic gardeners, plowed soil is completely ill-suited for vegetables. Those grown with chemicals are all but tasteless as well. In fact, you can hardly even call them vegetables. They are more like counterfeit vegetables.

Only a good, organic bed will yield genuine vegetables—often two or three harvests per year. There are many

---

* *Gley*—a layer of sticky, muddy clay containing very little air. It is formed by chronic waterlogging and is typically a blackish-blue color.

possible methods for growing them. Permanent beds, once established, are very easy to work with over the years. Compost allows for the use of vertical supports for vines, in a way transforming raised beds into gigantic flowerpots. Organic matter affords a broad diversity in the garden.

Vegetable bins: ten years later

I'll build a house of stone
And sow radishes there.
On Chrysanthemum Day,
When I give them to my mother-in-law,
Will she serve me sake?

Japanese folk tanka

In essence, a raised vegetable bin is, indeed, an enlarged "flowerpot." The walls can be made of bricks, logs, milled lumber, or stones, measuring about 3 feet (1 m) wide and any length you like. The height is as needed—anywhere from 12 to 30 inches (30–80 cm). Placed directly onto the grass and framed with flagstones, rock-walled bins are magnificent (Photograph 10). They are excellent for mixed plantings and can include some kind of framework or trellis* along the middle for cucumbers and tomatoes to climb on. It is best to use drip irrigation in bins and, ideally, to cover them with a transparent roof made of plastic or polycarbonate. This helps protect vegetables from fungal diseases. The bin can also have openings in the sides for trailing plants—strawberries, bush beans, nasturtiums, or petunias—and a small tank can be attached to one side for irrigation with

* *Trellis*—a structure to support climbing plants or to train trees on.

sun-warmed water (Photograph 9). Do not put concrete on the bottom. A direct connection with the ground allows for normal moisture exchange.

The bin is filled up in layers. Dirt is added to each layer—about half the total volume—and, if possible, some food wastes, too. Aim for a quarter of the volume to consist of porous materials: sand, loessial soil,* perlite, or vermiculite—whatever you have available. It is good to disperse about 12 ounces (350 g) of Terawet** evenly throughout the entire contents. The soil surface should be mulched during summer.

Coarse, partially-decomposed organic matter—rotting stalks, chipped brush, or decayed wood—is spread over the bottom. You can also add some nitrogen fertilizer to aid decomposition, and it never hurts to throw on some tufa,*** brick rubble, or clay pellets as well—they help conserve moisture. The middle layer consists of unfinished compost, partially-rotted manure, straw, corn husks, and other plant residues. At this point, it is important to include more sand than earth. The top layer is fully decomposed compost mixed with earth and sand.

Over the next year, this "stuffing" will settle about 6–8 inches (15–20 cm), so it is best to pile it high and lay drip irrigation over the surface. When it finally does settle, add

---

* *Loessial soil*—a very fine-grained, buff to gray silt or clay, usually calcareous, formed by glaciers and deposited by wind. [trans]

** *Terawet*—an efficient acrylic polymer which is very water absorbent. It swells up to 400 parts of water that resists evaporation but readily releases moisture to roots. It creates a reliable water reservoir in the soil. Innocuous and inert, it works in the soil for up to ten years.

*** *Tufa*—a soft, porous sedimentary rock consisting of calcium carbonate formed by the evaporation of water. [trans]

another layer on top. After that there will be very little set-tling, and your usual fall application of organic matter is all that will be required.

Raised bins have many advantages: a) they are beautiful, and create less mud and muddle; b) they are very comfort-able to work in, since you don't have to hunch over so much; c) they maximize space by utilizing trellises for climbing vines, the surface area for regular plantings, and the sides for hanging plants; d) they contain large amounts of nutri-ent-rich compost which require less watering and fertiliz-ing; e) when initially filled in the spring, raised bins heat up through decomposition and are also quickly warmed by the sun, providing a ready-made hotbed for early vegetables; f) they require no tilling and very little weeding; and g) they take up a minimum of space.

On the other hand: a) you have to build them, which entails time and money; b) they require large amounts of organic matter; and c) the organic matter has to be high-quality and nutrient-rich. These three minor shortcomings have kept bins from becoming more popular. However, my friends who have built classic bins under clear plastic roofs are very satisfied with the results: cucumbers and tomatoes have fewer diseases and keep producing all the way up until frost, and working in them is very easy. One of my clients who was wasting away after a severe heart attack saw this idea—and took heart! He built several bins, established a "Kurdyumov-style garden," and never tires of telling me that it saved his life. His creations are pictured in Photographs 7 and 8.

Basically, bins are miniature vegetable factories, and it makes good sense to build them!

Drip irrigation tape is the best method of watering bins. However, tape is very difficult to find in Russian rural areas. Somehow we always manage to resolve such issues, and we have come up with various home-made alternatives.

For instance, burying plastic containers perforated with holes. One- or two-gallon (5-L) plastic water bottles work well. If you fill them in the morning, and then again in the evening, they will provide sufficient water for a week. You can also punch holes into a hose with a screwdriver and lay it under mulch. Plug the far end of the hose and, whenever watering is required, attach the near end to a water barrel or hose, turn the water on low, and let it flow for 15–20 minutes. It is very important not to forget to turn off the faucet on time!

Soil containing large amounts of organic matter and moisture will actively convert and release nutrients to plants. Therefore, bins respond well to compound fertilizer applications. These should only be applied once a month in May, June, and July.

Roofs made of transparent plastic or double wall polycarbonate have many advantages. Experience has shown that under roofs there is little dew—the main cause of disease.

Therefore, tomatoes are rarely "burned" by blight, nor cucumbers by downy mildew. Moreover, roofs create a favorable microclimate, disperse sunlight, and protect plants from hail and downpours which often occur here in the south of Russia.

Trellises are best constructed out of metal as in Photograph 9. They should be very sturdily made—first, to withstand high winds, and second, to bear the weight of climbing plants, which in the summer can be as much as 35 pounds per running foot (50 kg/m).

In the spring, raised bins warm up quickly—rock walls especially collect heat well. If you orient them north to south, both walls will heat up evenly. In the winter, raised bins freeze through faster than other types of beds, so are not as good for perennials.

If a bin is covered with plastic, cucumbers and tomatoes can be directly sown in place along the center line. In April and May, bins will yield a harvest of radishes, garden cress,

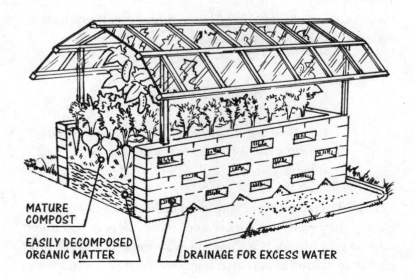

MATURE
COMPOST

EASILY DECOMPOSED
ORGANIC MATTER

DRAINAGE FOR EXCESS WATER

and lettuce. Towards July, tomatoes and cucumbers start bearing fruit along the central trellis. However, they grow so vigorously on the compost that it is best to pinch them back more than usual and remove all side-shoots. After harvesting early vegetables and removing the lower shoots of the tomatoes and cucumbers, carrots and kohlrabi can be planted along the edges. In the fall, there is still time to grow a crop of lettuce, leaf mustard, and late radishes. Finally, the bin is covered with straw and plant residues for the winter. In early spring of the following year, you just add a fresh layer of well-rotted compost.

Easier still, for some crops you can simply utilize the natural vitality of your spring compost pile, not constructing a bed at all. You only have to attach an extra section to the compost bin. In the spring, unfinished winter compost is piled into it and hilled up. Squash, pumpkins, and cucumbers are sown there. Sometimes vegetables will even sprout up on their own from seeds in plant and kitchen wastes. Their development is usually a good month ahead of my transplants, and they spread more rampantly than those in beds receiving the very best of care!

Raised beds

And if you tire out while constructing raised beds,
it is quite comfortable to lie down and take a nap
in them.

Raised beds are especially good for wet and northern regions—they warm up earlier and, when there is too much rain or groundwater, do not get waterlogged. People who garden in upland areas can manage without them, but many areas with clay soils, especially former croplands and rice paddies, become overly saturated in rainy seasons. In these places fruit trees should be planted on mounds and vegetables in raised beds. Even in normal years, the soil is very compact. A thick upper layer of organic matter, dragged under by worms, in time will loosen and aerate the soil. Raised beds are truly a saving grace on my alkaline soil.

A raised bed is permanent with sides made of lumber, concrete, or other materials. My frames are constructed from boards and logs (Photographs 11 and 12). Sides are an ingenious feature. They precisely delineate the area to be cultivated, which suddenly appears very small! Beds are about 4–6 inches (10–15 cm) high and each year are filled to the top with compost. Cucumbers and cabbages can have manure buried underneath them. Beds are always mulched with a thick layer of loose organic matter.

If raised beds are 30–50 inches (80–120 cm) wide, it does not matter which direction they are oriented to—vegetable rows can extend along or across the bed—but the rows themselves should always be arranged north to south. In this way plants will receive sunlight evenly. Narrow beds,

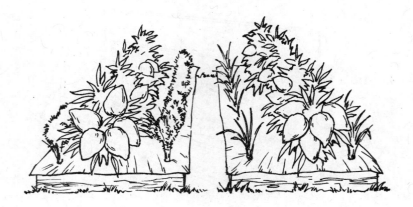

15–28 inches (40–70 cm) wide, should be oriented north-south, too, but we will examine them separately.

Like bins, raised beds can have trellises for cucumbers, tomatoes, and beans, plastic roofs, and drip irrigation systems. In this case, raised beds are simply low bins. Not as much organic matter is required to fill them, and they will not freeze solid as easily in the winter—these are pluses. But they are not raised as high off the ground, so working them is not as convenient—this is a minus.

When establishing a bed, dig the soil deeply one time, adding organic matter, sand, and Terawet. After the bed has been filled, never again allow it to be trod upon by human feet! Only organic matter and hands will go into it. Add a substantial top layer of mulch and a barrel to the side for liquid fertilizers, and you are done.

If the soil is fairly loose, you do not even have to dig it. This is much better for the worms. After the first year, the organic matter and worms will have loosened up the bed to about 8 inches (20 cm). In spring, I dump 2–3 wheelbarrows of compost onto the bed without digging it in. Then I sow or transplant directly into the compost. When the plants

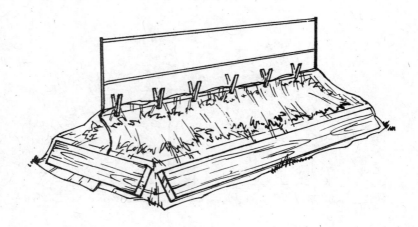

sprout up, I lay down a mulch of grass, seed hulls, or straw. Very few weeds come up, and any that do are easily pulled out by the roots.

As in a bin, you can grow 3–4 harvests of various kinds of vegetables in a raised bed from early spring through late fall. Intensive drip irrigation and vigorous plant growth require substantial amounts of nutrients, so it is good to fertilize beds once a month with a solution of organic or organo-mineral fertilizer. Using arched wire or a simple frame, the bed is easily transformed into a cold frame. Seedlings for transplanting can be grown in it during the spring.

If you live in a cold area, it is better to modify the design to make a special bed which will quickly warm up. It should be oriented east to west and inclined to the south—the southern edge is lower, and the northern edge about 6 inches (15 cm) higher. Every degree of incline toward the south adds as much warmth as if you moved the bin 60 miles (100 km) to the south! Russian gardeners have been making such "solar beds" since olden times. They are described in detail in books by Pavel Frankovich Trannua and Alexey Alexeevich Kazarin.

Narrow beds and narrow bins

In this day and age, narrow beds reflect the breadth of outlook of the gardener!

Narrow beds have proven to be the most rational and productive of all forms of beds. They are generally about 16–28 inches (40–70 cm) wide, and the pathways between them about 3 feet (1 m). Each bed can grow two rows of bush vegetables, planted along the edges and staggered in a dense planting arrangement, or 3–4 rows of lettuce, greens, or root crops.

This configuration harbors a huge reserve of productive capacity. Gardeners have long observed that the outermost plants of beds develop nearly twice as vigorously as those that are in the middle. There is much more light and space available in their outside position, since they do not have to compete as much with their neighbors—i.e., "bump elbows" with them. In narrow beds, all plants are located on the outside!

The wide pathways between beds are exactly what plants need to receive maximum sunlight and space. In the summer, bush vegetables spilling over the sides of beds almost completely fill them.

The narrow bed method was originally proposed and developed by Jacob Mittleider, and his ideas have spread throughout the world. In Russia, Tatiana Yurievna Ugarova was one of the first to master Mittleider's vegetable growing system. Her book *Home Vegetable Gardening on Narrow Beds* is very popular and has been reprinted many times over.

A narrow bed can be made without a frame, delimited by its earthen banks. If irrigation is applied directly to the roots by a drip system, water will not drain off the beds. The pathways are kept clear of weeds with a subsurface cultivator or razor hoe, or even better, by laying down a compact mulch as in Photograph 5. A trellis may be constructed for tall vegetables.

You can (as Mittleider did) fill a narrow bin with sawdust, sand, or clay pellets and grow vegetables by continuously irrigating them with liquid fertilizers. But why kill the soil with unholy doses of chemical fertilizers? We organic growers renounce such fertilizers almost completely, because we know that living soil is all that a plant needs. Pathways are covered with a thick organic mulch or cardboard, or even old linoleum. Worms thrive under them, and there is always an abundance of nutrients and moisture which can be fully assimilated by roots. All the ground is utilized, but only a third is cultivated! And the harvest from this third is more than you would normally receive by cultivating the entire area.

You can enclose narrow beds with boards and fill them with organic matter, turning them into narrow bins. These are much more convenient to work in. For instance, I like to prop a board on top of the sides of bins and work sitting down. What bliss!

According to the logic of chemical fertilizers, the less the volume of a bed, the more important the role of nutrients, making it imperative to provide frequent supplemental feedings. According to Mittleider, narrow beds should be watered every day. With organic matter, however, this is not the case. If both beds and pathways are covered with mulch, watering twice a week is sufficient. Here drip irrigation works especially well—one line, or at most two suffice for each bed.

Trenches are narrow beds for hot climates

In order to find less expensive options and to adapt various techniques to our southern climate, we are combining together the various merits of different types of beds.

If your plot never becomes waterlogged, it is best to sink narrow beds into the ground. I dig a trench directly into the sod two shovels wide by one shovel deep. Then I spread manure and humus over the bottom, topping it off with finished compost mixed with soil. Into this I plant two rows of tomatoes, cucumbers, beans, cabbage, or peppers. After they germinate and start growing up, I pile the trench high with straw or cut grass. My neighbor, Sergey Kladovikov, mulches his trenches with shredded cardboard (Photograph 6). It doesn't look bad at all!

After this, the only work left to do is to water twice a week, or even less if it rains. Sometimes you may have to pull up a few particularly brazen weeds. In the past, I used to mow the pathways several times through the summer— and the grass flourished. In the end, though, I covered the paths with thick black plastic covered in hay and seed hulls. The edges of the plastic were buried along the sides of the trenches. Two years later, I removed the plastic and started covering the pathways with straw. Now there are almost no weeds at all.

Vegetables in trenches grow very well, and with regular watering and feeding are utterly amazing. Each year the bottom of the trench becomes deeper and more friable—worms

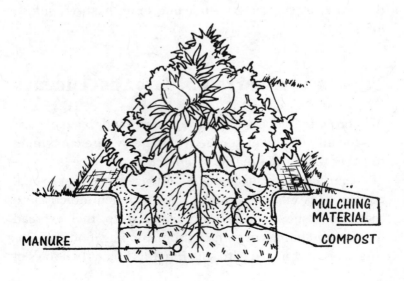

drag the compost deep into the soil. The main advantage of trenches is that they are excellent at retaining moisture, and so they hardly ever dry up. Plants do not become stressed even with moderate watering. You can, however, take this useful method to extremes—there is really no reason to dig trenches for squash, melons, and cucumbers!

Holes—the apotheosis of lazy vegetable gardening

I would strain every nerve, move entire mountains, just so I could sit around and do nothing!

In the first Russian edition of this book, I included a picture of a type of "raised mini-bed"—a barrel of vegetables. It was a good idea, but in practice did not pan out so well. In our hot weather the barrel needed a thick layer of mulch to protect it from the sun as well as constant watering—drip irrigation worked best. After this experience, I decided to "sink" the barrel into the ground!

Now I dig a hole—the "barrel"—approximately 2 x 2 feet (60 x 60 cm) and two shovels deep. Two buckets of organic matter are then dug into the bottom. Next I spread another wheelbarrow of any kind of organic matter, adding dirt and sand, and on top of that a wheelbarrow of compost. I lay black plastic all around the hole, burying the edges along the sides, and pile straw over the plastic.

Six pumpkins and the same amount of corn are sown in each hole. They shoot up like crazy. The only work left is to water by putting a hose in for ten minutes once a week. Summer squash grown in such a hole will feed us through the summer all the way up to the cold weather. In two holes, over 200 pounds (100 kg) of pumpkins will grow with very little help from me—this comes very close to perfection!

I tried the same method for melons. With these it is best to water using buried plastic bottles perforated with holes. After the third year additional organic fertilizer should be provided. This is easily done. In the fall I just empty out a couple of biotoilets, and in spring add a few buckets of kitchen waste and cover everything over with cut grass—that's it!

Arbors, fences, and southern walls

If you have a mesh fence which is fairly sturdy, you already have an excellent trellis for tall and climbing vegetables. You simply need to dig a trench along the fence and fill it with organic matter. A net is especially suitable for beans and cucumbers. There is one minor drawback, though: in the fall you have to clean the vines off the fence. If you do this before they dry out, it is not too difficult. The advantages of fences are great: you do not have to build a trellis, and the bed takes up hardly any space.

In the same way, you can encircle a garden arbor with a small trench. It will look beautiful braided with decorative or fig-leaf gourds (*Cucurbita ficifolia*), asparagus beans,* runner beans with red and white flowers, and hyacinth beans (*Dolichos*) with purple flowers. Cucumbers are the only vine not worth planting around an arbor—they quickly become diseased and lose their attractiveness.

---

* *Asparagus beans* (*Vigna unguiculata* subsp. *sesquipedalis*)—"Chinese long beans" or "cowpeas" are a bean variety with long (up to 2 feet), slender pods. They are described in the section "Beans" (see Chapter 13).

South and east-facing walls give plants a considerable amount of additional warmth and reflected sunlight which accelerates their development by 8–15 days. Instead of laying down flagstones at the base of walls, I make small beds out of sand, compost, and rocks. Or I trellis grapes along them. In the past, I planted beans and asparagus beans next to a wall with cherry tomatoes beneath them, but now all the vegetables have migrated to the garden, and along that wall I have grapes, various flowers, and some native plants (Photograph 29).

Pyramids and umbrellas

Pyramids and umbrellas are nothing more than a planting hole with a frame for climbing plants built on top. Cucumbers and beans are especially suited to them. Growing

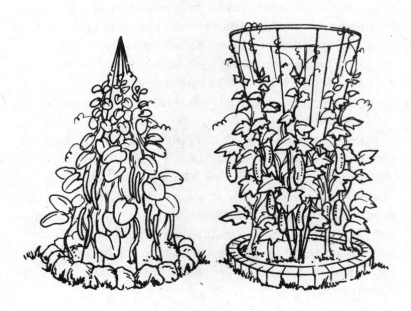

twenty vines of cucumbers on one square meter is a lazy person's dream! Another advantage is that it is easy to cover a pyramid with fabric or plastic fastened down with clothes-pins for early-season frost protection. Finally, these structures beautifully decorate the garden, and there is hardly any work to do except watering and tying up plants at the beginning of summer.

The bottom line

Shit or get off the pot!
It's time to harvest the plot!

Although we are still far from drawing definite conclusions, general ideas are beginning to take shape. The lazy gardener should:

    a) use a configuration of narrow beds more often;
    b) sink beds into the ground on dry plots and in the south, and raise them up in wet areas and in the north;
    c) never skimp on filling beds with organic matter, and mulch thickly during the summer; and
    d) whenever possible, compress beds into trenches, holes, and pyramids.

All open areas on a plot should be kept mown. This naturally transforms weeds into a diversified turf. The pathways between rows are best covered with organic matter and topped with straw, cardboard, old woolen carpeting, linoleum, or anything else you can find. In hot, dry regions, it is good to install drip irrigation in trenches and raised beds, or to bury plastic water bottles perforated with holes. Tanks are useful for nutrient teas and solutions.

By moving gradually in this direction, we are able to endure droughts without worry and raise a successful vegetable garden where the most difficult task is gathering the harvest! And soon we may be able to streamline this task as well!

The foundation of intelligent gardening is permanent narrow beds. For this reason they deserve closer examination. In the following chapter we will look at the "concise fundamentals of narrow-bed vegetable gardening" with commentary.

Did you know?
This book is printed on *100% organic matter*!

Chapter 5

Narrow Beds and Trenches

or

A Garden With Almost No Problems

It's the very narrowness of this method that expands its possibilities!

Why do I combine various kinds of vegetables in a single wide bed? It's more fun! But mainly I am trying to harvest more food from the same amount of space. Unfortunately, I do not succeed in this nearly as much as I would like! Maybe I used the wrong variety or poor quality seeds; there was an unexpected frost or my timing was bad; or I forgot to weed, became distracted, or was just too lazy—and the plants which were supposed to lag behind suddenly took off and overwhelmed those which should have advanced ahead. They are forced to compete for sunlight and space, and the losers become stunted for life.

Narrow beds completely eliminate this problem of planting arrangement and intercropping. I only have to monitor spacing within the row. Plants are set out in two rows, which enables each to "face" towards a wide pathway and joyfully stretch out towards freedom. This allows them to thrive to their fullest potential. Ovsinsky sowed his plants exactly in this way: "Wide pathways between rows are indispensable to ensure plants the required amount of sunlight and to incline them to form heavy kernels (or fruit) in expectation of falling over onto free space."

The average width of a bed is 20 inches (0.5 m), and the path—40 inches (1 m). In the south (Zone 6), if there is less space, the paths can be narrowed to 30 inches (80 cm), but only in an open area where there is no shade. It may seem that the ground in the pathways is not being used. But it certainly is! On a hundred square foot garden, the beds take up only about 35 square feet. This means that beds will receive more water and attention with less work. As a result, narrow beds yield not less, but as much or even more produce per square foot than normal gardens. Working them is easier and more enjoyable, and the garden is beautiful and delightful to the eyes.

In this chapter I will draw upon many of the recommendations and data found in the book *Home Vegetable Gardening on Narrow Beds* by Tatiana Ugarova. Ugarova is a true master of narrow beds, and her advice is based on actual experience. However, it is important to realize that Ugarova works under conditions found in the Moscow Region (Zone 4). Moreover, she precisely follows the methods of Mittleider, applying copious amounts of mineral fertilizers and watering daily. Here I will discuss a natural version of gardening on narrow beds using organic mulch, limited amounts of mineral fertilizers, and very infrequent watering. After all, the average gardener in Russia works in his garden only on weekends!

Building narrow beds

Beds should extend north-south in a sunny location.

They can be laid out using two parallel strings stretched out at a width of 18 inches (45 cm). At this point, there are three variations:

1. A strip 18 in (45 cm) wide is fertilized with organic matter, dug in thoroughly, and raked smooth. Next, the soil on the pathway is raked into the row, forming sides 3–4 inches (8–10 cm) high. From this point on, watering will be done only in the interior of the bed between the hilled up sides. If the soil is fertile, has abundant organic matter, and is covered with mulch, this variant works just as well as trenches filled with organic matter. If you water with a hose, though, you still have one problem: you must carefully level the bed crosswise, so that water does not flow off to one side or settle into puddles—making it perfectly level can sometimes be quite difficult! It is better to install a drip irrigation system from the beginning.

2. Using the strings as guides, dig out a trench one shovel deep. There is no need to painstakingly level it out or to deepen the bottom. Only the walls should be even. To keep grass from growing into the trench, cover the pathways with plastic, lowering the edges over the sides of the trench about

3–4 inches (7–10 cm). The plastic is covered with the excavated dirt, which in time will be trampled down into a thin layer. Weeds will not grow here since it will be too dry. The trenches are filled with organic matter—on the bottom with manure or plant residues, sand, dirt, and mineral supplements (potassium, phosphorus, and calcium), and on top with a layer of finished compost.

3. Boards secured by stakes are laid down to form narrow raised beds, which are filled with organic matter as with trenches. You can smother the weeds by covering the bottom with paper. Or, if you want to loosen the upper layer of soil to receive maximum benefit immediately, spread compost over the bottom of the bin and dig it in.

If the plot is prone to waterlogging, you should construct bins—in trenches plants will become swamped after a heavy rain.

Of course, if your garden has rich, friable black earth, you can generally get away with not adding any additional organic matter. The soil is already so rich that all you have to do is water! But in the case of poor clay or waterlogged soil

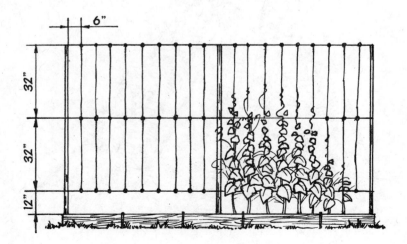

(as I have), organic matter is absolutely essential. Without it, even mineral fertilizers will barely work at all. On the other hand, in the presence of organic matter they yield a beneficial effect in even the smallest doses.

Supports should be set up under tall vegetables. You can, of course, also stake the tomatoes. Because beds are permanent, it is best to construct sturdy, long-lasting trellises. Place the lower crosspiece or wire about 15–17 inches (40–45 cm) high—it is easier to attach plastic to it with clothespins for covering the bed in spring (see illustration). The upper crosspiece should be 6–7 feet (1.8–2 m) high. It never hurts to run another middle wire at a height of 3–4 feet (100–120 cm)—tall tomato plants usually reach this level. I run binder twine or wires between the upper and lower crosspieces; the growing vines simply wind around them.

Water along the center of the bed. If mulched, a trench only needs to be watered once a week; a bin—twice. With drip irrigation, you can apply fertilizer at the same time. Unlike a hose or watering can, "drops" do not compact the

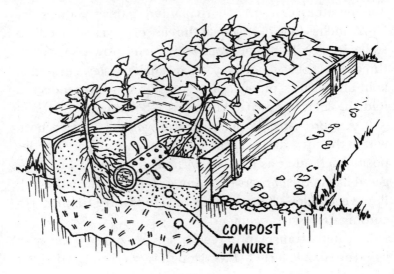

COMPOST
MANURE

ground, which allows soil creatures to pull humus down into the soil, so the fertility of trenches increases quickly.

If you do not have drip irrigation, though, you can make a homemade watering system. Bury one-gallon (5-liter), perforated plastic bottles into beds at 3-foot (1-m) intervals. Just fill the bottles with water, screw on the lids, and everything is watered (see illustration). To fertilize, you can sprinkle a teaspoon of a compound or chelate fertilizer (in Russia—Kristalon, Akvarin, etc.) into the bottle top.

Sowing and transplanting in narrow beds

1. Both seeds and transplants are grown in two rows along the sides. Two-row plantings are the overriding trump card of narrow beds—all plants face outward. In Mittleider's system, fertilizers are applied along the center of the bed. However, in an organic bed we use the center line for other reasons as well: a trellis can be built there for cucumbers, beans, and tomatoes; or a row of corn planted sparsely about every 23–27 inches (60–70 cm). I eat the ears of corn and grind the stalks into mulch. Root crops and greens grow very well in three rows: lettuce, watercress, arugula, parsley, coriander, kohlrabi, carrots, onions, garlic, beets, and winter radishes. Radishes may be sown as closely as 2–3 inches (5–7 cm).

2. A more sensible planting arrangement is used both within the rows and over the entire bed—plants are not opposite each other as if in the corners of a square, but staggered like in the corners of a triangle (in a "zigzag pattern"). Row vegetables—lettuce and root crops—are thinned according to this arrangement.

3. To make transplanting easier, some people use a strip of wood about 3–5 feet (1–1.5 m) long as a marker. It is divided

into intervals of 3, 6, and 12 inches (8, 16, and 32 cm), each designated by its own color. This yields a system of planting which is dense within the row but wider between rows—very similar to Ovsinsky's planting arrangement.

Can the density of plants be increased? Probably, yes. A two-row, V-shaped trellis can be made for climbing vegetables, increasing their density in the bed by one and a half times. Or if vines are planted in one row, then the surface of the bed can be used for sparsely planted smaller crops. In this case, you remove the lower runners and leaves from the vines. For example, I have combined a row of trellised cucumbers and two rows of cabbages in a single trench with good results.

With 4–5 hours of shading—that is, under a trellis overgrown with vines—the following crops will not perform well: bulb onions, garden peas, cauliflower, Brussels sprouts, and iceberg lettuce (it will not form a head). Tomatoes, peppers, eggplants, and squash will produce just a few stunted fruits.

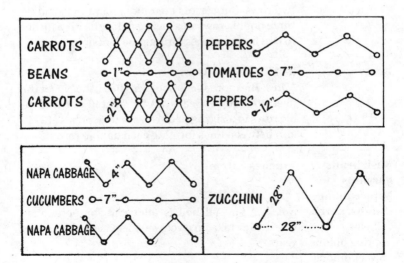

Table 1. The approximate spacing in the row between the plants
Except where noted, all vegetables are planted in two rows with plants staggered between rows in a zigzag pattern.

Pole beans	**1–2 inches** (3–4 cm) *Notes:* In the Caucasus they traditionally let beans climb up sticks which are stuck in the ground—"poles." Three or four seeds are planted at the base of each pole, which are spaced every 6–8 inches (15–20 cm).
Garden peas **Radishes, spr.** **Parsley** **Watercress** **Arugula** **Dill** **Basil, sweet** **Coriander**	**2 inches** (5 cm) *Notes:* These plants can be planted in three double rows in a zigzag pattern (see illustration on the previous page).
Carrots **Onions, bulb** **Leeks**	**2–3 inches** (6–7 cm) *Notes:* Bulb onions especially love sunlight and will not tolerate any shading, so it is best to plant them in two rows. But carrots are more tolerant of shade—three double rows in a zigzag pattern with 2 inches (6 cm) between lines forming each double row.
Beets	**3–4 inches** (7–10 cm) *Notes:* The more space between them, the bigger the beetroot will be. Beets can be planted in two double rows in a zigzag pattern with 5–6 inches (12–15 cm) between lines forming each double row.
Bush beans **Parsnips** **Napa cabbage** **Onions, peren.** Chives Spring onions Sweet onions	**4 inches** (10 cm) *Notes:* A special bed is allocated for perennials where they take up a very small space but for many years.

Celeriac **Celery** **Daikon** **Kohlrabi** **Swiss chard** **Tomatoes, trellised** **Cucumbers, trellised**	**7 inches** (17 cm)

Hot peppers **Rutabagas** **Turnips** **Winter radishes** **Lettuce,** leaf and head **Cucumbers, spreading** **Potatoes**	**10–12 inches** (25–30 cm)

Bell peppers **Eggplant** **Chinese cabbage (bok choy)** **Cabbage,** early **Tomatoes, bush**	**12–16 inches** (30–40 cm)

Cabbage, mid- and late-season **Cabbage, red** **Cauliflower** **Broccoli**	**14 inches** (35 cm)

Ground cherries (*Physalis*)	**20 inches** (50 cm)

Brussels sprouts	**24 inches** (60 cm)

Planted in a single row:

Squash **Zucchini** **Scallop squash**	**28 inches** (70 cm)

Pumpkins	**40 inches** (100 cm)

Garlic, leaf lettuce, napa cabbage, green cabbage, Swiss chard, root crops, and most herbs grow fairly well in partial shade. However, you should plant them with one-and-a-half to two times more space within the row.

The principal care required for narrow beds is removing old and sick leaves, occasional watering, and fertilizing. Additionally, vines and tomatoes must be tied up, and top and side shoots pinched back. The more serious work is harvesting at the proper time, not allowing the fruit to linger too long on the plant. But I think we can deal with that.

* * *

We can now envision the various types of bins, beds, pits, and trenches. If we view the garden from above—maybe not a birds-eye view but at least from a roof or nearby tree—what do we see?

Chapter 6

Intelligent Gardening— A Bird's-eye View

or

An Attempt to Combine the Rational With the Beautiful

We are all one.
But each one *is different from all the rest!*

You can find showcase landscape designs in any garden magazine depicting an ideal arrangement of flowers, trees, and garden beds. But I have no idea how anyone could possibly use them. After all, each garden has its own very specific conditions—the climate and microclimate, direction of the sun, availability of light, slope, type of soil, and groundwater and moisture levels. All of these aspects are essentially unique to each plot.

Moreover, every gardener has his own personal goals as well as a particular layout of buildings and other physical features to start with. Everyone raises different crops—each to his own desire. Not to mention that every person wishes to be the creator of his garden. I cannot imagine anyone who would want to exactly follow someone else's plan. But mainly there is a difference in available resources. No European could imagine how widely resources vary among

Russians. There are some people who have everything while others have just enough—and still others have pretty much nothing at all! What do we have to fall back on? Just one thing: the constant development of intellect, ingenuity, and common sense. Truly, we Russians have little choice but to remain a great yet enigmatic country!

In principle, the power of our labor-saving ideas should have already transformed our gardens into a heavenly paradise. But suffering from a collectivist syndrome, we often direct our thoughts outside ourselves, trying to change anything but our own lives. It is as if we are striving to improve society and bring the government to its senses, so that, being more enlightened, it will suddenly show up to improve our lives—on its own without any effort from us. Unfortunately, this arcane logic is clearly unsuitable for the gardener. Neither society nor the government has the slightest idea how to improve your garden in a way that *you* would appreciate. Therefore, as I have already said, a garden is a good testing ground for success. It should both yield vegetables and bring you enjoyment. It should be beautiful to you, and a comfortable place to relax in. For this reason, I do not intend to offer you a set plan for laying out your plot; instead, I will share various rational principles of garden design and maintenance which I have gleaned from long years of observation.

How many and which kinds of beds you need

Everyone can't have everything, since there's lots of everyone, and not enough of everything!

Only a highly experienced and thoughtful gardener knows the optimal number of beds to make, and how best to arrange them in order to receive the amount of vegetables required for an entire year. Do you know the total yield of each vegetable which will grow in your beds? Or how much of each you will need to plant? This is often a mystery to me, too! Truly, our gardens are a reflection of how well we understand what we want.

Recently, I made this humble discovery: the majority of us work in our gardens and orchards not so much for the sake of the harvest but for the enjoyment of seeing everything flourish and mature. We love to admire the beautiful plants, the even rows of our beds, the luxuriant greenery, and, most importantly, the ripening harvest. If it is a "bad year," we are somehow completely innocent, but in a good one—we did it ourselves. We created all that abundance! We are exalted by the harvest, but if it suddenly rots from rain or is destroyed by hail, for some reason we don't suffer all that much.

Our real requirement for vegetables is, in fact, what we can actually manage to eat, including produce stored and preserved. However, what we require for joyful gratification and serene contemplation is *anticipation*. In my view, our anticipation is ten times larger than our actual need.

"What are you saying?! The more vegetables, the better!"

Really? And what about all the extra land you will have to dig up? That's why your time and energy manage to last only for the beginning of the growing season. In spring, when the beds are still empty, we are filled with anticipation. It comes in the form of hope that somehow everything will grow well—all by itself. We take great delight in this, but for some reason we don't feel like working too hard for it. And then a month later, everything changes. The plants sprout up out of the ground, but the seedlings may not turn out as we had expected; and then weeds and drought kill off our hope completely. Our enthusiasm fizzles out. Tired of hoping, some of us rush to the opposite extreme: less is better! I believe that if we can find that golden mean—our actual need—it will give us a good starting point from which we can proceed calmly and consciously.

Let's look at the data of Tatiana Ugarova on crop productivity from ten square feet (1 m^2)—or *from six running feet (2 m) of a narrow bed*, which is essentially the same thing. Considering our level of mastery, quality of seeds, etc., we have decreased her figures by half. Based on this realistic minimum, we will calculate the harvest by primary crops. Two additional columns of the table could be "pounds of vegetables needed for your family" and "running feet of narrow beds required." Fill them in yourself, right here, with a pencil.

Table 2. Number of plants and yields from 6 running ft (2 m) of narrow bed

Crop	Plants	Harvest: "realistic"–high	
Cabbage, early	12	26–52 lb	(12–24 kg)
Cabbage, late	12	44–48 lb	(20–40 kg)
Broccoli	10	13–26 lb	(6–12 kg)
Beets, garden	60–80	33–66 lb	(15–30 kg)
Tomatoes, vine & bush	12–22	33–66 lb	(15–30 kg)
Beans, pole and bush	80	9–18 lb	(4–8 kg)
Carrots	80	18–36 lb	(8–16 kg)
Squash and Zucchini	6	44–48 lb	(20–40 kg)
Lettuce, head	20	13–26 lb	(6–12 kg)
Cucumbers, trellised	22	44–48 lb	(20–40 kg)
Onions, bulb	80	13–26 lb	(6–12 kg)
Radishes	160	9–18 lb	(4–8 kg)
Garlic	80	9–18 lb	(4–8 kg)
Potatoes	14	22–44 lb	(10–20 kg)

Notes:
1. Experienced gardeners know the yields of their crops and can correct any inaccuracies in the table.
2. The data on onions, garlic, and radishes are my own.
3. Potatoes in narrow beds are a good option. Trenches covered in straw work especially well and increase harvests.

How does this work out in practice? For example, my family loves vegetables and eats them at almost every meal. Combining the most extreme demand (about a ton per year for five!) with very modest—I would say, even terribly low—harvests, we can raise enough vegetables on just 1,000 square feet (90 m²), or 600 running feet (180 m) of narrow beds or trenches. For this we require only 3,000 square feet (270 m²) of land! Coincidentally, our garden is just about that size. Considering that vegetables grown on beds rich in organic matter tend to give much higher yields, and that beds can always be utilized more rationally, plus not everyone needs nearly that many vegetables, the average garden can probably be half as small. Isn't this at least worth trying?

After all, there is no harm in dreaming a little. For instance, it would be great to grow the same vegetables which Jeff Dawson at the University of California had at his disposal when he calculated how many plants were needed to feed one person through the summer season. He came up with these figures: beans—8 bush plants, plus another 3 pole plants; cabbage—2 heads; peppers and eggplant—2 plants each; potatoes—12 plants; cucumbers and staked tomatoes—2 plants each; 3 melons; 2 pumpkins; 10 beets; 15 carrots; 3 lettuce plants per week; 10 radishes for each lettuce; 12 onions, and an equal amount of garlic and herbs. You may think that this is a very small amount. I tried calculating it out myself, multiplying everything by four to cover the entire year. As it turns out, even using standard varieties of vegetables, this would be more than you could possibly eat! Isn't it one of our biggest mistakes that *we plant five times more than we actually need, and then give up because we don't have the energy to take proper care of everything*?

What size garden did you end up with? Perhaps now, after calculating how small your actual need is, you are wondering what to do with all your remaining land?! Don't worry. Boldly put it into grass turf with several small flowerbeds. Or plant a berry patch. From my experience, there are far too few of them in the world. Or you can plant a small grove of trees. On one fifth to one quarter of an acre (800–1,000 m²) you can arrange everything quite sensibly. Look at me! I have close to an acre (3,500 m²)—it's crazy! I would rather die than cultivate all that!

Now grab a pencil and paper, and draw out a plan for your *intelligent garden*. We already know approximately how large it should be. All that remains to do is take into account certain rules.

Basic design principles for gardens

Students! Pay attention and write this down!
An ellipse is a circle inscribed in a two-by-four
square.

An ill-considered arrangement of beds, pathways, and water sources causes an unbelievably huge amount of stupid work. And most gardeners obediently submit to this inexhaustible outlet for workaholism. I am by no means an exception. My garden is still far from perfect, but every year I change something, considering carefully how things can be improved. In this section I will share what I have learned.

1. Plant in zones. This is a very important principle! It wouldn't hurt to repeat it. The more attention a crop requires, the closer in it should be planted. "Vegetables will be grateful if you can see them from the kitchen window." This is very true! And they are especially grateful if there is a water source nearby. Walking down a pathway hauling a bucket or hose is tedious and uncreative. Moreover, it's hard work. And what if you are tired, sick, elderly, or depressed? The farther you have to haul water, the less interest you will have in gardening. Hence this law: watering the farthest bed is always put off until tomorrow.

Generally, if beds are located behind trees and bushes at the back of our lot , we do not take them as seriously—even if there is a faucet right there next to the beds. Out of sight—out of mind! Except for the most irrepressibly enthusiastic people, we are just like that. Do not berate yourself, but rather use this to your advantage: arrange vegetable beds which require more tending near your house, and put those which need less attention farther away. The closest plantings will be lettuce and early radishes, beds for cucumbers, tomatoes, and greens, and a greenhouse for seedlings right at your backdoor. Also, your water supply should be at hand. Root crops, peppers, eggplants, cabbages, and beans can be a little farther off. Perennials, pumpkins, and potatoes even farther; it is good to have a water source near them as well. At the very back is the orchard. Within individual beds, too, it is best to sow plants which require more commitment and work on the closer side!

Photograph 27 was taken from the doorway of my home. It is obvious what is most important to us—the flowerbeds and ornamentals!

2. Nothing bears fruit in the shade. Almost all vegetables require direct and continuous sunlight. Even in our southern sun, they yield 2–3 times less in the partial shade of scattered treetops. It is better to establish flowerbeds and a lawn in these places! You can, however, grow cucumbers next to trees. In the south they love the partial shade, are less diseased, and take up very little space. You can also plant rhubarb, sorrel, garlic, leaf lettuce, greens, perennial onions, and scallions in partial shade. However, solanaceous plants (tomatoes, peppers, eggplants), pumpkins, squash and zucchini, beans, and crucifers (radishes, daikon, black radish, and cole crops) cannot tolerate shade. Strawberries also bear fruit poorly in partial shade.

3. Arrange all beds, trellises, and frames to maximize exposure to sunlight. If a trellis runs along the center of a bed, it should be oriented north-south; otherwise, only the sunny side of the bed will be functional while the shaded half will fall out of the production loop. If the trellis runs along a wall or fence, it should extend east-west. Then all the plants in front of it will have maximum sun exposure.

The very beauty of narrow beds is in how they stretch the planted space lengthwise. Ten square feet (1 m²) is a square with 3-foot-2-inch sides (1m x 1m), or a 10-foot strip which is 1 foot wide (3 m x 0.33 m). In this case, we are referring to a 6-foot (2-m) strip which is 20 inches (50 cm) wide. Or consider a 12-foot (4-m) long strip which is 10 inches (25 cm) wide. Presumably, these "square inches" would be even more productive—of course, with proper watering and fertilizing, and a wide space between rows. A bed 5 inches (12 cm) wide and 24 feet (8 m) long is really more like small-scale hydroponics—i.e., vegetables grown in peat blocks arranged along a pipe and watered with a nutrient solution.

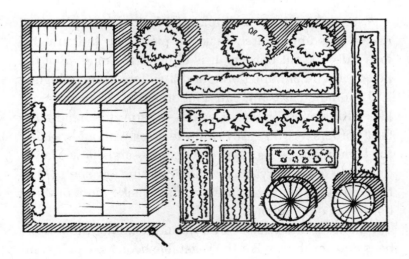

4. Make beds permanent. With permanent beds you continually add more organic matter and fertilizer, and you water only the bed itself. You do not walk on it, so you never compact the soil. You just need to weed a small area—and there are fewer weeds with each passing year. It makes more sense to fertilize the actual growing area rather than the entire plot, saving much time and effort! And these are not the only advantages of permanent beds. You can elevate them to prevent waterlogging. Plant grass in the paths, and pave larger walkways with flagstones. And you can do all this beautifully, interconnecting the vegetable garden with flowerbeds. Finally, once you have become accustomed to your personal arrangement of beds, you will quickly learn to estimate and predict the yield of your plantings.

Once everything is arranged perfectly right, will you become bored over time by the monotony? Not at all! You can still vary the selection of plants, cultivars, and how they are arranged in beds. And keep adding new flowers and shrubbery.

5. Use borders to delineate beds from uncultivated areas. This immediately makes a plot clear and straightforward! Without borders, it is difficult to conceive of the bed as a self-contained unit, and it suffers from ambiguity and sporadic care. You can "emborderate" it however you like: with stones, bricks, or wood—whatever is handy. The best borders let you easily trim the grass without breaking the trimmer line—e.g., logs and boards—and allow a lawnmower to mow everything without missing any spots (Photograph 30). I am constantly trying to make more of these borders in our garden.

I mark off and enclose everything including the flowerbeds and shrubbery. For the vegetable beds I use poles and boards, and for the flowerbeds—stones, magically trans-forming them into rock gardens. I really couldn't care less about what grows outside of the borders—I simply use a trimmer to mow it all down (Photograph 1). It is truly a joy to see how little soil I have under actual cultivation!

6. Use walls, arbors, and fences for climbing plants. North and west sides of structures are not suitable—there will be few flowers and fruit, and much disease.

7. Designate a corner for composting organic matter. Make your compost pile in a shady part of your plot as close as possible to gates and garden beds; also, assign an area for buckets and containers, and perhaps a tub for water stor-age. If you plant shrubs around them, or build a trellis for vines, they will not spoil the view of your garden.

8. Take plenty of time to construct suitable paths and walkways—especially those which lead from the house, the water source, and the corner set aside for the compost pile. You should be able to move a garden cart or a lady friend in stiletto heels on them with equal ease. If you do not have defined pathways, your nerves will be jangled and energy wasted by always having to trudge "cross-country" through the garden! As soon as they are properly laid out, you will immediately understand what I mean.

9. Do not spare expense on installing a water system. This ensures sufficient moisture and saves time. It will pay for itself many times over. In a later chapter, we will cover drip irrigation in detail.

10. Do not restrict yourself to straight lines and right angles! If it is more convenient, crook, shave, or round out beds. Be bold! Use your imagination! For example, a permaculture bed in the shape of a "keyhole" is well-suited for greens, perennials, and herbs. The bed is compact and looks beautiful, more like a flowerbed. If you are dragging hoses or use a wheelbarrow, a "herringbone" garden may be suitable—there are no right angles which can be so annoying to friends strolling amongst the beds. Have you ever noticed how people, contrary to the best laid plans of city engineers, tend to take diagonal shortcuts in parks and squares? Sergey Kladovikov has 6,500 square feet (600 m²) of "herringbones" (Photograph 31). It's a shame that this garden could not have been photographed from above!

You now have all you need to design your own plan. Sketch the borders of your lot first. Next: a) draw in your house and any other structures as well as trees and fences; b) mark areas shaded at noon when the sun is due south. The size of the shaded area will be half the height of structures or trees. Crosshatch over these shady zones where vegetables will not grow well; and c) in the same scale as your plan, cut out paper strips, rectangles, circles, and squares to represent beds, trenches, holes, pyramids, and bins. Their total area should be equal to the required growing space which you calculated earlier. On each piece write the name of a vegetable, or two if you are planting the bed twice per year. You can use different colors according to the color of the harvest, or draw a symbol for each type of vegetable. All that is left to do is arrange the pieces of paper on the plot, taking into consideration the principles given above.

A garden's beauty is in its purposefulness

*An unsightly garden transforms a human being
into a workaholic. A beautiful one transforms a
workaholic into a human being!*

Fact: nothing in nature is ugly. Every living creature,
plant, community, and landscape has its place within the
whole collection of aesthetic masterpieces. We understand
this all the more vividly thanks to modern photographic
art. Through photography we can see that everything in
nature—absolutely everything—is supremely rational. Every
speck, every tiny patch of reflected light is vital to the
survival and advancement of life. Nature is the embodiment
of purposefulness. In this sense, beauty and rationality are
synonymous.

Humans may create artificial forms of beauty, but the essence
remains: everything rational and constructive which
enhances life is beautiful. In fact, you could say that beauty
is our sense of living abundance. At the same time, humans
are the only beings on earth who can make their lives worse
by acting irrationally. We are capable of creating the worst
ugliness. Is your garden beautiful? And even more important,
do you have enough energy left over after working in it
to appreciate its beauty?

What makes a garden beautiful?

First, the **vigor and abundance** of the plants themselves.
A good harvest caresses the eyes, and then delights
the tongue. Seeing the color photos of luxuriant vegetables
on seed packets, we reach into our pockets for money without
reservation. In the garden, we admire the most vigorous
plants and largest vegetables. It's the same at produce
stands. Actually, this is a type of dependence which has its

downside, too. We end up purchasing beautiful yet inedible produce, forgetting about flavor and healthfulness. We should be smarter than that! Of course, it is important that plants are vigorous, but why judge them by their outer gaudiness rather than what they taste like within?!

Second, a garden is beautiful as a **combination** of rows and beds of vegetables. It is especially impressive if plantings are diverse, accentuating differences between various plants (Photograph 13). A variegated garden caresses the soul—in fact, this is diversity, and diversity is abundance. The combination of tall, trellised plants mixed in with lower, humbler ones is inherently attractive. It is a pleasure to watch how they thrive in harmony with each other.

And third, in order to really appreciate the beauty of garden beds, a **contrasting backdrop** is indispensable. The traditional backdrop of a garden is bare ground scraped perfectly clean. But I consider bare ground a deformity—it is unheard of in nature. What should soil be covered with? A mulch of organic matter is a good top layer for beds, but you do not need to cover the entire plot with mulch. Gravel is rather expensive; and in time sinks into the soil and becomes overgrown with weeds. The single, most ideal covering of open ground is grass sod, or more simply, a lawn. Against this backdrop a garden looks fabulous. Your garden becomes transformed into a park!

A cover of diverse grasses is the ideal contrasting backdrop for all other plants. It is beneficial in every way. Grass sod structures the soil and protects it from drying up. It is hygienic, eliminating mud and dust which are unhealthful for vegetables. You can comfortably walk and push a wheelbarrow over it. Turf is ecological, enhancing biodiversity and decreasing pest populations by giving shelter to their enemies. It is sanitary, suppressing the growth of weeds, replacing them with a beneficial meadow community of grasses. Finally, grass sod is the laziest method for maintaining ground in good condition—I would even say the very best possible condition. With just four or five mowings during the summer, we obtain an abundance of nutrient-rich grass mulch for our beds—and what's more, it's not so much work as sheer pleasure.

Nothing is more rational than **turf** composed of a variety of wild grasses—I repeat, wild grasses. For most gardeners in Russia, sterile, manicured lawns are too expensive to maintain, and they are very labor intensive: mowing twice a week, frequent watering, monthly feeding and thatching, re-seeding after severe winters. Such a lawn requires as much attention as a bed of cucumbers! And what's wrong with the natural turf which grows wild in our fields and wastelands? Absolutely nothing! You don't even have to sow it; Nature Herself creates it.

The fact is that weeds cannot tolerate mowing, especially frequent mowing. Weeds are a product of our traditional agriculture. It is humans who over thousands of years of crop cultivation have selected them for their tenacity. Weeds are the offspring of our plows. They flourish—and are only truly ineradicable—*on cultivated soil.* They cannot grow anywhere else.

This is their Achilles heel! If you do not rend the earth with steel, but instead suppress weeds by mowing, then their song is sung. They are the exact opposite of meadow grasses. In fact, grasses have been adapted to mowing. Constantly grazed by animals over eons, they conceal their growth point below the level of the turf. Moreover, mowing stimulates their propagation by offshoots which spread off in every direction. And their seeds can germinate in the turf, since they are able to work their way down into the soil.

Any stand of weeds contains sufficient seeds of meadow grasses. You should mow weeds every time their green mat reaches a height of 8–10 inches (20–25 cm)—in May about every two weeks, in June every three weeks, and once a month in July and August. With each mowing, meadow grasses will proliferate and become stronger while weeds are suppressed. In July you should allow grasses go to seed— wait until the seed heads begin to turn yellow. A community of mown turf changes every year, and weeds disappear right before your eyes.

If you want to cover everything in grass quickly, scatter seed right into the mown spring weeds and mulch with a 1-inch (2–3-cm) layer of humus, or a mix of peat moss and soil. Water well with sprinklers 3–4 times and keep mowing everything that grows. By autumn the weeds will have wholly succumbed to the grasses.

The best grasses for shady areas—for instance, in a mature orchard—are creeping bentgrass (*Agrostis stolonifera*) and Supina bluegrass (*Poa supina*). Nowadays, you often

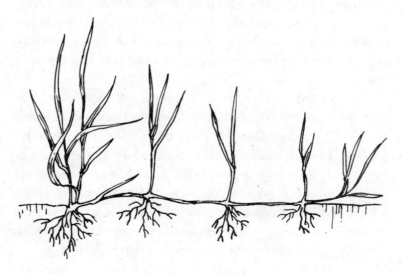

encounter gardens covered in these grasses. They put out a mass of side shoots which quickly turns into a soft mat of extraordinary fluffiness. The soil becomes thickly overgrown and is remarkably friable beneath the turf. A rootlet sprouts from each joint, so you can transplant them into the ground singly or in bunches. Plant bunches every half meter, water, and the area will be covered over by a lush, green mat within a year. In the summer, bent grass may turn brown, but after a rain this "hay" will green up and grow again as if nothing happened. Even when dried up and withered, bent grass produces rootlets from the nodules on its runners!

Bentgrass seeds cannot be confused with anything else. They are very tiny, no longer than one and a half millimeters. It is very difficult to even see them. They are commonly added to "shade" grass seed mixtures.

Tools needed for establishing turf grasses are a trimmer and lawnmower. In Europe these are in every shed, like rakes, but in Russia they have only become popular in the last decade. When I first used a trimmer and saw how cheerfully grass shot out from under the cover, I realized that I could create my very own park! And so my garden has now become one (Photograph 27).

I intersperse small flowerbeds among the grasses—tiny "buttons" slightly elevated with seasoned compost and surrounded by stones. I plant flowers as thickly as possible, so that there is no empty space, and give preference to perennials—I don't have to resow them, and they require very little care. This results in a very lazy and exceedingly pleasant little garden. I just keep adding more new plants, and spend most of my time altering and constructing new vegetable and flower beds.

I even transform the ring around tree trunks into flowerbeds. I surround them with stones, fill them with rotted compost, and plant flowers, or sometimes vegetable greens. It is good for the trees, and makes us happy, too (Photograph 28).

I try to cover all walls and fences with vines. Decorative gourds, multicolored beans, hyacinth beans (*Dolichos lablab*), bindweed, and perfoliate honeysuckle (*Lonicera caprifolium*) are all very good. In recent years, we have become enamored of clematis. In five years or so, our front yard will probably look quite beautiful (it alone occupies about 6,500 square feet, or 600 m^2!). My book *Growing Fruit with a Smile* covers grasses in much greater detail.

Purchase a mower, and you will never want to dig again. There are times, though, when I wonder if I'm getting too carried away—sometimes I just want to cover the entire garden with grass! Don't fall into this trap! Remember: the less you are forced to work in the garden, the less you will want to!

Photo 1. My laid-back garden.

Photo 2. Cucumbers break free into the light and flourish.

Photo 3. Grass clippings make an ideal mulch.

Photo 4. A new bed for yams.

Photo 5. Continuous blanket of mulch on Vladimir Antropov's farm.

Photo 6. Sergey Kladovikov mulches trenches with cardboard.

Photos 7 & 8 *(above)*. A patio garden can be quite productive and , importantly, very convenient to work.

Photos 9 & 10 *(right & below)*. Raised bin designs.

Photo 11. Log bins are very long-lasting.

Photo 12. These bins can convert into cold frames.

Photo 13. Orach beautifies any bed.

Photo 14. Onions and carrots make good companions.

Photo 15. Radishes managed to mature between tomatoes and beans.

Photo 16. After radishes are harvested, strips of lettuce remain.

Photo 17. Cabbages between rows of potatoes in June.

Photo 18. Beets and garlic get along great together.

Photo 19. Late tomatoes wait for the bed to become free.

Photo 20. Cucumbers are planted here as radishes leave for the table.

Photo 21. Cucumbers love growing on corn! (Photo by Stanislav Karpuk.)

Photo 22. Asparagus beans, cabbages, and corn.

Photo 23. Tomatoes successfully set fruit next to young strawberry plants.

Photo 24. These flowers will arrest development of the entire plant.

Photo 25. Light sprouts are miniature plants.

Photo 26. Leaf tubers in the hands of Andrey Udovitsky.

Photo 27. Flowerbeds are closest of all to our house!

Photo 28. Flowerbeds ringing tree trunks are both beautiful and good for the trees.

Photo 29. Grapes and a rock garden along a south-facing wall.

Photo 30. No need for a trimmer here—the lawnmower does it all.

Photo 31. Diagonal pathways are much easier to walk on.

Photo 32. This is what living soil looks like.

Photo 33. Remove the wheels and you get a first-rate weeder.

Photo 34. Fokin hoe.

Photo 35. Cultivator of Sergey Koliada.

Photo 36. Clay spattered on the plastic prevents overheating.

Photo 37. This cold frame is simple and very practical.

Photo 38. A solar vent opener is a great addition to any greenhouse.

Photo 39. Intelligent greenhouses of Vladimir Antropov.

Photo 40. Yummy Chinese yams.   Photo 41. A still-life for lunch.

Photo 42. Only a head like this deserves to be called lettuce!

Photo 43. Titan pumpkins, as-   Photo 44. Mramornaya squash is
paragus beans, and hot peppers.   a healthful culinary marvel.

Chapter 7

How to Make Plantings Denser

or

Considerations for Those Who Love Combinations

All in all, all is in all.

Wisdom!

Important: if you already know how to raise healthy vegetables and are satisfied with the results, you do not have to intercrop anything. It is also likely that this technique is suitable only for those who are inclined towards creativity. It is not easy to develop a successful method for intercropping. You have to think things through, develop strategies, and take detailed notes. In other words, it's not for everyone.

However, there is much to be said for intercropping, also known as companion planting. First, it enables you to squeeze two beds of vegetables into one. The harvest of carrots on a narrow bed may be good, but to grow cucumbers on a trellis along the middle at the same time is still better, even if you only receive an average harvest of cucumbers. Most Russian dacha gardens are 4,300–6,500 square feet (400–600 m²), so we are compelled to be creative whether we like it or not! Second, plants can protect each other from

199

pests, which do not feel as at home in intercropped beds. Intercropping allows you to avoid virtually all poisonous substances. This is very important if you are trying to transform your plot into a stable, balanced ecosystem. Third, intercropping allows for a more consistent and dense plant cover which is better for the soil. Finally, it's fun to experiment! Truly, intercropping is a highly interesting way to garden, full of fascinating discoveries.

Successful intercropping is much easier in theory than in practice. I have certainly made my fair share of mistakes. The most difficult issue is to decide when to sow which vegetables. You have to ensure that plants do not crowd each other out. For example, if you transplant cabbages and cucumbers at the same time, the cucumbers will lag hopelessly behind, and over time the cabbages will smother them completely. Among plants there are "sprinters" which shoot out ahead and "invaders" which impetuously take over an entire area. Moreover, these plants behave differently on different soils and under various weather conditions. Ultimately, you just have to work everything out based on your own experience.

The first thing to understand about intercropping is that on a single square foot you will obtain the most vigorous and productive plant when it is growing alone with no plants nearby to compete with it! So, intercropping is essentially a compromise between the freedom of plants to grow without restriction, the size of the garden, and the desire to not work too hard. The most perceptive gardeners understand that intercropping is, in fact, the art of utilizing sun and soil to the utmost.

On the whole, *cultivated plants cannot bear close neighbors*. Finding themselves surrounded by other plants, they sharply curtail their growth, and the more sun-loving they are, the more they lag behind. However, once they have broken free into the light, many will quickly regain strength. This is true of lettuce, staked tomatoes, cabbage, and the cucurbits (cucumbers, melons, and squash). Cucumbers and pole beans maintain their vigor if their tops manage to stick out above other vegetation. Thus, in order for plants to receive what they expect and give back what is expected of them, *sufficient time is even more important to them than space.*

It is easier and more sensible to intercrop vegetables on narrow beds by planting them in two rows. You can use three rows, if the middle row is a trellis. However, for wide beds there is another good variation: I have found that it is much more convenient to interplant rows or strips rather than different plants within the same row. Even simpler is to interplant "spots"—10- to 15-square-foot (1–1.5-m^2) stands of various vegetables. In the south, gardeners sometimes also use the "amphitheater" method. Following are some observations about intercropping which I have made over the years.

Some thoughts on the "Square Foot"

This method of intercropping—or, more exactly, of *understanding intercropping*—was developed by the American Mel Bartholomew. His book *Square Foot Gardening* has been translated into numerous languages.

Mel proposed an extremely simple unit for intercropping beds—one square foot (30 x 30 cm) planting areas. In this tiny space, it is easy to intercrop several plants of varying heights, and by observing what happens, learn how various plants get along together. For example, a pepper plant may be planted in the center, four carrots in the corners, and between the carrots four parsley plants.

I work with *20-by-20-inch squares* (0.5 x 0.5 m) which better suit us here in Russia. You can fit more vegetables in a space of this size. For instance, a tomato in the center—or a couple cucumbers or four bush beans—on a single vertical support (the stalks are stripped of leaves on the bottom as soon as possible), four beets or four clusters of three carrots in the corners, and between them, along each edge of the square, three or four parsley, cilantro, cress, or radish plants.

You can extend the productivity of squares through time as well. First radishes are planted underneath—30–40 plants in five rows at a spacing of about 2 inches (5 cm) in the row. Later transplant cucumbers, also sowing either carrots or beets. After harvesting the root crops, sow lettuce or radishes in September.

I tried making 3-by-12-foot (1 x 4 m) arrays out of these squares—but suffered total failure. The plants in the center lagged behind and hardly grew at all. Again, narrow beds won out! From this experience, however, I can share the

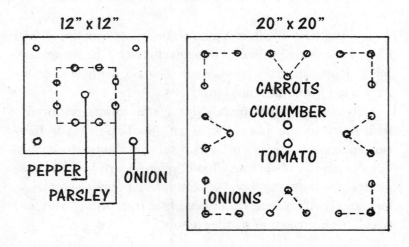

following observations with people who like the concept of planting squares.

1. Fact: a framed square filled with humus works best when it stands all by itself with nothing else growing around it. Then all the plants develop well. This leads me to conclude that it is best not to combine squares of vegetables into a larger array. But you can arrange them in a long strip one square wide. In this case, however, the central, taller row of the strip should not be crowded with smaller plants. This essentially transforms it into a narrow bed.

2. Plants located on the northern half of the square will be stunted by the shade of the central, taller plants. This means that tall plants should be planted on the northern side of the square, creating a tiny "amphitheater."

3. If a wide bed consists of squares, it is better to plant only low-growing vegetables and flowers. Squash, pumpkins, Swiss chard, and all cabbage family except kohlrabi are not suitable for dense intercropping—they crowd out one and all with their huge leaves.

4. Squares with wide-branching plants which need more time to grow should be staggered. If a flowerbed is laid out in squares, it is better to transform it into a "checkerboard" with the "light" squares planted in mats of bentgrass, sedum, or other unpretentious cover crops.

5. It is good—especially with flowerbeds—to delineate the squares with frames made of beautiful, light-colored strips of wood, forming low "boxes." It is easier to plant such a network, and you can see better what you are doing. It looks very elegant!

The square method is good for experimenting to help you understand intercropping. It is especially suitable for winter gardens, sunrooms, and patios. Squares also work well for small, rectangular flowerbeds which are adjacent to walls where the most compact plants are usually placed. In a regular garden, they are less likely to be useful. A strip of squares may be used, but this is essentially a narrow bed.

Triangles are better

This section is about how to fill up a *planting area* rationally.

Farm equipment can sow, transplant, and cultivate only at right angles. For this reason, we have become accustomed to "square" plantings. However, this is not the most sensible arrangement. In nature there are no squares; rather there are hexagons which use space more rationally. In Russia, the agronomists Vladimir Petrovich Ushakov and Petr Matveevich Ponomarev have done extensive research on this, and biointensive gardeners have long condensed plantings by positioning vegetables in hexagons.

Plants placed in the corners of squares strive to be round but feel pressure from their neighbors in all four directions (see illustration). You only have to shift the rows in relation to each other by approximately half an interval, and the

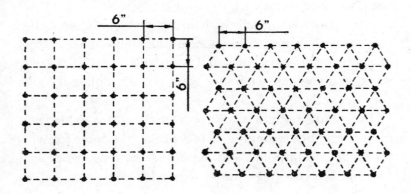

plants magically become arranged in hexagons. The space around each plant is increased, the pressure from neighbors is decreased, and there is less unoccupied space. In narrow beds this is especially recommended for bushy plants—cabbages, peppers, eggplants, and squash. It never hurts to plant other vegetables and transplants in this arrangement as well. With potatoes, for example, the effect can be substantial. On an equal area under the same conditions, you can squeeze in nearly 20% more plants, and there will be much less room for weeds; that's nice, too!

It is best to arrange rows of plants like an "accordion"—in a zigzag pattern of two rows. If the strip of plants faces out to open space in both directions, then you can offset the accordion more, with nearly right angles between plants (see illustration). In free space (for instance, along a pathway), it is always more sensible to plant in two offset lines rather than in a single line.

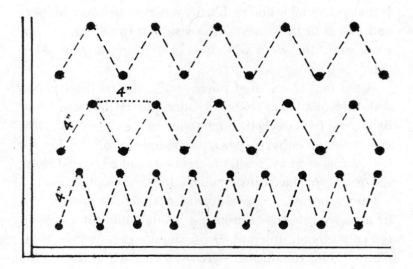

Interplanting vertically

Doctor! Prescribe me a pill to cure greediness.
More and more and more of them!!!

Theoretically, you not only can efficiently cover the surface area of a bed but also achieve maximum *volume*—both above the bed and down the sides of it. Just look at all that airspace going to waste! This idea is so fascinating to me that I am constantly conducting experiments to utilize the entire space.

In a narrow bed, you can interplant two or three different kinds of plants. Cabbages, beets, carrots, napa cabbage, lettuce, peppers, and bush beans are planted along the sides in a zigzag pattern. On the center line you can grow sweet corn, cucumbers, tomatoes, pole beans, or asparagus beans on a trellis. Three types of plants in a narrow bed deter pests better than two. For instance, dill can be planted along one side of the trellis, and carrots on the other. The main thing is that you quickly and ruthlessly remove the lower runners and leaves of the vines. Otherwise, interplanting will not work well—the vines will choke everything out on either side.

If the bed is oriented north-south, the trellised plants should be planted at 1½ times wider spacing than usual. The light must pass freely through them, or else the rows of low vegetables on either side will be shaded for half the day. If a bed is oriented east-west, the trellis should be placed along the northern edge, transforming it into an "amphitheater."

One important issue to consider is that the central trellis usually grows the sun-loving plants while side rows often contain cold-tolerant crops. Therefore, early vegetables planted along the sides in March and April will choke out the climbing "southerners" planted later. Finding themselves under the gloom of cabbage leaves, cucumbers or beans simply stop growing, hopelessly falling behind. Even among carrots, cucumbers will sit quietly waiting to be freed. Tomatoes are a bit more tolerant; they will eventually break free, but their growth will be delayed.

How then should this be done? 1) First sow the "small fry": radishes, cress, and cilantro. Next transplant vines in the middle, sowing the side rows after the center plants have

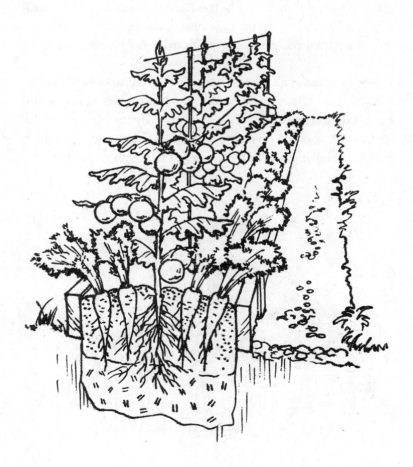

begun climbing up the trellis. 2) Make sure that the side rows are sown as far as possible from the trellis—in narrow beds 8–10 inches (20–25 cm) to either side. 3) In the center transplant only high-quality seedlings with undamaged roots, so that they will shoot up quickly. 4) At the proper time, carefully thin out the side rows, so that their growth is not retarded.

Finally, it is better to interplant climbing plants with vegetables which can be sown throughout the summer—i.e., those which will not bolt in the heat of summer: beets, radishes, bush beans, napa cabbage, daikon, carrots, lettuce, kohlrabi, turnips, peas, Swiss chard, and various cooking herbs.

Bulb onions are a special case. They generally do not tolerate any shade from their neighbors, but we have even found a good neighbor for them. Once onions become established, we sow carrots between the rows. After the onions are harvested for eating, the carrots are left to finish maturing.

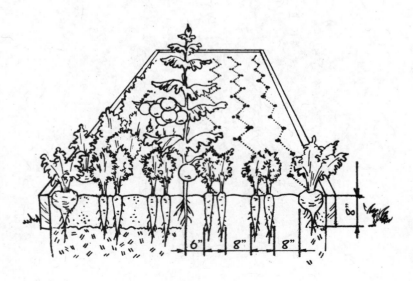

Provided that trellised plants are decisively outstripping the side rows, cucumbers, winter and summer squash, broccoli, and bush tomatoes are well suited to plant along the sides. Bush beans are particularly good near a trellis.

It works very well to sow the side plants as late as June, after the early greens along the edges have been harvested. The lower leaves of the central vines will then have been removed, and the bed is essentially free. At that point, you can plant the various quick-ripening vegetables normally grown in the summer—they are listed above. Ensure vigorous growth by frequent watering and a thick layer of mulch.

Interplanting rows lengthwise in a wide bed is much more difficult than in narrow ones. The main thing to understand is that in any arrangement of plantings the spaces between rows should never be less than 6–8 inches (15–20 cm). For example, on a bed 4 feet (120 cm) wide, you can fit three rows (or strips) in each direction from the center line. Those nearest the trellis—dill, sweet basil, marjoram—should be pruned back ruthlessly, so that they do not intermingle with the side rows. Peppers or carrots squeezed into the middle will not yield a good harvest (see illustration); plant them along the edges.

An "amphitheater" of vegetables

Intercropping three different kinds of plants on a wide bed is even more complicated. The easiest method is to arrange plantings by size: a) the bed should be oriented east-west which exposes it to sunlight "from the front"; b) the trellis must stand on the northern side of the bed; and c) vegetables are of varying heights. The bed resembles the grandstand of a stadium.

The primary "rule" of an amphitheater is that plants in the higher, back rows should always be ahead of their shorter, front neighbors (see illustration). First, vegetables are planted along the trellis—this is the "balcony." Once they have taken off, sow or transplant the mid-sized plants—the "amphitheater." Finally, about ten days later, sow the "orchestra pit." By that time, the radishes, cress, or coriander—which had been occupying the space of the orchestra pit in the interim—have been harvested.

Peppers (sweet and hot), eggplants, staked bush tomatoes, and herbs like sweet basil, catnip, and dill are the only vegetables suitable to the middle of the amphitheater. They

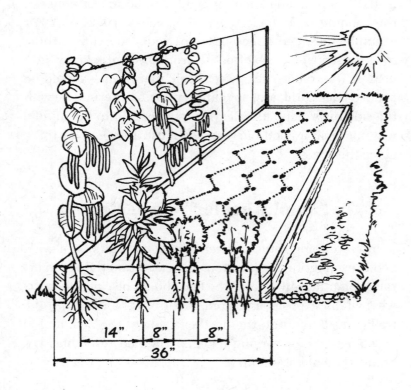

14"   8"   8"
36"

are set out when cucumbers or beans have begun sending up their climbing runners. Tomatoes planted with beans will at first choke them out, but peppers will not. Asparagus beans and certain kinds of pole beans are so heat-loving that they only start growing tall during the hot days of June, although they germinate at the same time as bush beans. Tomatoes and cabbages grow earlier and more vigorously than anything else.

Rows of vegetables in an amphitheater are best spaced at 12–16 inches (30–40 cm). The tall, back row runs along the very edge—there's no reason to leave room for weeds. The middle row is 12–16 inches (30–40 cm) forward, followed by a row of carrots or beets yet another 8 inches (20 cm) further in front. Plant bush beans only along the near edge. They require a large amount of free space and will sprawl down onto the pathway. Onions should also be planted along that edge; they need full sun.

The yield of an "amphitheater" is really no more than with monoculture. All the same, they are extremely productive beds. And they are very beautiful. For this reason, an "amphitheater" is best located near the house. A semicircle facing southwards, surrounded by stones, is absolutely gorgeous!

Strips are easiest!

In practice, of course, we are not always patient enough to plant beds exactly as they should be. We use all the above variations, depending on when space is freed up by an earlier crop. Yet we keep longing for something simpler—to just wave our hand over a bed, and have everything magically fall into its proper place!

The closest I've come to such simplicity is planting "strips" in wide bins. Mostly this applies to the "little guys"—greens, lettuce, root crops, onions, and bush beans. Beds are sown by section in rows running across the width of the bed as in Photograph 16. A couple feet of radishes here, a foot of lettuce there—and when space is freed up, you simply sow something else. Ten rows of beets, ten of carrots, six of onions, three of parsley—it is all very easy and sufficiently variegated to deter pests. You only have to ensure that one crop does not choke out its neighbors by leaving sufficient space at the borders of "strips," and by utilizing the edges of beds to the utmost. In such a system, even perennials along the sides of the bed get along nicely.

The simplest interplanting

A simple "wave of the hand"—like Vasilisa the Wise does in the Russian fairytale—is the dream of the laid-back gardener! And I have accomplished this. There are almost no weeds on my compost-rich beds, and I really do not mind thoroughly weeding once. In the spring around the end of March, I break up the surface of a bed with a rake and cover it with plastic. After a week or two, I cut down the mat of emerging weeds with a multi-purpose hoe and a few days later simply broadcast seeds of radishes, cress, cilantro, or lettuce over the bed. I work them in with a rake, water, and again cover them with plastic. After a couple of weeks, I sit down comfortably on a board and, without hurrying, weed and thin out the seedlings. All that remains to do is periodically harvest the young greens to eat—first of all from the center strip, where cucumbers and tomatoes will soon be transplanted.

But do they want to live together?

Relatives are people not connected in any way to each other, but who periodically gather together to be accounted for and eat heartily on occasion of changes to their number.

Andrey Knyshev

The more diverse a community, the more stable it is. A diverse environment makes it difficult for pests to function. It is harder for them to find host plants because there are so many unpleasant and frightening smells all around and a multitude of enemies. However, plants themselves also strongly affect each other—they shade one another out and produce offensive volatile compounds and root secretions.

This brings up the experiments of Lenz Moser. He explicitly demonstrated that certain plants stimulate the growth of grapes while others suppress them—*no matter what the age of the grapes and given a steady supply of nutrients and water*. It is a proven fact that plants actively communicate with each other both chemically and by means of electromagnetic signals. There is even a scientific term for this—allelopathy. However, there is such a huge mass of data—and it is often contradictory—that it is very difficult to apply anything in practice. I have tried to gather the available information in a single sack, shake it all together, and squeeze out whatever conclusions I can. This is what I came up with:

1. Certain plants definitely do not get along together: a) plants of the same height and leaf size which are planted densely; and b) members of the same family—that is, relatives. This is only natural since they have the same requirements, and produce similar excretions. As with us, relatives

are often the worst companions. Umbelliferae—dill, parsley, celery, parsnip, lovage, and cilantro—clash particularly violently with each other. Only carrots retain allegiance to their kin.

2. Fennel and wormwood suppress everything without exception.

3. Onions and garlic are offensive to legumes and cabbage family.

4. Carrots, beets, cucumbers, and tomatoes basically couldn't care less.

5. Lettuce and spinach exude substances which vitalize the roots of other plants and shade the soil. They are outstanding community helpers and providers!

6. The following plants protect others from pests: beans, parsley, and cooking herbs in the mint family—lemon balm, sweet basil, savory, thyme, catnip, hyssop, and sweet marjoram. Also, pungent ornamental flowers: calendula, nasturtiums, marigolds, chrysanthemums, zinnias, and cosmos. Onions and garlic suppress fungal diseases.

7. Corn, Jerusalem artichokes, sorghum, and millet provide shade, protect against wind, and create a beneficial microclimate. Sunflowers, on the other hand, can be offensive to many other plants. It is better to plant them along the edge of the garden.

Tatiana Ugarova cites several pairs which help each other to withstand pests. These plants can be grown in neighboring rows. Carrots and onions protect each other from the carrot rust fly and onion root maggot. Celery deters cabbage worms from various brassicas. If planted between each cabbage plant, it will flourish after the cabbage is harvested. Cucumbers and dill get along excellently in the same space—on the condition that there is not too much dill. Sweet basil and tomatoes also collaborate well. Kohlrabi and lettuce are good neighbors in the same row; the lettuce is harvested before the kohlrabi. Cucumbers love climbing up corn and sunflowers, producing all the way until frost. Pole beans get along very well sharing a row with spreading cucumbers or tomatoes. Finally, it is always good to sow radishes where zucchini, squash, or other summer vegetables will later be planted.

This brings us to interplanting through time.

A conveyer belt of vegetables

"Zhenka actually got a tomato to ripen!"
"Really?! Let's have a shot before the cow gets it!"

If we learn how to gather 3–4 harvests from every bed, then we can eat fresh vegetables from early spring through late fall without complicating our lives with intercropping. Here in Southern Russia (Zone 6), we keep beds covered with plants from April to October, and with the help of plastic or Spunbond—from March to November. Furthermore, cabbages, lettuce, parsley, mustard greens, coriander, and leeks can overwinter under plastic and will even continue to grow a little.

This being the case, I feel it's a shame not to interplant through time. Even without plastic during a cold spring, I can easily grow radishes and cress followed by lettuce and carrots on the same bed; in the late spring tomatoes are transplanted in the middle and peppers along the sides. In July napa cabbage is transplanted into any free space, and at the end of September, after clearing off the bed, more radishes and greens are sown. Before winter, I sow lettuce for an early spring harvest.

Table 3. Planting times and days to maturity of garden crops

Sown early with long days to maturity

Cabbage, late *200 days*	Leeks *180*
Cabbage, red *180*	Cauliflower *160–180*
Brussels sprouts *180*	Onion, blackseed *200*
Savoy cabbage *130–150*	Jerusalem artichoke *150*
Broccoli, sprouting *100–160*	Black salsify *dug until winter*
Parsnips *150–180 (can overwinter in the bed)*	

Occupying beds permanently

Parsley	Onions, perennial:
Sorrel	Chives
Rhubarb	Siberian garlic chives
Lovage	Spring onions
Mint	Chinese chives
Tarragon	Altai onions

Sown early with short days to maturity

Lettuce *40–60 days*	Kohlrabi *60–70*
Napa cabbage *50*	Cilantro *40*
Radish *20–40*	Mustard greens *40*
Cress *20*	Onions, green *20–40*

Sown late with long days to maturity (140 days)

Tomatoes	Broccoli
Cucumbers	Corn, sweet
Beans, pole	Chicory for winter forcing
Peppers	Asparagus bean
Eggplants	Cucumber, white
Pumpkins	Sweet potatoes
Squash	Bitter melon (*Momordica charantia*)
Zucchini	Chayote
Scallop squash	Other tropical vegetables

Will mature when planted at the beginning of September or later

Radishes *30–50 days*	Kohlrabi *60*
Lettuce for spring harvest	Napa cabbage *50*
Mustard greens *40*	Cilantro *40*

Will mature under plastic

Lettuce	Endive
Swiss chard	Shallots
Spinach	Carrots
Salad chicory	Potatoes

Sown early for summer harvest

Carrots *100 days*	Shallots *120*
Turnip *60*	Dill *100*
Broccoli *100*	Cabbage, early *110*
Kohlrabi, late *70–90*	Carrots, bunch *90*
Peas *90*	Endive *90*
Spinach *60–90*	Potatoes *60–120*

Sown late for summer harvest

Soybeans *100 days*	Herbs:	
Beans, bush *70–90*	Cilantro	Catnip
Beets *110*	Sweet basil	Dill
Onions, from sets *120*	Hyssop	Celery

Sown in summer

Salad chicory *100 days*	Parsnips, winter *150*
Radishes *100*	Napa cabbage *80*
Daikon *100*	

Potatoes, late, planted at the end of August will mature around the middle of November

Sown from spring through the end of July

Cucumbers	Rutabagas
Squash	Spinach
Zucchini	Cauliflower, early
Scallop squash	Broccoli, early
Carrots	Kohlrabi
Beets	Peas
Lettuce	Swiss chard
Beans,bush	Soybeans
Napa cabbage	Endive
Turnips	Herbs

As for timing, there is some wriggle room even in Siberia (Zones 2 and 3) and Central Russia (Zone 4). If we classify plants according to planting times and days to maturity, and roughly arrange them through the growing season, a rather illustrative picture is revealed (see Table 3). It becomes clear how best to fill up a bed with vegetables throughout the entire year. I collected the data on the previous two pages based on my own and other people's experience, on the classical study of Valentin Bryzgalov, and on Tony Biggs's book *Growing Vegetables*.

After mastering intercropping, ingenious gardeners can no longer picture a bed with only one vegetable growing in it. It is utter nonsense to them!

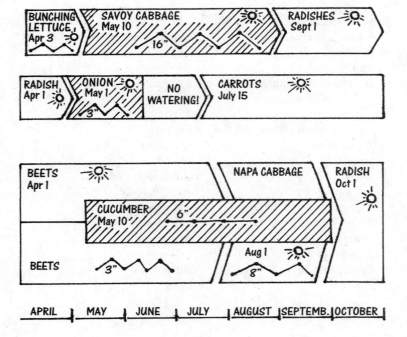

Examples of successful intercropping

In Russia and the republics of the former Soviet Union, we have many ingenious gardeners, each of whom has found his own variation of efficient intercropping, receiving two, three, or even more harvests from a single bed every year.

Photographs 17 and 18 show the garden of Alexey Kazarin outside of Pskov in Northwest Russia (Zone 5). Notice how he raises cabbages with potatoes, and beets with garlic—even his second harvest usually produces high yields.

Then there is the garden of Sergey Kladovikov of Kuban in Southern Russia (Zone 6). He consistently replaces harvested plants with other vegetables. For example, he interplants garlic with currant berry seedlings. In June, garlic is harvested and currant transplants dug up and sold. Next, the bed will be sown in cucumbers and corn. In Photograph 19, peas and garlic will be soon harvested, and tomatoes are just starting to grow up alongside the carrots—the young plants are visible to the right of the irrigation pipe. In Photograph 20, you can see dill reaching upwards and bushing out after the lettuce was harvested. Along the center of the bed cucumbers are growing, covered with cloches.

Stanislav Karpuk, president of a local natural gardening club in the southern city of Dnepropetrovsk (Zone 6), manages to grow as many as eight different kinds of vegetables on a single bed! Pictured are some of the combinations he has worked out so far: early cabbage–cucumbers–corn (Photograph 21) and beans–corn–cabbage (Photograph 22). He also does onions–carrots–cucumbers and much more besides.

Boris Bublik, a gardener and writer from the Ukrainian city of Kharkov (Zone 5), has developed a two-year intercropping system—a truly acrobatic feat! Here is an example of his methods:

At the end of August, wheat is sown sideways in strips across the bed. A couple weeks later, garlic bulbils* are sown between these strips. In the spring the wheat is cut, replaced by two bush tomatoes planted on either side of the bed with a single sweet basil plant in the middle. At the end of summer, before removing these plants, coriander and mustard green seeds are broadcast. Some of these greens are for the table, and the rest cover the bed through the winter. The following spring, the garlic, having overwintered as bulbs, vigorously sprouts up in its strips. Early greens are sown between them: radishes, lettuce, cress, and napa cabbage. The greens are harvested, and tomatoes and sweet basil again replace them. The garlic is dug up continually. Towards the fall, the tomatoes are harvested and vetch or oats are sown. The bed passes through winter under their protective "blanket."

Here is another example of a system based on garlic. In the middle of September, garlic is planted in the bed, and soaked oat seeds are scattered on top for green manure. In the early spring, the bed is covered with winterkilled oat straw, and the garlic sprouts up right through it. Next, parsnips are sown in the spaces between the rows. In June, the garlic is harvested, and in their holes dragonhead or zinnias are sown; they will cover the bed through the winter. The parsnips are dug up all through winter as needed.

You can invent many other similar systems—if you are willing to give it some thought!

---

* *Bulbils*—mini-bulblets which garlic develops instead of seeds in their flower head. In the first summer after planting, each bulbil will grow into a single, small bulb. In the second year, this bulb becomes a normal garlic head divided into cloves.

You have already seen many pictures of my garden, but here are a few more. In Photograph 23, strawberries raised from seeds are growing alongside trellised tomatoes, which manage to produce an excellent crop in the same bed. In Photograph 2 peas interwound with cucumbers are nearly ready to relinquish their space to two rows of late carrots. Among the pea vines, small cucumbers ripen very well, but be sure not to sow peas closer than 8 inches (20 cm) apart— the lateral shoots of the cucumbers have to be able to easily break free. In Photograph 15 you can see how radishes have succeeded in intermingling with the tomatoes and beans. And in a different combination, sea-lavender flowers (*statice*), sweet basil, eggplants, and black walnut transplants all get along just fine. Everything is doing very well together!

I continue to experiment and learn how to transform my beds into productive conveyer belts of vegetables. I soon hope to develop the combinations best suited to my own situation. This means that the garden will take up even less of my time and effort. After all, predictability is highly energy efficient.

But now let's take a short break from vegetables!

Chapter 8

Freedom Lost

or

A Tale About Digging Down to the Roots

Humans would be much happier if we weren't always banging up our knuckles by knocking on wood.

On Lake Tanganyika they have a very simple way of catching fish. Two dugouts are connected by a rope—strung with wooden blocks like beads on a necklace—and paddled out into the middle of a cove. They separate, stretching the rope out between them, and head back towards the shore. As they move forward, the fish in front of the beaded rope are herded into a hoop net which awaits them. They all but leap out of the water to escape the wooden blocks! Why? Because they put off a shadow, and the fish perceive this shadow to be solid—like a net. So in order to save themselves, they flee from the shadow towards the shore right into the hoop net, and so into the frying pan.

According to Hans Selye, the originator of stress theory, "stress is whatever a person chooses to perceive as stressful"—i.e., our problems derive from how we view ourselves, our own self-appraisal. Our opinions about ourselves, our vanity, and our values are all part of this imaginary network, a devious trap of the mind. We have created it ourselves, yet we recoil from it. Our loss of freedom arises directly from our own personal beliefs!

Consider two women who are both pretty: one of them enjoys her life while the other is unhappy. The difference is in their beliefs. The unhappy one is certain that she is not beautiful; she has ensnared herself in her own self-created mental trap. Yet all she needs to do to become free is to change her point of view. If she could just alter her outlook, she would realize that actually she is pretty in her own way—or that it really doesn't matter how she looks. In fact, this is what everyone around her thinks! But the woman stubbornly clings to her conviction.

What is freedom? Freedom is the absence of mental traps. It is the ability to change your beliefs, to look at life from varying points of view. More precisely, freedom is the capacity to avoid fixating on any one particular point of view. Why is this so difficult?

An examination of how we have lost our freedom is a vital component of the science of success. An entire book on this topic has been ripening in me for quite a while, but here we will touch on the most salient points.

An anatomy of our problems

What will be will be,
So let it be, let it be!

"That's not true! Our beliefs are sacred! In fact, our very self-respect is based on these beliefs. It's the loyalty to our personal convictions which defines our worth as human beings." Stop right there! We have arrived at the first mental trap. Whoever said that adherence to our beliefs is some kind of higher calling? In my opinion, what matters most is the *quality of our beliefs*; they should be constructive. But loyalty? Life is constantly changing. Yesterday's personal values may lose their meaning today. What is right in Russia may make you an outlaw in Thailand. How often I have encountered unhappy people whose "principles" are destroying their lives! Since when do we need values which make our lives miserable?!

Why do we stubbornly cling to our beliefs?

The answer is simple: *we want to be right.* To believe that we are right, that we are behaving and thinking *properly*, is a fundamental human requirement—much more important than food, sleep, or sex! Consequently it becomes a major tragedy for us to change our beliefs. If we abandon even the most ridiculous principle, we feel that we have literally "betrayed ourselves." No way are we going to let that happen! We would rather find a scapegoat for our problems. In fact, this is what we do throughout our lives. Whenever our principles do not work out as expected, we immediately blame those around us for not understanding, or for being dishonest. This is the easiest method to "be right"!

Take any problem. How do we typically deal with it? The simplest way is to denounce the people responsible for it as being wrong. Or we may try fighting the problem—i.e., battling against ourselves. Sometimes we turn to expert advice; this shifts the responsibility onto another. Or we just resign to the problem and humbly bear our cross. What is the bottom line? In all four instances, the problem is preserved—in fact, it prospers and multiplies! But in exchange we are able to maintain the illusion that we are right! Our beliefs-problems thus turn into our values.

Eventually, we become so accustomed to having problems that we can no longer live without them. If someone tries to remove one from us, we staunchly resist. We have all experienced how difficult it is to counsel a friend who constantly complains about his accursed life. The most straightforward answer to the question of why we have so many problems is that *we want to have them.*

You don't believe me? Take a closer look at any one of your problems. Suppose you are suffering from a sore foot (liver, lower back, etc.). Let's pretend that we can just wave a magic wand over it, and by tomorrow your problem will have disappeared. How does this change things? First off, it means that you will have to modify your beliefs about doctors, your way of life, and the "blessings of civilization." From now on you will take better care of your health—eat wholesome foods, take up sports, even forget about medicine completely. Secondly, there will be no more bellyaching, whining, or looking for sympathy! No more complaining to everyone, playing hooky, or slacking off at work. Your family and relatives will now simply be your friends, not soundboards for your grumbling, moaning, and righteous indignation. Since you have become free, no one owes you anything. For example, you can simply choose to work in your garden by yourself. Nobody feels sorry for you anymore; you are fully in charge! And if you do start complaining again, you will always get the same response: "Your problems are nothing compared to mine!" Are you ready for this?

Once your problems are gone, you are no longer the person that you were before. Now you are healthy, strong, and free. Horrors! Your husband (wife) will suddenly feel unneeded and afraid, your children's eyes will bug out in amazement, and arguments will break out everywhere. And what will your friends think?! You will always be explaining everything to everyone. In time you may start developing interests of your own. "But this means abandoning my friends and family. I would never do that! How could they get along without me? It's better to just keep things as they are."

I can hear your denial. You don't need sympathy! And you certainly want to be healthy! You *want* it. Right. But what do you *do* to make it happen? What *actual actions do you take*? Everyone has the desire, but what about the intention?

At most, any action you do take only increases your struggle by "trying to solve the problem." But you are not being honest with yourself. Actually, there is no problem if you aren't thinking about it and fighting against it. *Struggle is a way of holding onto problems.* Do you have a problem with green grass, fresh air, or your favorite pastime? The plain truth is that you either choose to have problems, or choose not to.

You can do away with a problem for good by simply letting it go, *by changing your attitude towards it.* Wouldn't it be wonderful if the woman mentioned earlier suddenly realized that she is, in fact, pretty? Poof! The problem evaporates; it's gone! Think about it. Has this ever happened to you? Reaching the end of your rope, finding yourself at the brink of a precipice, you suddenly realize that things aren't so bad as you thought. You were just stuck in an old tape loop. It's crazy! But then relief comes—and a huge load is lifted from your shoulders. You could even laugh at yourself: "What a fool I've been!" And poof! The problem ceases to exist.

At the root of every problem is fear—fear of being wrong or bad. For this reason, letting go of a problem can be like leaping out of an airplane with a parachute—at first it's scary, but then—what an amazing feeling of soaring!

Essentially, every problem is a mirage, an illusion. An autopsy of the beast reveals its primitive organization—it merely consists of two contradictory intentions. Both exist in us, but we are completely unconscious of one of them. For example, I want to be thin, but I also want to eat rich food. I understand that it is unhealthy for me, and I resolve to avoid it—but all the same keep scarfing it down! Or I want a wife, but I don't want to get married. I want to have a beautiful garden, but I don't want to do the work. I want to water the beds, but I'm not in the mood. And so it is with everything, every day—and, of course, the blame always falls on somebody else.

Inasmuch as these are merely illusions, we have the power to instantly dispel them. If we boldly take a problem by the horns and lay it down flat for all the world to see, examining it thoroughly and *making a conscious choice*, it will immediately disappear. It does not even matter which choice you make! The main thing is to conscientiously decide on a particular line of action—to get married in good faith, or not get married in good faith. Choice gives us the opportunity to act, because *choice is freedom*. What characterizes strong,

self-confident people? They know what they want. It doesn't matter whether everyone around them likes it or not. They choose their own path, and for this reason they have to be reckoned with. On the other hand, they are easy to understand and reliable to work with. However, if a person does not make a choice one way or another, we see him as "slippery," two-faced, and unreliable—a wimp. It is difficult to understand him, and nearly impossible to help him.

I believe that the most practical knowledge is to be aware of the way our minds work. In the following pages, I will present a brief selection of typical, false beliefs—something like "A Short Course in the Science of Dogmatic Thinking" or "Fundamentals of Narrow-mindedness."

Life is struggle!

Teach your children well...
And everything goes to hell!

Efim Samovarshchikov

From our earliest years we are taught to struggle. And we continue struggling throughout our lives—against enemies, relatives, the government, our bodily aches and pains; against drought, pests, and our depleted soil. We struggle for civility, sobriety, culture, and the environment; for love, children, and the conquest of evil. We struggle and search; we discover—and for some reason we never quit! We just keep struggling, often receiving the exact opposite of what we are striving for, and ever refusing to acknowledge this. Obviously, yet another trap!

The fact of the matter is that struggle is a despicable and devious thing which, if we probe deeply enough into it, turns out to be an instinctive reaction to danger. Most often the threat is imaginary, intentionally trumped up by someone—or by ourselves. Struggle is wholly destructive and exists only for its own sake. In essence, it is our inability to manage without it. Its effect is to frighten us, to wear us down, to drag us into controversy, or to compel us to pay dearly for "help." However, it is never the intention of struggle to achieve a constructive result by eliminating the problem! This is an entirely different matter; enterprise and creativity are the opposites of struggle.

Struggle never solves the problem, just as no poison will ever deliver us from pests, and no kind of punishment will ever eradicate crime. Struggling for our health will not make us healthy, because struggling actually inflates our problems and allows them to flourish. In order to be delivered from a problem, we must discover and understand its underlying causes. What compels us to struggle? What ideas push our buttons? And most importantly, *who created the problem* which initiated the struggle, and then cashed in on the "solution"?

If you realize this truth, refusing to support struggle, then the problem will go away since it no longer will generate a profit.

Disorder is also an insidious myth. We believe that it arises on its own, but this is not true. Disorder is created. We create it ourselves—for instance, by giving in to struggle. A classic example is protecting plants by chemical means. If from the very beginning we took care of the soil and created a stable ecosystem in our garden, our harvests would go through the roof, and pests and diseases would be so minimal that we could completely ignore them. But we prefer to get angry at pests! This battle cry against these silly insects

has given rise to an entire "war industry." Yet it is obvious that we created these pests ourselves. Monoculture,* weakened plants, and the systematic destruction of beneficial predatory insects are principal reasons why pests invade our gardens. These problems never occur in nature.

Here's how it happens: first, we create disorder, and then we struggle against it, which only makes things worse. The more we wear ourselves out in this struggle, the greater the disorder. After all, we never stopped creating it! We must understand that *struggle against disorder never leads to order.* It merely *masks the creation of more disorder.* You can see how horrendously abominable struggle is? It's simply incredible!

Whenever you realize that you are struggling, just slow down and take a breath. You have been duped; you have bought into a scam. Ask yourself: "What am I struggling against?" Answer honestly, and then ask: *"How did I create it?"* This time answer with even more honesty. After that,

* *Monoculture*—when a single crop is grown over a large area.

you can simply stop creating disorder, and start creating a completely new order—without the struggle.

Sometimes we try to rearrange our lives, but is that ever difficult! Tired out by the struggle for some new breakthrough, we finally give up and go back to business as usual. There is a fundamental law regarding this: whenever a new order of things is introduced, temporary chaos will follow. But if you start struggling against it, a new order will never be instituted! You can only achieve success if you boldly *ignore opposition and interference*; just don't pay attention to it.

This is why struggle against evil never uproots evil. In order to eliminate evil, you must institute something good—a new, intelligent design. Then the focus moves off of evil and onto good. After all, "what is evil but good tormented by hunger and thirst?"

Stability equals reliability

"You know, Petrov is seriously in the black."
"So, how do you think he'll wash all that black off?"

We trust in stability* because we accept that the "higher powers" will take care of us—for instance, a just government, the social safety net, or insurance. Most of us do not like change since it might only make things worse. But times are changing, and it is becoming clear that, in fact, we create

---

* *Stability*—here: when nothing is changing. Actually, a state of suspended growth which indicates that decline is about to set in. Only when stability halts decline can it be considered a good thing, but if growth does not subsequently follow, then decline will again ensue.

our own reality. With each decade the world keeps trans-forming beyond recognition. We have come to realize that what does not change will only get worse. Stagnation inevi-tably leads to decline.

Life is continuously preoccupied with its own prosperity. That is its nature. Every creature exerts itself, striving with all its might to keep growing in some way. No sooner has one creature slowed down than others immediately move in to take its place. The only safe and reliable condition of life is steady growth. *This is the norm.* As long as a person is do-ing something creatively, he grows. Every good decision and every problem solved is a victory and is growth.

But when growth ceases, that's where problems arise! Of course, this does not happen on its own. Somewhere you must have dropped the ball. And if you foul up even more, that's it—everything will surely go downhill. A "stable" con-dition is really *an emergency situation*! It is as if all the en-gines of an airplane suddenly shut down at takeoff. If you have stopped growing, you must raise the alarm and ur-gently search for the cause of the breakdown! Then you can eliminate it by sensibly changing your life—and, of course, by ignoring struggle.

Not changing is a symptom. It is a sign that we have *stopped creating*. Creativity is always changing, growing, and prospering. But if growth stops, this means that noth-ing new is being created. Expect that decline will soon fol-low. With this in mind, you might want to check out what's happening in your garden.

It may seem that many things exist in and of themselves—for instance, our work, health, family relations, and the har-vest. But these things only exist when you are actively cre-ating them, seeking them, improving them, giving them all your attention. If you no longer care about improving your work and are merely serving time, then in reality this is no longer truly your work. I have often noticed how after the wedding a couple immediately stops creating their love— and it evaporates! They begin living as separate beings, and the family essentially ceases to exist.

If your garden is a burden to you, it indicates that you have stopped being creative. This situation cannot last. Either you will fall ill, or—more sensibly—you will sell off your plot. Knowing this, I am always creating and altering my garden a little bit at a time—it's the only sure way to have a problem-free garden!

Circumstances are stronger than we are

Hey! Don't even think of complaining to me about your happiness!

In trying to break free of such a "stagnation crisis," to restore order and resolve problems, we are hindered by our "rose-colored glasses"—namely, the belief that results are not dependent on us. We prefer to push responsibility onto something or someone else—i.e., "outer circumstances." But let's be honest here. In almost any situation, we could have behaved differently. We could have anticipated what was coming, made the extra effort, or done something else entirely; we could have shown up or gone away, accepted or refused; or we could have seen and understood. Could have? Yes, we could have. The specific circumstances are not to blame. We failed to do what was best because we did not know how to deal with the situation properly—or, as is usually the case, because we did not want to or were afraid.

We always have the option to make our own choice. To choose means to take responsibility. The main point is that, if a person takes responsibility, then "circumstances" have no role. Realizing that he receives what he truly desires, he has nothing to regret.

Circumstances are not beyond our control! In fact, they are the same as our intentions. The real problem is that we usually do not realize our true intentions, just as a lover rarely realizes his true motives. Most often being in love is simply the need to receive—a burning desire to gain someone's attention, to feel cool, or to sacrifice oneself for someone. But there is no way we're going to admit *that*—after all, we have been brought up to believe that "egotism is wrong— and sacrifice is right." So a person becomes convinced that he loves "for the sake of the beloved."

To search for causes outside of ourselves is also symptomatic, a sign that we refuse to make our own choices. We want someone else to decide for us—and to be responsible for the result. This is easy to see whenever life starts falling apart. We find a thousand reasons for our misfortune! They creep into our mind every time we try to make a decision. Excuses are so tempting, so logical and alluring, that we are even prepared to give up success for their sake. It is a hundred times easier to find an excuse than to attain victory! Excuses are one of the main traps we fall into.

If, however, you can manage to summon up your courage, there is a mental instrument you can utilize which will help you outwit excuses. You simply need to ask two questions: "What did I do to make things worse?" Eliminate that from your life! And: "What did I do to make things better?" Incorporate that into your life! What made you feel better? "Things I enjoy doing, love for my wife, and healthy food." Incorporate this! And what made you feel worse? "I got pissed

off at my wife and stuffed myself with junk food." Reconsider the situation, eliminate what is harmful, take responsibility—and life comes naturally back into balance.

It is crucial to comprehend why we would possibly want to get sick. The greater truth about our circumstances is that *the only things which happen to us are what we actually want.* It does not matter how we feel about them. What happens to us exposes our real intentions. What are we buying?

And in what currency are we willing to pay? It is difficult to understand this, but awareness is freedom. Consider what you have—and you will understand what you truly desire!

Endurance and hard work grind stones into dust

Pecking away all day long,
The woodpecker wasn't lazy,
But it drove him crazy.

Masterpiece

This moral principle is beaten into us from birth. We endure and we work hard. We grind our gardens into dust, not to mention millions of hectares of fertile steppe lands, or even the once beautiful Aral Sea!* In time we may grind down all of nature, including ourselves—if we don't come to our senses.

We believe in hard work, encouraging zealous perseverance, and then we are surprised that things turn out poorly. We do not want to recognize that it is not a matter of fervor! Rather it's about *results*. Ultimately, thoughtless zeal causes more harm than hard work brings benefit. Life is not improved by fervor but by success. *It is not zealous work, but rather productive work which is successful!* If we look at two workers, the more successful one expends less time, effort, and resources to achieve the same result.

---

* *Aral Sea*—located in Central Asia, this lake was formerly one of the largest in the world but was subsequently reduced to less than 10% of its original size after the rivers feeding it were diverted to large-scale irrigation projects. [trans]

It is often said in Russia: "Without hard work you won't catch even the tiniest fish in the pond."* Really? I would say that perhaps you do not need to go fishing at all. What if we came up with a way to make fish leap out of the water by themselves right into our hands? And not just puny little fish, but sturgeon and salmon!

Engels wrote that: "Labor transformed ape into man."** Really? I cannot recall, though, if he specified whether this was intellectual or physical labor.

It would then follow that all those apes who were not transformed remained forever as "slackers." And what would you expect from wild beasts? However, I can assure you that, seeing how zealously we dig, plant, and cultivate the soil, and whitewash our trees, year after year, sweating our guts out and ending up with the same poor harvest, the apes would surely die from laughter watching us! No other living being in nature slits its own throat. Only mankind—the "master of nature"—acts so completely ineffectually, basing his activities on faith, other people's opinions, and advertising. Even bunnies know to chew off only the tips of shoots, so that new ones will grow back more quickly. We watch an ant dragging along a twig. If we set it on a dish, it will continue to drag it full-circle. We get all excited, thinking: "It has no brain—just instinct!" But the truth is that each year these same ants steal away half our harvest. They herd aphids up trees, and then kick back and take it easy—despite all our efforts to thwart them. They don't struggle, nor do they engage in endless warfare—they simply institute their own order. So, who are the "brainless" ones here? If we remember that work should result in prosperity, we will realize that actually we are way behind the apes: *we have invented unproductive labor*—labor which produces an inverse result.

* A popular Russian proverb, similar to *No pain, no gain* in English. [trans]

** Reference to Friedrich Engels's work *The Part Played by Labor in the Transition from Ape to Man* which was an integral part of Soviet ideology. [trans]

How did we come up with this value which separates hard work from personal success? It's simple: throughout history we have paid for it, rewarded it, and praised it. Those few people who knew how to think were ignored or condemned—sometimes even killed. Hard work is the trait of average citizens which is most advantageous to the government.

This is a fundamental law of management: *rewarding poor work and not rewarding productive work leads to the breakdown of all work.* Or more simply: as you reward, so shall you receive. Work which is not rewarded ceases to be performed. This is how relationships, companies, economies, and agriculture fall into decline. We are paid when we are sick, so we become sick more often. We are paid to be unemployed, so why should we work? Are your children naughty? You might consider which behaviors you are rewarding with your attention and reactions. Are your plants developing poorly? Perhaps you are not rewarding their healthy development! But what reward should you give them? Only they can show you that. You must observe more attentively. All they want is your reward; they have no need for your hard work!

"I live for the sake of others..."

I love them all, but they don't love me. And for that I hate them!

How dare I challenge these morals! Please forgive me, you who "live for the sake of." I do not want to infringe on your values. I am simply trying to sort things out. Why is it that those who "live for the sake of" are so unhappy? Why do they woefully lament the ingratitude of the people whom they live "for the sake of"? Russians frequently say: "Do no good, and you will receive no evil in return."

It's very simple. Why do we live for the sake of others? Ultimately, so that they will be better off. But why do *we* specifically have to do this? So that we will be better off, too. In actuality, we are "living for the sake of others" for the sake of ourselves. And by so doing, we are trying to be happier, more important, and more accepted.

You don't believe me? Look at everything we do "for the sake of" our children, grandchildren, and loved ones—without their needing it, even without their consent. Tell me, who gains from our constant anxiety over our children? Certainly not our children! They accept our care as an inevitable fact of life; they take it for granted—often, unfortunately, as an unavoidable evil. This is not help; this is abuse! Why? Because we want so much to be their saviors, their benefactors, and to hear their words of gratitude.

It is *we* who need to care for others. It is *we* who have this compulsive urge to feed our children, and keep supplying them with produce and preserves long after they have become adults. It is *we* who want to force our children to appreciate us. It is *we* who are afraid of living honestly—that is, for ourselves. They want just one thing: to see us happy, healthy, and self-sufficient. Not that we "live for the sake of them," but simply that we *live*. Why can't we do *this* for their sake?

Are you convinced yet?

Well, imagine someone suddenly showing up to live only for *your* sake. He gives you everything and thinks and worries about you all the time. Anything you do, every change in your life becomes a part of his experience, if not his tragedy. "For your sake" he is willing to fall ill and die. You want to see him happy, but he is fatally unhappy—simply because

you have some kind of issue. You want to be happy but constantly feel that you are the cause of his grief! Imagine this very clearly, and you will see that such a life is a nightmare.

The fact of the matter is that the **law of reciprocity** underlies any relationship or cohabitation. Symbiosis is a fair exchange. Not receiving anything in return, the giver becomes weakened—and both perish.

Any normal person feels discomfort, anxiety, and ultimately even danger if he receives significantly more than he can give back. This is true without a doubt. We subconsciously refuse handouts so as not to weaken our environment. In this way, we protect those around us and their proper relationship to us. This is sensible. In giving, we must offer the opportunity for the receiver to give back, since a person who cannot give back feels inadequate. He feels indebted and will not be thankful to you. Not understanding this, he will search for the cause of his problem—and it will be *you*. This is the secret of the saying: "Do no good, and you will receive no evil in return."

Who is the egotist? The person who since childhood has been forced to take without giving back. It was too satisfying for his parents to be "good" and to "live for the sake of."

There is no contradiction between egotism and altruism. Both represent our need and our desire. Live for the sake of others, yet allow them to live for your sake, too. And realize that you are doing this for yourself as well, since by sacrificing and always being unhappy you become a burden to everyone.

"I am with you so that life will be better for me. And you are with me so that life will be better for you." Relationships built on this basic agreement are honest, straightforward, enduring, and easily created. Straightforward accountability for your altruism lifts a heavy load from your shoulders, liberating your soul. Fearlessly providing yourself with enjoyment does not make you an egotist! To the contrary, it increases your health and appeal. But most importantly, you will discover that people begin to respect you, and the lives of those near and dear to you will immediately improve. After all, you want to live for their sake, don't you?

Science is smarter than we are

A scientist is a person who solves his own problems by studying those of others.

Fact: if science were smarter than we are, then all our problems would have been resolved long ago. But they have become even greater, and usually we end up resolving them on our own. We somehow manage to cope with them much better than any scientist ever could.

The achievements of science are undeniable. It is just that its goals do not correspond to our own. Modern corporate science operates for profit, either its own or another's. But it is the opposite for us: we want to improve and bring ease to our own lives. And it is precisely this that science neglects to research. The majority of its achievements come about at our expense—not for our benefit!

Modern science increasingly serves the manufacturers of all kinds of products. It may seem that developers of shampoos and toothpastes are working hard to resolve our problems—but this is an illusion. *A problem is resolved when we don't have to spend any more money on it.* Science does not offer the elimination of problems, for its very nature is to invent and exploit them. No one shampoo will save us from dandruff forever, and no brand of toothpaste has ever done away with tooth decay. No single farm implement or fertilizer has conserved the soil, no antibiotics have produced healthy food, and no poisons have ever protected the harvest. Today is no different than a century ago: we still lose about a third of all we grow. Only now our losses come at a much greater price!

I will share with you a terrible secret: an overwhelming majority of scientists are not any smarter than ordinary people. We too know how to think! Some of us much better than scientists. After all, they toil over a single, narrow topic while we live in free flight. In order to resolve our problems, we often invent incredibly brilliant tools and techniques—for instance, those cited in the first chapter. All science ever really does is appropriate the right to decide whether these inventions are good or bad. If clever people could manage to disseminate their successes, science would lose its authority. In any case, so science seems to think.

Plainly speaking, anyone who has figured out how to make something which serves the job well has created genuine, undiscounted scientific knowledge and know-how. It does not matter if he is recognized by the scientific establishment. Perhaps some will argue that it is not really scientific. Fine! Let's call it *practical experience* instead. We will use it for our own benefit—because it works! God grant that science will manage to keep up with our practical experience!

And God grant that science will bring us as much benefit as our common sense and inventiveness have. In developed countries respectable scientific institutions have finally begun studying organic farming, narrow beds, and mulch. But here in Russia, all we have are intelligent farmers and gardeners with a wealth of practical experience. We know that "we cannot wait for favors from science. It is our task to win them ourselves!"*

Gardening myths of our times

The garden clearly needed its owner's care. And the more care the owner can get, the better...

Judging by the deep divide between scientific recommendations and our actual yields, contemporary gardening should be considered a kind of religion. It is based almost wholly on faith. There are strict ritual ceremonies complete with requisite props—for example, whitewashing the trunks of mature trees in the spring, ritual spraying with any and all kinds of poisons, scraping the soil free of weeds wherever anything green sprouts up, cultishly digging up the soil twice a year, pruning off the central leader of vigorous fruit trees, and so on.

We zealously perform what ultimately causes more harm than benefit, feeling great satisfaction in fulfilling "our duty." As I see it, the average efficiency of our gardeners looks like this: 10% of work is for the benefit of plants (and

---

* Rephrasing the much-cited words of Ivan Michurin (famous Russian plant breeder): "We cannot wait for favors from Nature. It is our task to win them ourselves." [trans]

themselves!), 30% is in fact harmful, and the remaining 60% goes for struggling against that 30%. This is the ritual behavior of a true believer!

And where there are rituals, you will also find cult objects. The main one is the shovel, which over time has evolved into the motorized plow and rototiller. As for poisons and various other miracle concoctions, I would estimate that 80% of these are cultish. Mesmerizing us with their labels, they are usually applied incorrectly and therefore have no effect. We Russians are also prone to bowing down to imported equipment. For example, a "hand-held electric cultivator" with a revolving disk at the end. Actually, it is much quicker and easier to loosen soil with a regular hoe (not to mention a razor hoe!). Our garden stores are so pleasing to the eye that they put to shame the most ornately decorated temple.

The primary gods of the garden pantheon are Science and Hard Work; also Order, in the sense of tidiness and being "like everyone else." Isn't it time, brethren, to call these gods to account and to reexamine their doctrines? Here are some of the absurdities they have taught us:

"The more digging and cultivating you do, the better your soil will be." This is not true for most soils. The best soil structure is created by organic matter, roots, and small creatures. Shovels only help on heavy soils, and even then only by digging once every 4–5 years. In all other cases, the truth is that digging and cultivating are merely a struggle against the loss of structure which results from digging and cultivating.

"Well-tended soil is soil with nothing growing on it." Just the opposite is true! Bare land is dying land. It is more logical to call land "cultivated" when it is covered with plants which you have sanctioned to be there. And it is up to you to decide which ones to sanction. Permanent beds made directly on top of a lawn, an undisturbed woodlot, or a meadow which you consciously decide to maintain in its natural state—these are truly well-tended ground.

"The only source of nutrients is fertilizers." If this were true, plants in nature would have died out long ago. The main thing that chemical fertilizers do is swell up artificial veggie-broilers with an excess of water. But these plants are so sickly and unhealthful to eat that they are not even worth mentioning—at least for gardeners who grow food for their own consumption.

"Chemicals will solve our pest and disease problems." In reality chemicals support and exacerbate these problems. There are two elements which allow us to ignore pathogens: ecological diversity in the environment and high immunity in plants. Chemicals are powerful poisons which destroy life. They should be used very cautiously and only in the most extreme circumstances. More details about intelligent—and foolish—plant protection can be found in my book *Meeting Pests with a Smile*.

"Roots suffocate under mulch!" On the contrary, roots suffocate without mulch due to compaction from digging and cultivating the topsoil.

"The chemical industry can guarantee high yields." This is a half-truth. Chemicals can help yields if they are used wisely and appropriately. But they do not produce soil fertility, nor will they ever do this. All great civilizations have perished for one simple reason: they used up and destroyed the fertility of their soils, and in the end were left with no food. If we do not restore soil fertility, we will repeat their fate on the scale of the entire planet. I have devoted two books to restoration of soil fertility and intelligent farming: *Classics in Soil Fertility* and *Growing with your Garden*.

"Genetically-engineered plants will feed the world."
Feed—possibly, but it is very questionable whether we can
survive this type of feeding and stay healthy. It has been
demonstrated by many independent researchers that GM-
plants may cause the destruction of vital organs and degradation of offspring. The truth is that in nature genes can be
transferred asexually; such transference has been scientifically proven. The consequences of GM foods have not been
studied sufficiently and could be disastrous for our entire
biosphere.

A look at the myths of recent decades would not be complete without mentioning the commonly-held conviction
that all purchased seeds are viable and properly graded by
variety. This depends on a nation's seed market. I can only
hope that, unlike in Russia, Europe and the United States
utilize strict standards.

As I have already mentioned, our thinking has the habit
of reaching to extremes: if it is not this, then it must be the
opposite. Please, do not succumb to this kind of black-and-
white thinking! Usually both ends of the spectrum are in-
correct—the truth is somewhere in between. For example:
"pesticides will solve—or will not solve—problems of plant
protection." Obviously, total rejection of chemicals is as one-
sided and false as unflinching belief in them. The real solution is to grow vigorous and resilient plants. The basic practices for achieving this are soil restoration, enriching the
ecosystem, and intelligent care. But I would not exclude the
reasonable assistance of chemicals in years of severe pathogenic outbreaks.

This brings me to the sermon I gave in my book *Growing
Fruit with a Smile*.

"My dear parishioners! Let us confess together that the
cunning deities of our pantheon for some unscrupulous

reason are neglecting their duties: they shun practical work, ever slacking off and going on wild drinking binges for whatever reason, or for no reason. But mainly they are shirking their responsibility (the sin of gods!). And as a result, if you look back on the reporting period of the past fifty years, our gardens seem less like the Garden of Eden than some form of purgatory. For this reason, I consecrate all who desire this into a new faith. Do not believe, brothers and sisters, anything except what your hands and eyes tell you! Do not believe anyone except those who are successful and truly happy. And more than anything else, *trust yourself.* Invite Intention, Experience, Interest, and Observation into your pantheon. These young gods will never allow you to sink into everlasting boredom! They are innately good because it is nearly impossible to turn them into objects of mindless devotion.

"Truly, we receive according to our faith! As for success, this is something you must work out on your own. Amen."

Chapter 9

Fertilizing and Watering Intelligent Beds

or

How to Feed and Water Plants Without Causing Harm

Bibo ergo sum.
I drink, therefore I am.

Watering and fertilizing are important elements of gardening. Yet when not done sensibly, it can bring harm to plants. Let's consider this more deeply.

Water should be applied so that:

a) soil remains consistently moist;

b) water is uniformly distributed throughout the root zone;

c) moisture levels are stable, not fluctuating between sporadic watering and severe drying;

d) water applied to beds is utilized efficiently by plants and not wasted;

e) watering does not compact the soil and destroy its structure;

f) water is not too cold, causing temperature fluctuations in the soil;

g) fertilizer is supplied with the water; and

h) most importantly, all the above should take up as little time and effort as possible.

Fertilizer should:
a) be suitable in composition to the given circumstance, not randomly applied "just in case";
b) be used only according to recommended dosages;
c) be applied only when soil conditions help plants to maximally assimilate nutrients—that is, in the presence of moisture, soil structure, and microbes;
d) not degrade the soil under various weather conditions—i.e., cause acidity, alkalinity, etc.; and
e) once again, not take up too much time and effort.

Finally, fertilizing and watering should not be expensive. This is our goal!

On fertile, living soil, plant development is dependent on two primary factors: moisture and nutrients. So to ignore any one of the above points can transform all our labors into a Sisyphean task. Believe me, I hear people say the same thing over and over: "I fertilized with this and with that, and still nothing grew!" So what is the most rational system for watering and fertilizing? To begin, we should familiarize ourselves with the work of Kliment Timiriazev, *The Struggle of Plants Against Drought*. By the word "struggle" he actually means adaptation—i.e., automatic mechanisms of compensation. But most importantly, Timiriazev was able to see drought from the viewpoint of the plants themselves—a rare gift of scientific genius!

Why plants transpire water

*Man should imitate plants in overcoming the
hostile powers of nature
a) by lessening transpiration without hindering
feeding, and
b) by achieving this through automatic adjust-
ment to conditions.*

Kliment Timiriazev

Vegetables transpire 400–800 or more parts water to create
one part dry matter. This amounts to about 2.5–5 gallons to
produce one pound of plant biomass (20–40 liters per 1 kg),
and often less than half of that makes up the harvest. On the
southern steppes and black earth soils of Russia, only in the
best of years does this much water fall as precipitation.

Williams tells us that on bare unstructured soil only a
fourth or fifth of total precipitation is utilized by plants. The
same is true of our irrigation attempts, especially on bare
soil in the summer heat. A bucket poured onto 10 square feet
(1 m^2) of dug and compacted soil saturates only the top 1–2
inches (3–4 cm). All that water will evaporate away on the
first day, and in a dry wind in just 2–4 hours. Rather than providing roots with moisture, we are zealously watering the air!

Plants cool off their leaves by transpiring water. In a wind
they transpire 2–3 times more water than usual, and in the
sun even more than that; otherwise, leaves would wither
away in the heat. The classical experiments of Schlössing
demonstrated that plants in the open air transpire 800 parts
water for one part dry matter, but, when grown under glass,
transpiration was nearly five times less! Also, protected
plants accumulated only half the salts yet produced twice
as much organic matter. We can see this for ourselves in

greenhouse cultivation. This demonstrates that transpiration of excessive amounts of water is completely unnecessary for plants. It is more like an unavoidable evil. Then why don't plants simply decrease the surface area of their leaves? For over a hundred years, Russian agricultural science has answered this question based on the conclusions of Kliment Timiriazev on atmospheric feeding of plants.

The answer seemed obvious to Timiriazev: a large leaf area was necessary to absorb carbon dioxide gas—a primary element of plant nutrition—from the atmosphere. After all, it makes up only 1/4000 part of air but in plants constitutes up to half of their total mass! For this reason, plants are compelled to broaden and increase their leaf mass—annuals cannot allow themselves the same lethargy shown by leafless cacti. And as far as cultivated plants are concerned, they are obliged to grow very quickly!

Plants must constantly "pump up" leaves with water; otherwise, they would instantly wither and droop like old rags. But having so many large leaves causes a problem: they have to transpire huge amounts of water through these leaves! Timiriazev concluded that the need to increase leaf mass and, consequently, to absorb so much extra water for transpiration is, as mentioned above, an unavoidable evil, a curse to which plants are compelled to agree for the sake of carbon dioxide gas which is in such short supply.

However, since when does nature ever tolerate an "unavoidable evil"? Nature is the embodiment of rationality!

I am not one for lofty scientific discourse, but I do care about finding the truth. Recently, one of our more curious scientists began questioning the "atmospheric feeding" of plants. He and I discussed this question seriously with several other organic farming scientists. Together we made a number of interesting observations.

1) Pressure of carbon dioxide gas in the cellular fluid of plants is much higher than in the atmosphere. Therefore, it cannot be absorbed; it can only be released. As it turns out, carbon dioxide gas is discharged through leaves both day and night.

2) Carbon dioxide gas dissolves in water 150 times better than nitrogen and 70 times better than oxygen. Any open water, even falling drops of rain, will quickly become saturated with carbon dioxide gas.

3) The higher the concentration of carbon dioxide gas, the more is dissolved into water. Under decomposing organic mulch, where microbes are breathing intensely, there is up to 500 times more carbon dioxide gas than occurs in the atmosphere. Under such conditions, as much as 1.5 grams of carbon dioxide per liter of soil moisture passes into solution—that's a lot!

Our conclusion was that, under normal conditions of a living soil, plants absorb almost all their carbon through their roots in the form of carbon dioxide solution in the soil. The single mechanism of root uptake gives the plant *everything it needs*: carbon, hydrogen and oxygen, minerals, leaf elasticity, and cooling. So here it is—the rationality of nature! Only on lifeless soil lacking in organic matter are plants forced to starve, desperately pulling carbon dioxide gas out of the atmosphere. This process is treated in greater detail in my book *Growing with your Garden*.

So how can we help our plants? 1) Provide them with maximum amounts of soil carbon dioxide gas and water; and 2) reduce excess transpiration.

To do this, you must first create a benign microclimate. Plant a dense belt of trees to block summer winds. Also, plant rows of corn, pole beans, sorghum, and sugar cane in the garden—they will moderate the wind and, to some extent, reduce solar radiation. Calm air saves plants at least half the total water which they require! Moreover, a permanent cover of organic mulch over living soil is the only source of carbon dioxide gas on the entire planet. It not only helps accumulate and retain moisture in the soil but also returns to plants the carbon they require.

Timiriazev also proposed various technological solutions for irrigation. In France, simple devices for elevating water—Mouchot and Tellier pumps—were already well-known (see

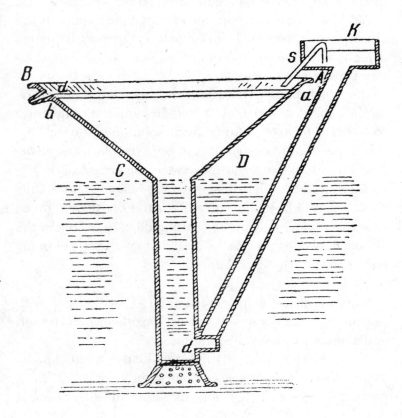

illustration). The Mouchot pump is solar driven. The sun heats up a membrane which serves as a lid to a funnel. The warm air forces water into an upper tank. The water collects around the membrane, cooling it down, which causes the water to drain out into a collector. Then the membrane warms up again, drawing in the next batch of water. Once set up, it can pump water maintenance-free for many years, elevating water up to 5 feet (1.5 m).*

The Charles Albert Tellier pump is more complex. The solar heater (the roof of a chicken house) is filled with ammonia. Heated to evaporation, the ammonia powers an ordinary gas engine. It is then cooled off in water and returns to the

* Augustin Mouchot's book *La Chaleur Solaire et Ses Applications Industrielles* (*Solar Heat and Its Industrial Applications*) was published in 1869. *The Clutha Leader*, a New Zealand newspaper, reported on December 17, 1880, that Mouchot's "apparatus worked a pump, raising water at the rate of 264 gallons per hour one yard high. The pump was kept going from 8 a.m. to 4 p.m., and neither strong winds nor passing clouds sensibly interfered with its action." [trans]

heater. With a heating area of 750 square feet (70 m²), the pump can raise 60 tons of water per hour to a height of 33 feet (10 m)! In other words, in an hour this pump can supply a thousand square feet (100 m²) of soil with all the water it requires for an entire growing season. It did for Tellier during the summer of the unforgettable drought year of 1891. And nearly for free!

A century has since passed. Our skilled craftsmen have invented many similar pumps which do not require electricity. Of course, even today they are still not produced commercially, since they are not in line with the goals of the "national economy."

I hope that some day these devices will be brought into mass production. But what can we do ourselves?

What we can do

"Ale to the Fatherland!" sang the salesgirl at the beer stand.

1. We can train ourselves to mulch. Remember that bucket poured onto 10 square feet (1 m²) of ground which evaporated in half a day? It's no laughing matter!

Russian horticultural research centers have been studying mulch for at least 70 years, and organic matter, too. Following are some of the results from Valentin Bryzgalov's classic work, *Vegetable Production.* Mulch provides these benefits: a) uniform distribution of moisture is maintained throughout the soil up to the surface; b) abrupt changes in moisture levels are essentially leveled out; c) soil moisture under mulch is 3–4% greater (that's a lot!); d) there is no crusting of the soil surface; e) soil aeration (breathing) under mulch is doubled; and f) structural porosity (the ability to absorb and conduct moisture) is five times higher. All these conditions increase nitrification—coming into autumn there is 6–8 times more nitrogen under mulch, and average levels during the growing season are four times higher. Furthermore, mulch smothers weeds. We can only conclude that *watering without mulch is unproductive labor*, a kind of "watering syndrome." We end up using three times as much water to achieve one-third the result!

2. The most important point is that **we can decrease the watered area.** Take the experiments of Schlössing: with an equal supply of water, plants in small pots grew well while in big pots they died from lack of water. Small-scale hydroponics demonstrates the same thing: a 3-by-3-inch (8 x 8-cm) peat block, if kept constantly moist, will provide roots with all the water they need. Plants look absolutely splendid in the holes I plant, and they only need 2–3 buckets of water each week. In this regard, beds and trenches are both rational and convenient—you water less, yet the soil retains more moisture.

On the assumption that beds are permanent and mulched, let's now consider the various alternatives for watering.

Watering with a hose is very common among our gardeners, but in reality it is the most barbaric way to water. It severely compacts the soil, requiring that the soil be loosened, destroys topsoil structure, reduces nitrification, and leaches away organic matter and nutrients. If water pressure is low, it can take forever, and if it is strong, it washes everything out. An ingenious solution was invented by Jacob Mittleider: cover the hose end with a small bag made from several layers of burlap. Then you can turn it on to any pressure!

Various hose nozzles or "watering guns" are not much better. These toys may add to your enjoyment, but soil is washed away just the same. This includes the "rain" setting on guns—the pressure is too strong. They are appropriate for lawns and flowerbeds but not for vegetables.

Watering with a watering can is no better than using a hose with a spray nozzle, and takes much more effort. This method works well only for very small gardens and very athletic gardeners—a desperate measure for people who do not have a faucet on their plot. To drag a watering can to an unmulched bed is not only a Sisyphean task but, indeed, a form of masochism!

If you pump water from a well, set up a large container nearby, even a tub. It is easier to fill up a container, and then water peacefully from it, rather than to do both at the same time.

Watering with a wick is the most frugal but certainly not the easiest method in actual practice. It is more suitable for large potted plants, winter gardens, small greenhouses, and germination beds. To install a wicking system, bury a 3- to 5-gallon (10–20-liter) container "up to its neck" at each end of a bed which is no more than 6 feet (2 m) long (or bury

one every 6 feet in a longer bed). Or you can dig a hole and line it with plastic, but this type of cistern must be carefully covered so that the water does not evaporate. The wick consists of a twisted strip of cloth forming a thick braid about 1 inch (2–3 cm) wide. Both ends of the wick are submerged in the container, and the rest is buried in the bed 4–6 inches (10–15 cm) deep. The uncovered section of the wick should be wound with plastic to prevent evaporation. The soil itself "sucks out" moisture through the wick by capillary action. The flow of water depends on the dryness of the soil and the width of the wick. With a 1 inch (2 cm) wide strip, a moist bed will "drink up" approximately a liter per day. With a wider wick, the water flow is greater (see illustration).

The disadvantages are that wicks must be changed every year, containers must be dug in, and, of course, you have to regularly fill the containers with water. Advantages are that it is easy to fill containers, water is warmed up before entering the soil, and soil and roots are maintained at ideal moisture levels. Plants themselves use only as much water as they require. It is important that wicks be made from material which will not rot and which conducts water well.

Watering with containers is imperative for those who do not have a reliable source of water. This kind of system is easy to install. As has already been described, 1- or 2-gallon (5–6-liter) jugs are buried neck-up at a depth of 10–12 inches (25–30 cm) every 28–32 inches (70–80 cm) along a bed. The bottom and lower third of each container is pierced with a thin knife 20–30 times. This kind of watering works well with a hose. You pass by and fill up each bottle, screwing on the lid—and then don't worry about it for 3–4 days. You might even add a little fertilizer sometimes. As with a wick, this kind of watering is much more effective under mulch.

The era of homemade watering systems in Russia is ending as drip irrigation systems manufactured in Israel are becoming more common. They lack the defects of the "first generation" of drip systems and combine most of the advantages mentioned above.

Drip irrigation can be attached to a water faucet or to a large container elevated above ground level. This is the easiest and most rational system for a family garden which has running water, a well, or is adjacent to a body of water set up with a pump. Water is supplied directly to the roots very efficiently, and can even contain small doses of fertilizer (*fertigation*). Water consumption and waste is reduced by two-thirds, and uptake efficiency is doubled. In fact, since switching to drip systems, in less than a decade formerly arid Israel has been transformed into a green, food-exporting nation. Nowadays, many other arid countries are also moving in this direction.

You can assemble a small system in your garden, too—about 1,000–1,600 feet (300–500 m) of tape will suffice for all your beds. The system requires minimal maintenance: a simple filter at the front end and flushing out in autumn. Assembling and dismantling is elementary using standard fittings, and you can easily install your irrigation system yourself. In the winter, all you do is raise the main pipe up off the ground, resting it on supports right there above the bed.

Hose drip systems are much more durable than tape. Flexible hose will last 4–5 years, and more rigid hose up to 15 years, which is less expensive in the end. These systems can be assembled just as easily but in the winter should be completely dismantled, and the hoses coiled up and stored away from mice.

Drip irrigation tape, on the other hand, is very inexpensive but not at all durable. In field conditions it is essentially non-reusable. Lately, it has been pushed aggressively onto the Russian market more than any other systems. T-Tape produced in France is especially easy to use. It releases water through tiny slits which run along the entire length. It can be buried in the soil, but we just cover it with mulch. In an hour a meter of tape discharges up to 2.5 gallons (10 L) of water. The amount of time to water is easily determined by experience. You simply push aside the mulch and evaluate soil moisture.

Israeli farmers abandoned "tape" long ago; they now prefer the more expensive but longer-lasting line system. Moreover, it is important to them "not to water the weeds," instead precisely watering only the plants. But for us it is not so clear-cut. Our plots are small. In a garden, irrigation systems do not have to extend for many hundred feet while maintaining proper pressure. Plantings are fairly dense, and generally water is not scarce. If an emitter becomes clogged, it's no big deal to clean it out. It's not difficult to cover tape with mulch to protect it from the sun, or to flush out and carefully coil it up for the winter. To install a simple filter at the system's entry point is also not a problem. In this way, the durability of tape can be significantly increased. Without any special care, my tape lasts two, and with repairs even three years. Its main advantage is that it saves a huge amount of nonproductive work—watering and cultivating. When you turn on the faucet and feel the entire garden being quietly watered all by itself, you experience that exquisite joy of laziness. At the price of 2–3 cents per foot, it makes good sense to install drip irrigation!

Although gardeners cannot purchase drip irrigation tape in every region of our vast Motherland, they can roughly construct a similar system. An old water hose is pierced every 6–8 inches (15–20 cm) on two sides. The holes are made

with a screwdriver or awl—not with a drill! Otherwise, a large portion of the water will flow out of the first few holes, and there will not be enough pressure at the end. The far end of the hose is plugged, and the hose is laid under the mulch. The water source is connected to the front end. It is better to make a network and supply water to several beds at once. This is how I water my raspberries and flowerbeds.

The best way to provide supplemental feeding to plants is to add organic fertilizers in liquid form. Russian gardeners have known this for at least three hundred years. Both in southern and northern regions, villagers water vegetables with an infusion of manure and ash. However, the question of fertilization deserves a more thorough discussion, which we will undertake in this next section.

What plants eat

Let's begin by reviewing the fundamentals of plant nutrition. Agrochemistry teaches that plant nutrients consist of soil minerals, but by focusing exclusively on minerals we have lost sight of the most important element: organic matter. In order to understand what *really* feeds plants, we need only examine *what they are made of.* This is no secret.

Plants are **50% carbon** which they absorb through roots and leaves in the form of carbon dioxide. Additionally, they consist of **20% oxygen** and **8% hydrogen**. Plants receive these elements from the air and water. Another **15%** of plant mass is **nitrogen** which they receive from soil organic matter and various microbial symbionts. I would not be surprised if "suddenly" it was discovered that leaves absorb nitrogen, too, directly from the atmosphere. We do know that all soil nitrogen originally came from the atmosphere. Compared to these big four, mineral elements (ash) are hardly noticeable, representing just 7% of plant biomass. Plants are so kind as to take in only 1/15 of their nutrients from the earth's crust! Thus, in a strict sense, plants do not subsist on minerals, but rather on *nitrogen, carbon, and water (hydrogen and oxygen).* Minerals are important, but only as a supplement, much like vitamins are for us.

It now becomes much more clear what we must provide to plants for their primary sustenance.

Do we need mineral fertilizers?

I repeat, comrades: a loaf of bread is no loafer!

I am convinced that, if there is sufficient organic matter in the soil, and mulch maintains optimal aeration and moisture, then mineral fertilizers are not needed at all. They only destroy the naturally established, stable ecosystem of the soil. However, there are very few soils which perfectly meet these criteria, and we want the harvest right now.

Therefore, I am not completely against mineral fertilizers. Extreme positions rarely serve us. Our main task is to "feed the plants, not the soil." But in practice it is usually the other way around. Most often, in fact, we feed the soil. While reading labels with the magical words "boosts and increases," we forget to take a pill for greed—and sprinkle anything and everything onto our beds. The word "useful" translates in our minds as "the more, the better." We start believing that fertilizers are the primary food of plants. Unfortunately, the plants themselves do not know this!

Even when applied using soil test data, no more than 30% of chemical fertilizers are actually assimilated—the rest become bound up, precipitate out, leach into the subsoil, and wash away into the sea. Solutions of mineral salts often become antagonistic, destroying the pH balance and hindering absorption of other elements. With insufficient water, solutions become concentrated and even poisonous. In the plants themselves, nutrient elements are physiologically linked to each other—a lack or surplus of one may block assimilation of another. Piling up on one thing, which we commonly do, rarely brings benefit. Generally, in our inexperienced hands mineral salts are just plain nasty.

In the end, you cannot envy plants. One moment they are suffering from salinity and hunger, and the next they become bloated through overfeeding! In either case their resilience is weakened. Having gorged themselves on nitrogen, plants become less resistant to frost and drought, and they suffer more acutely from aphids and other pests—their tissues are overly soft. On fertilized beds, plants suffer much more severely from lack of water—they don't want to grow, their leaves are pale and randomly blotched, their fruit underdeveloped, their tissues coarse, and their life expectancy significantly reduced. Think about it: symptoms showing an obvious deficit of nutritional elements are found only where chemical fertilizers have been applied!

The conclusions are self-evident: 1) providing the right minerals to plants is an art rarely mastered; and 2) *the most important rule for mineral feeding is to create suitable conditions for nutrient assimilation.* This requires the same elements as always: organic matter, carbon dioxide gas, water and air, and a properly structured soil.

In the beginning of the 1950s, the Russian academic Trofim Denisovich Lysenko (an extremely interesting and unorthodox scientist!) introduced an *organic mineral blend*— fifty parts by weight of compost or rotted manure combined with five parts lime (chalk, ground limestone, or dolomite* powder), and one part superphosphate. The lime is required for beneficial bacteria, which feel more at home in

---

* *Dolomite powder* is ground up dolomite, a mineral which contains calcium carbonate (limestone) and magnesium carbonate. Ground limestone is ordinary chalk.

an alkaline environment. Experiments have demonstrated that the effectiveness of these fertilizers in combination is three times higher than when they are applied separately.

Also during that time, "artificial manures" were used with positive results. Straw, hulls, and leaves were spread in 6- to 8-inch (15–20-cm) layers interspersed with mineral fertilizers: one part urea, one part superphosphate, and three parts lime—18–22 pounds (8–10 kg) of minerals to a ton of organic matter. Each layer was thoroughly wetted. After 3–4 months the "manure" was ready, and turned out to be three times more effective.

In the middle of the 1990s, the organo-mineral fertilizer Sveklovichnoe came onto the Russian market. It has proven to be two times more effective than chemical fertilizers, since the mineral elements are combined with humus to form organo-mineral compounds. Furthermore, nitrogen and calcium are prevented from leaching out, and phosphorus is converted into an easily assimilated form.

Our conclusion is simple: organic matter increases assimilation of chemical fertilizers by 2–3 times. Nowadays agrochemists are moving away from simple saline forms of mineral fertilizers towards complex organo-mineral "cocktails." Their effect is multifaceted: feeding, stimulating, and increasing immunity and tolerance to stress.

Let's compare various types of fertilizers.

Saline inorganic fertilizers were first-generation fertilizers. They are messy, inefficient, and harmful both to the natural world and to human health, yet they have held out for a full hundred years because they are so easy to apply. Their greatest, incomparable advantage is that "you don't have to think!"

Public policies promoting mass application of chemical fertilizers have played a part both in the degradation of soils and in the advance of new diseases. Yet there are people who have mastered their use. One of them is Dr. Jacob Mittleider. His methods are a good example of mineral-chemical intensive horticulture which is very difficult to achieve, and nowadays ecologically unacceptable. But in order to better understand the potential of plants, it is worth reviewing his research.

Dr. Mittleider was an amazing vegetable grower. His narrow beds alone were a breakthrough in vegetable gardening. Besides this, he was a pioneer in creating **compound fertilizers**, developing and testing mixtures adapted to plant requirements which were superior to individual mineral salts applied separately. These mixtures are easy to prepare yourself.

Mixture #1: calcium and boron are applied together as a basic fertilizer prior to planting. The role of this mixture is to regulate soil acidity thereby ensuring assimilation of other nutrients as well as to provide calcium. Adding mixture #1 to rotted manure or compost—approximately 1 ounce per cubic foot (1 kg per m³)—will significantly improve nutrient quality.

For acidic soils you should use dolomite or lime; for alkaline or neutral soils—gypsum. Carefully combine 5.5 pounds (2.5 kg) of lime (or gypsum) and 0.7 ounce (20 g) of boric acid powder. If gypsum is used, the mixture must be stored in airtight bags—gypsum will absorb moisture and clump up.

Mixture #2: nitrogen, phosphorus, potassium, magnesium, boron, and molybdenum are applied before planting and for periodic feeding throughout the summer. The role of this mixture is to provide primary nutrients to plants.

According to Mittleider, the proportion of N-P-K for vegetables should be about 1.5-1-1.5. Following established conventions, these figures relate to the proportion of N, K_2O, and P_2O_5.

The mixture is a blend of 6.5 pounds (3 kg) of ammonium phosphate 16-16-16 or ammonium nitrate phosphate 17-17-17 (the numbers show the relationship of N-P-K and are given on fertilizer bags), 1 pound (450 g) magnesium sulfate (bitter or English salt), 0.2 ounce (5 g) boric acid, and 0.2 ounce (5 g) of any molybdenum salt.

Mittleider's fertilizing strategy brings to mind the fattening of a Christmas goose. He raises vegetable-broilers—huge and tender—which require constant protection, and the bloated plant tops must be trained. The main "seasoning" is about 1 ounce per square foot (300 g/m²) of both the above

mixtures followed by 0.7 ounce per square foot (220 g/m^2) of mixture #2 three times per month throughout the summer. On top of this, you must attentively watch for signs of nutrient deficiency (!!!), which are ameliorated by supplementary corrective feedings!

When carried out precisely, this "hydroponics in soil" method yields a very good harvest. But at what cost?! Beds should be saturated with water daily—or even better twice a day—at a rate of 2 gallons per square foot (6–7 buckets per m^2). The bloated plants must be provided strict chemical protection from pests. All weeds are shaved off clean, leaving beds completely bare, and about 2–3 pounds of fertilizer mixes must be applied on 10 square feet of narrow beds in a single season (1–1.4 kg/m^2)! Salinization of the topsoil is reduced by the heavy watering, but where do the unassimilated salts go? There is a Mittleider demonstration farm not far from us. You cannot drink the well water in neighboring villages because they are so polluted with fertilizers! But most important, the vegetables themselves are barely edible.

Mittleider could not have been unaware of this. He knew that organic farmers also achieve excellent results. So why did "Uncle Jake" stubbornly advocate a narrow, chemical method for growing vegetables? It is notable that his books are filled with advertisements for his proprietary mixtures. Having converted his gardening method into a business, he went all the way with it.

Thank God, agrochemistry has moved forward. It seems that old-fashioned chemical fertilizers have at last reached their final years. Developed countries no longer use them at all. First, they were replaced by compound chemical fertilizers—mixtures of NPK and trace elements balanced in the required proportions. Such were the first generations of Kristalon, or in Russia—Rastvorin. Since then they have become much more efficient. Scientists have researched the optimal relationship of elements for different crops at various stages of development, but the incompatibility and low assimilation of salts by plants has remained problematic on depleted soils. Only organic matter can cope with that! So again scientists turned to it for solutions. Organic compounds of nutrient elements were discovered—*chelates* which are assimilated much more freely and easily.

Chelate compound fertilizer is a part of natural soil structure. Soil organic matter and microbes supply nutrients specifically in the form of chelates. Essentially, they are humates and compounds of other organic acids. They do not destroy the chemical qualities of the soil, are natural for cell metabolism, and are rarely antagonistic. They provide plants with the same bioactive substances which they usually receive from microbes and from organic matter itself.

Nowadays chelate fertilizers—like modern Kristalon, and in Russia Akvarin—are produced by the world's major agribusiness corporations. They are highly water soluble, so are generally applied through irrigation systems (fertigation*) or as foliar sprays.

The potency of these substances is very high. For instance, chelates of iron, cobalt, and copper are 1,000–10,000 times more active biochemically than in their saline forms. With applications of Akvarin, the intensity of photosynthesis in wheat, potatoes, and clover is increased by 36–82%. It could even be proposed that chelates function more as growth regulators.

---

* *Fertigation*—watering with supplemental fertilization through an irrigation system.

Foliar sprays with chelate fertilizer are also very good. Leaves quickly assimilate dilute chelate solutions, and effects may be evident as soon as three days after application. Plants should be sprayed in the early evening, saturating the entire leaf surface. The effectiveness of chelates applied in this way is approximately 15–20 times greater than chemical fertilizers worked into the soil. Twenty grams (0.7 ounce) of Akvarin sprayed onto leaves increases biomass up to 23 pounds on 1,000 square feet (10 kg on 100 m^2). To achieve the same result using chemical fertilizers, you would have to apply over 1 pound (500 g), and then take special measures to assure uptake by plants!

Ashes should also be mentioned at this point. This natural mineral fertilizer is more sensible than even the best manufactured mineral mixture. First of all, they are balanced—after all, ashes were formerly plants. Furthermore, they contain potassium, calcium, and phosphorus which are often deficient in soils. Second, the charcoal, too, is valuable—it loosens up soil and is a good source of carbon. And third, ashes are alkaline—they moderate acidity in soils.

Any intelligent fertilizer should also contain lime to increase assimilation of nutrients, supply plants with calcium, and create a proper environment for soil bacteria. These all significantly strengthen a plant's resilience. It's no coincidence that grapes which receive regular applications of ashes virtually stop becoming diseased.

Organo-mineral bio-fertilizers are fertilizers of the new era. Finally, scientists are turning their attention to microbes and attempting to recreate solutions of decomposing organic matter. These solutions are extremely complex, and it seems that new beneficial substances in them are being discovered weekly. They are primarily extracted from composts and biohumus,* from fermentation products, and from processed manures and other organic wastes. Mineral components and living beneficial microbes are also often added. Of course, they are no replacement for genuine organic matter but will significantly accelerate disintegration of plant residues and strengthen plant immunity and root vitality. Examples of such "cocktails" are products of the companies Agromaster, Nutritek, and Kemira. Many are now being produced in Russia: Humistar, Humisol, Darina, Biovita, Agricola, Sila Zhizni, etc.

* * *

I personally believe that the very best way to feed plants is a combination of green manures and organic matter. To be on the safe side, only small amounts of the most essential fertilizers should be used—mainly for supplemental feeding by spraying. Even if you unabashedly love chemical fertilizers, you should still sow green manures at the end of summer. Green manures are natural soil buffers and good providers of nutrients. They quickly absorb top-dressings and distribute them deep into the soil through their root systems. They convert fertilizers into compost and humus. And they draw up potassium and phosphorus from soil depths. Finally, they improve soil structure. *Green manures create conditions for improved assimilation of nutrients.* In this type of system, you can also pamper plants with supplemental feeding—i.e., with a balanced complex of chelates.

* *Biohumus*—compost obtained utilizing earthworms. It is very rich in composition and highly fortified with microbes.

In the natural world, plant nutrition cannot be separated into mineral, organic, and microbial—these are rather various aspects of a single living process. In general, the biosphere does not divide itself into "ours" and "theirs," right and wrong, harmful and beneficial. Lord help *us* to learn to live this way as well!

Fertilizing, stimulating, and watering— all at the same time

In the chapter on compost, I mentioned an organic infusion which can be applied with irrigation. Its effectiveness can be increased by improvising on the recipe to be more diverse and complex.

Begin with a 50-gallon (200-L) container filled with water. Dump in a pound (0.5 kg) of any compound fertilizer containing trace elements—or even better, half a gallon (2 L) of dried bird droppings. Next add a half-bucket of compost and another of rotted straw to provide humates and microbes for incubation. You can include some fresh grass and leaves, too. Pour in half a liter of ashes or lime, then 2 pounds (1 kg) of sugar and a couple buckets of rotting fruit (or some 2 quarts of old preserves), and finish with a pinch of any kind of yeast. The yeast quickly multiplies in the sugar, and the fertilizers intensely accelerate reproduction of one-celled algae. Soon the water will "bloom."

The "brew" will be ready in about a week: the yeast will have multiplied but not yet overpopulated and died out. At this point, it never hurts to add lactic acid bacteria to the barrel by pouring in a liter of curdled milk. The resulting concoction will be inundated with nutrients, microbes, and stimulators. In essence, it becomes a crude, enhanced equivalent of EM.* Watering with this brew significantly invigorates plants and has a long-lasting effect.

Yeast is the basis of all our EM preparations. Once I decided to conduct some comparative experiments. I found that baker's yeast is an extraordinary stimulator, as good as any Russian-produced EM. I put half a cup of sugar or a cup of old preserves into three liters of water, added a pinch of baker's yeast, and after 3–4 days the "brew" was flourishing. I poured one cup of it into a bucket of water, which I used for watering a test plot—once a week on seedlings and transplants and twice a month on adult plants. The other test beds received plain water. On the plots with the brew, young plants developed nearly two times faster than those treated with EM and other store-bought stimulators.

In general, the more beneficial ingredients are combined, the better. Mix together greens, compost, half a dose of a chelate fertilizer, some form of sugar, lactic acid bacteria, and yeast, and you will get an effective and unequivocally harmless infusion. You could even call it the "drink of the gods"—nectar and ambrosia for plants. But even such "Herbalife" works only when it can penetrate into soil under stable moisture conditions. Otherwise, the microbes will die.

So, let's talk more about these microbes. How exactly do they benefit plants?

---

* *EM*, or *Effective Microorganisms*—various microbial preparations for accelerating decomposition of organic matter and also for treatment of water, municipal effluent, cesspools, and landfills. They were invented in Japan where they are still produced. In Russia, we have our own domestic versions of microbial preparations, generally calling them by the same name: EM.

Some microbiology

Show me your microbes, and I will tell you who you are.

A more detailed explanation about soil life can be found in my book *Growing with your Garden*, but I will cover the main points here.

When first attempting to understand the function of soil microbes, I found the advertising materials for Effective Microorganisms (EM) to be completely worthless! Instead, I had to read serious scientific tomes and endlessly pester microbiologists with questions, which over time led to an active correspondence with several interesting scientists and practitioners. I cannot depict the soil community in full detail here but can provide a general outline in layman's terms.

The main thing to understand is that there are literally hundreds of different kinds of soil microbes—bacteria, fungi, algae, parasites, and various other cohabitants of plants. Some of these collaborate directly with roots. Others convert minerals into available forms. Many fix atmospheric nitrogen in the soil. The majority of microbes and nearly all fungi decompose organic matter utilizing various enzymes.

Each microbe occupies its own niche, eats its own particular food (including each other), provides nourishment for other microbes, and competes and cohabits—in the end, a stable ecosystem is created. This ecosystem is a global "trade union" of soil workers. Their job is to return carbon and other necessary nutrients to plants. In accomplishing their work, they produce the primary "surplus value" on our planet: they transform plant residues and rocks into fertile soil.

Populations of various types of microbes are always fluctuating. For example, after all available nitrogen has been consumed, the numbers of cellulose decomposers decrease sharply. Then the nitrogen-fixers start to multiply, consuming the carbohydrates which were synthesized by the cellulose decomposers. These leave behind nitrogen, which allows the cellulose decomposers to again proliferate. In this manner, the composition of the microbial community is constantly "breathing."

Drastic changes to the environment—overwatering, cultivating the soil, fertilizers, poisons—will abruptly worsen conditions, impoverishing the living soil community. Frequent and repeated stress causes irreversible biological degradation. The more plowing, fertilizing, and pesticides applied, the worse and more impoverished soil life becomes— and the less stable the soil and its ability to produce and maintain fertility.

Plants cohabit directly with many microbes. A layer of microbes is constantly present around young, growing roots, providing exactly what they need at that particular moment. Plants themselves propagate them, excreting various organic compounds through their roots. Up to 40% of all products of photosynthesis are for the benefit of microbial symbionts! You can just imagine how important they are! Proliferating on the nutrients provided by plants, microbes respond quickly with their own products—hormones and biologically active substances, protective agents, and available forms of nutrients. In this way, plants direct a host of "service workers" which enable them to maximally utilize the potential of the soil for their own needs.

Scientists have recently begun to show more interest in these highly specialized microbes: *protective agents, decomposers of organic matter, and microbes which service roots.* The majority of microbial symbionts are multifunctional: while decomposing organic matter, they also excrete large amounts of phytoncides and antibiotics, and many of them fix nitrogen as well. Scientists are discovering more and more of these microbial symbionts, studying their efficacy, cultivating them, conducting selective breeding programs, and producing bio-preparations from the most dynamic strains. They are far from having discovered all of them, and known microbes still make up only a small fraction of what is there. In fact, it is highly unlikely that we will ever be able to understand fully the complete picture.

It is often said that humus is formed from the bodies of dead microbes, but it is very doubtful that this claim is true. After all, microbes do not simply die and vanish into nothing. Finding themselves in poor conditions, they either pupate as spores, or are consumed by other microbes. In a good environment, they proliferate, devouring all available food. On the whole, organic mass does not increase from this process—on the contrary, it becomes less. Microbes are living and so expend energy. This is why our compost piles are not "magical cauldrons" but instead shrink before our very eyes. Organic matter "combusts" like fuel which is utilized by microbes, insects, and worms.

This means that it is impossible to overdose plants with microbial preparations, especially those containing only harmless soil microbes. There is also no sense in increasing the dose—a heightened effect will not occur. Practice has shown that the effectiveness of microbial preparations depends not on the concentration but on regular and frequent application. To spray or irrigate with EM-preparations each week is the only way to support the microbial population when the environment is not conducive to them.

Where do scientists look for beneficial microbes? In living soils which are capable of suppressing the development of pathogens and quickly neutralize toxins—that is, in soils which are rich in organic matter, well-structured, moist, and teeming with microbes and fungi. If this is the type of soil you have, all bio-preparations already exist in it. If not, it is unlikely that they will proliferate there anyway.

Each microbe needs its own particular environment. After all, it must occupy a niche in order to survive. For this reason, bio-preparations are not a cure-all. Applied to the soil, microbes may experience pressure from competitors, lack of food, and other factors of distress. At that point their numbers decrease sharply. But we want microbes to live and multiply. *The effect and survival rate of microbes depends on environmental conditions.* Soil microbes need organic matter, mulch, and moisture—that is, fertile, living soil. In fact, it is living because of the proliferation of microbes in it!

But what about enhanced, selected microbial strains? They work more efficiently but are even more demanding on their environment. Their populations will not increase higher than what the environment will allow—even if you pour buckets of them onto the soil! Therefore, even for these enhanced strains the main requirement is good soil conditions.

Our conclusion is simple: *the culture of microbes is only a ferment, an accelerator for improving soils with the help of organic matter, mulch, and watering.* It is not an independent factor of fertility.

You can easily propagate certain beneficial microbes yourself. Nadezhda Naplekova, a Doctor of Microbiology from Novosibirsk, has worked out methods for making preparations at home. They are surprisingly simple.

Nitragin contains bacterial nitrogen fixers of the genus *Rhizobium* which live in the root nodules of legumes. Each species of legumes has its own type of bacteria. First, we prepare the medium: 2 pounds (1 kg) of soil mixed with a tablespoon of lime or chalk and a cup of sand—bacteria require a slightly alkaline base. This mixture is moistened well, placed in a half-gallon (2-L) container, and lightly tamped down.

Next, a handful of peas or beans is boiled in two cups of water and allowed to cool. This is the nutrient solution for bacteria.

All the *red and white* nodules from the roots of 5–6 legume plants in flower—for example, peas—are washed and mashed up well in a cup using a pestle or wooden spoon. The resulting pulp is mixed into a half cup of the nutrient solution and poured over the soil mixture. The container is then covered in plastic with a few small air holes, labeled "peas," and stored in warm darkness. In a week it will be ready. It can be used immediately, or dried out in the shade for later. To inoculate seeds with symbiotic bacteria, wetted pea seeds are rolled in the preparation and sown immediately—bacteria do not like the sun.

I can't help but throw in a comment of my own here. Obviously, if legume green manures are sown fairly often, seeds will be successfully inoculated in the soil itself.

Azotobacterin is a bacterial nitrogen fixer from the genus *Azotobacter* which lives freely in the soil. Besides nitrogen, it produces stimulators and vitamins, and suppresses growth of several pathogenic fungi. It is introduced with seeds or as a soil additive.

The initial soil medium is prepared in the same way, but 0.2 ounce (5 g) of ground superphosphate is added. This is spread into a 2- to 3-inch (5–7 cm) layer in a wide bowl, leveled out with a spoon to form a smooth, shiny surface, covered with plastic, and set in warm darkness. In a week, the soil surface will be covered in slime—this is the Azotobacter. The soil can then be dried in the shade and used the following spring.

Note: the conditions for making this preparation are very similar to those which occur naturally under mulch!

Subtillin contains the bacteria hay bacillus (*Bacillus subtilis*), which decomposes cellulose and lignin in plants, producing more than 70 antibiotics, a wide range of enzymes for breaking down organic matter, and a number of vitamins for plants. It is also a powerful protector against pathogenic fungi, especially root rot and powdery mildew. In Russia, the preparations Phytosporin-M, Bactophyte, and Rhizoplus are based on hay bacillus.

Most of all, hay bacillus is found in rotting grass hay—both in vegetative mulch and in piles of old hay. If hay is covered in mildew, it is not suitable, since this means that fungi are ruling the roost. First, 5 ounces (150 g) of rotted hay is boiled for 5–10 minutes in a quart (1 L) of water with a teaspoon of lime added. The spores of hay bacillus will survive. When left in the dark for three days, the bacillus will form a film over the surface of the solution. This is the stock culture, a concentrate.

In the garden, pour a bucket of hot water over 3–4 pounds (1.5–2 kg) of fresh hay, add the stock culture to it, and shelter it from the sun. After three days, strain it before spraying on cucumbers, berries, and grapes. If sprayed once a week, plants will be significantly less diseased. It is even better if you combine the preparation with micronutrients.

There is another beneficial fungus called *Trichoderma*, from which the preparation *trichodermin* is made, and also an excellent soil microbe *pseudomonad* which is used to make various preparations. It is good to propagate these microbes, but remember that *all beneficial microbes proliferate in a natural environment containing organic matter, moisture, and air.*

So what do we come to once again? *Mulch and organic plant matter*—that is, living soil! The beneficial microbes themselves and ideal conditions for their propagation have existed in it from the beginning.

Chapter 10

The Benefits of Plastic

or

A Tale About How to Deceive Winter

Announcer: "A vegetable garden for the entire year!—a program for people who have to work in the garden even through the winter."

In the summer of 2006, *Greenhouse Gardening with a Smile* was published as part of my gardening series. In it the innovative gardener Konstantin Malyshevsky explains clearly and in great detail why our greenhouses cause us so many problems—and often do not yield expected results. Here I will touch on only the most fundamental principles of greenhouse gardening through the experiences of several "innovative greenhousers."

Experience of American growers

In the mid-1990s, the Russian-American magazine *Novy Fermer** began publication in Russia, inspiring our minds

* *The New Farm*—a magazine published in English, and subsequently in Russian, by Rodale Press. [trans]

and hearts with the successes of innovative farmers in the US. I cannot resist revisiting its articles from time to time with my readers, since circulation of the magazine was small while the experiences and achievements reported were invaluable.

Steve Moore from Pennsylvania used to heat his greenhouses with gas. At one point he calculated that in ten days he consumed 180 gallons (675 L) of fuel! So Steve started experimenting. Over the next couple of years, he designed a very simple greenhouse made of plastic pipe and boards with a double-layer covering of UV stabilized plastic (which lasts 6–7 years). Pathways were constructed from bricks and concrete. Steve determined the optimal shape for the roof to be a "Gothic arch"—that is, not rounded but peaked—and he oriented his greenhouses east-west for maximum accumulation of heat. Ventilation is done by means of wide doors and vents at each end. Soils in his greenhouses are organic, so he has no particular problem with disease.

Inside are five long beds, each about 3 feet (1 m) wide. In the cold of winter, the beds are covered with old plastic stretched over arches made from plastic pipe (see illustration). The result is a 28-by-95-foot or 2,660-square-foot (8.5-by-29-m or 250-m²) greenhouse which can provide 130 families with vegetables. Soil temperature in the greenhouse never falls below 54°F (12.5°C). When air temperatures fall to -17°F (-27°C) at night, it is 18°F (-8°C) in the sheltered beds, and cold-resistant crops—cabbage, lettuce—do not suffer.

Steve raises many vegetables during winter—in particular, potatoes. Sowing the beds at the end of December, he harvests new potatoes in March. The same with carrots. Early carrots are exceptionally sweet and very popular with his customers.

Plants begin rapid growth in March, so plastic over the beds is removed to be used on cold frames outside. In the summer, the greenhouse is planted in tomatoes, peppers, and eggplants. His harvests are impressive: from 130 square feet (12 m²) he receives 608 eggplants weighing 170 pounds (78 kg), and from 100 square feet (9 m²)—923 peppers weighing 165 pounds (75 kg). This is 7–8 times greater than the US average. Steve also sows buckwheat, yarrow, and other herbs in the greenhouse to attract beneficial insects. He does not use any chemical substances, and his plants are completely healthy on the organic soil.

Eliot Coleman from Maine is an organic gardener and "wizard of winter vegetables." His books include *The Winter Harvest Handbook* and *Four Season Harvest.* Unfortunately, they have not yet been translated into Russian! His greenhouses are covered over with a single layer of plastic, but the beds inside are covered with Spunbond nonwoven fabric. "If we had started our winter operation with more elaborate systems, we never would have known if they were really necessary," writes Eliot. Spunbond is fastened down with ordinary clothespins to a frame made from wire arches, so that it does not sag under the weight of condensation (see illustration). This kind of double covering protects plant leaves from frost and is known as the "Coleman method."

One layer of plastic protects plants nearly as well as two. It may be 3–5°F (2–3°C) cooler, but light is increased by 10%, which is more important for plants than warmth. During the winter, temperatures may fluctuate from 19°F (-7°C) at night to 86°F (30°C) during the day. There is convincing data that cold-resistant plants react not so much to temperature *per se*, but rather to average daily temperatures. During winter in Coleman's greenhouses, averages range from 46 to

55°F (8–13°C), which allows him to raise many kinds of vegetables successfully.

Making two visits to one of our cold houses—one at dawn after a below-zero night, and the other a few hours later—provides a striking introduction to the winter harvest. During the dawn visit all the crops are frozen solid. Raising the inner covers, which is difficult because they too are frozen, reveals a spectacle of stiff, frost-coated leaves bleak enough to convince anyone that this idea is foolhardy. Yet a few hours later, after the sun (even the wan sunlight of a cloudy day) has warmed the greenhouse above freezing, the second visit presents a miraculous contrast. Under the inner covers are closely spaced rows of vigorous, healthy leaves that stretch the length of the greenhouse. The leaf colors in different shades of greens, reds, maroons, and yellows stand bright against the dark soil. It looks like a perpetual spring.*

Experience has shown that plant growth virtually stops when days are shorter than 10 hours. At the 44th parallel (Crimea and Kuban in Russia) this period lasts from November 7 to February 7. Coleman names this time the "months of Persephone," the daughter of Demeter who is goddess of the earth. Persephone was forced to spend the time of the "low-hanging sun" in the underworld kingdom of Hades, so each year Demeter, languishing for her daughter, denuded the earth. However, the most cold-resistant plants (spinach, lettuce, and beet greens) with root systems developed in the

---

* Eliot Coleman, *The Winter Harvest Handbook: Year Round Vegetable Production Using Deep Organic Techniques and Unheated Greenhouses.* Chelsea Green Publishing, p. 55. [trans]

fall continue to grow slowly even in winter under a double covering. And young shoots from November and December plantings will patiently await lighter days when they will hit their stride quickly, producing the very earliest harvests.

In winter, Coleman sells salad mixes, carrots, spinach, radishes, leeks, shallots, Chinese cabbage (bok choy), and cress. A bit more demanding of warmth and light are intermediate crops sold at the very beginning or towards the end of the winter season: baby beets, new potatoes, overwintered onions, broccoli, turnips, collard greens, and arugula (rocket salad).

Winter salad mixes consist of the truly winter-hardy crops: red and green lettuce, arugula, endive, Swiss chard, spring beauty (*Claytonia*), spinach, corn salad (*Valerianella olitoria*), cress, and red beet greens (arugula, spring beauty, and corn salad are not cultivated here in Russia and are totally unknown to me!). The young leaves of these plants withstand frosts better than mature leaves. The most "heat-loving" salad greens—tender leaf lettuce, arugula, and endive—are warmed slightly by a small forced-air heater during severe cold spells.

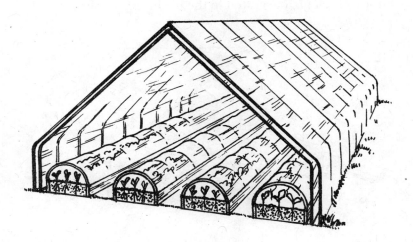

Late carrots sown in August are a very profitable crop. Eliot's greenhouses are portable and can be moved on skids. With the help of his ingenious design, Eliot can lengthen the time plants are shielded, which accelerates his vegetable conveyer belt. At the end of October he moves a greenhouse over his carrot beds. Carrots are harvested from November through February, becoming sweeter with each month. Winter carrots are a true delicacy in comparison with summer ones. They are sold with 1–2 inches (3–4 cm) of their tops retained, which makes them even more attractive and marketable.

Radishes are an excellent intermediate crop. The Colemans sow them at the end of September and the end of January, harvesting in December and March respectively. At this time the quality of root crops is at its peak, and the demand for radishes greatest.

Shallots are very winter-hardy, and onion sets, too, can be sown in August and overwintered—the bulbs will be ready as early as May. Superior quality beets with their tops attached sell well in late autumn and early spring. Cress is hugely popular in winter. The Colemans also grow new potatoes which are harvested in the beginning of May.

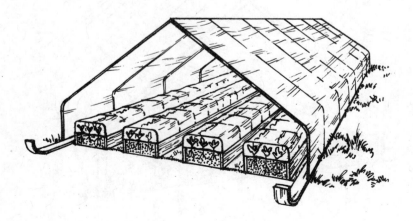

Eliot gets three harvests out of every square inch of his greenhouses. For example, after harvesting winter carrots, he sows early potatoes on March 15. He harvests the new potatoes around May 10, at which time he sows melons. The melons are followed by a green manure crop of rye and vetch. By October these plants have grown tall, and he moves the greenhouse off of them. The green manure will initiate a cycle of open-air cultivation. Another variant is to grow various winter crops into the early spring, followed by tomatoes transplanted into the beds on April 15. In September, a green manure of clover is sown right under the tomatoes. Eliot does not apply any animal manures, and only occasionally supplements the soil with high-quality compost.

Lynn Byczynski of Kansas has taken a similar route. Two of her greenhouses measuring 20 x 95 feet (6 x 29 m) paid for themselves two times over in the first year. The roofs of these greenhouses are rounded into arches. The large volume of air significantly lessens the threat of overheating, although it is still necessary to provide supplemental ventilation since some plants may become stressed by the heat.

Her greenhouses are also covered with a single layer of plastic and individual beds with Spunbond. When it is -17°F (-27°C) outside, it may be 5–8°F (-13° to -15°C) in the greenhouse. Lettuces and other cold-resistant crops can normally overwinter under the Spunbond cover. Flowers such as delphiniums and carnations also overwinter well. They become damaged by frost only if they lack proper drainage, but overwinter excellently on raised beds and flower very early. March plantings in the greenhouse yield early harvests of flowers as well. Bluebells, snapdragons, lisianthus, and decorative sunflowers grow fifty percent larger.

Byczynski sows greens—lettuce, spinach, arugula, and napa cabbage—in September and sells them as late as the middle of December. Her family eat greens throughout the entire winter. Spinach is harvested up to the hard frosts of winter, and then again in early spring. Leeks planted in October overwinter and are harvested in the spring. Early plantings of cucumbers and tomatoes are good sellers, too. They ripen 2–3 weeks earlier than in the field, the crop quality is outstanding, and they continue producing all the way into autumn.

I am truly spellbound by the efficiency of these gardeners. I will not describe their methods in greater detail here, because each system really deserves its own book. But they do work! This is what I really want to convey in this section.

Basic principles of "intelligent greenhouses"

Here is a preview of some chapters of the book *Greenhouse Gardening with a Smile.*

Konstantin Malyshevsky, a gardening expert from Krasnoyarsk (Zone 2) and head of the local Organic Gardening Club, makes small "intelligent cold frames." Having experimented with various greenhouse designs throughout his life, he has come to understand nearly everything about them.

First off, Konstantin researched daily temperature fluctuations in ordinary homemade greenhouses. He concluded that they usually caused more harm than benefit! If you do not constantly attend to ventilation—opening vents in the sun and closing them during cloudy weather—temperature fluctuations wreak havoc on plants. During the day they experience severe overheating, and at night they are as cold as it is outside. This kind of greenhouse does not fulfill its purpose, which is *to constantly maintain comfortable temperatures for plants*. On the contrary, it creates stress which actually weakens them. This is why greenhouse plants are so prone to disease.

He also demonstrated that it is very important how ventilation is provided. Side vents and doors cause harmful drafts—movement of cold air low over the soil. Hot air should move away by the shortest means possible, and cold air needs time to warm up, mixing with the hot. Only overhead ridge vents give this effect. Their overall length should be no less than half the length of the greenhouse.

In order to automate his greenhouse, Konstantin utilizes a simple mechanism—a "solar valve" or, more simply, an "opener" customized from an ordinary hydraulic cylinder (Photograph 38). As temperatures increase, it opens the vents, and when they fall, it closes them. After the book *Greenhouse Gardening with a Smile* was published, Russian manufacturers became very interested in this, and now similar openers are appearing on the market.

For watering, he uses a homemade, low-discharge drip system. The water faucet is regulated by the same kind of hydraulic cylinder. In the sun the water is turned on, and in overcast weather it is turned off.

Why do soils in greenhouses compact so quickly and lose fertility? It's very simple: because we water and cultivate much more than we do outside, and often we water with a hose. Under hot conditions with abundant air and water, organic matter decomposes much faster. We complete this destruction by compacting soil and washing away organic residues with a strong stream of water. The soil is quickly transformed into a dead substrate for chemical fertilizers.

However, for Konstantin it is the other way around. He utilizes drip irrigation, large amounts of organic matter, and a thick mulch of plant residues; he also releases homegrown earthworms into the soil to increase fertility.

He has identified an interesting and often overlooked process which causes a lot of heat to be lost: evaporation of water from bare soil. It takes a huge amount of energy to evaporate water! For instance, in just ten minutes at least 2 teaspoons (10 ml) of water can evaporate from 10 square feet (1 m²) of soil. For this process to take place, nearly 23 kJ of energy are consumed! If this energy was not used for transforming water into vapor, in the same ten minutes it would heat 70 cubic feet (2 m³) of air above the soil by almost 16°F (9°C). When we leave the soil bare, we allow the sun to remove both heat and moisture!

The solution is to mulch the soil. You can also convert mulch into a sort of "solar battery" by using black plastic. It should be sealed by digging the edges into the bed or pressing them firmly against the soil. It will heat up intensely, warming the air. The soil will warm up very little, since there is no greenhouse effect under black plastic. The plastic holds in soil moisture, preventing evaporation. At night this moisture condenses in the form of dew on the underside of the plastic and falls back into the soil. Watering is reduced to a minimum. Konstantin spreads black plastic on both pathways and beds—wherever it is convenient. For example, after harvesting radishes and greens, you can cover the whole ground with plastic and transplant tomatoes and peppers into small crosses cut into it, as described in the chapter on mulch.

Black containers filled with water also can be placed in the greenhouse to maintain warmth during evenings and in the night. They moderate nightly drops in temperature by

3–5°F (2–3°C). This may not seem like much, but plants do not have to expend any energy to achieve this benefit!

Konstantin attends to his greenhouses once a week. This is all that is required. One small, automated cold frame, chest-high, of just 65 square feet (6 m²) can feed an entire family with large, high-quality peppers from the beginning of June until late fall. For maintenance and harvesting, a portion of the roof can be raised and a section of one wall lowered (Photograph 37). Another cold frame, a bit higher and larger, provides his family with tomatoes, and yet another even taller one yields greens and cucumbers. It is very important not to transplant cucumbers and tomatoes into the same cold frame! They will both suffer. Cucumbers and peppers love heat and a lot of water while tomatoes and eggplants cannot bear heat and become diseased with too much moisture. Therefore, cold frames are adapted differently.

Finally, the type of plastic used is also very important. High quality materials have recently appeared in Russia— for example, Svetlitsa plastic manufactured by the Russian company Shar. It is a poly composite material and is very flexible—difficult to tear with your hands. It cannot be damaged by either sun or frost, and lasts 6–7 years on a greenhouse. Its light transmission and biological characteristics are significantly better than plastics based on polyethylene.

Multi-layer polycarbonate is an exceptionally good material for greenhouses, lasting for 20 years or longer. It is offered in double- and triple-wall with insulating layers of air sandwiched between. On a sunny day at -13°F (-25°C), the soil temperature in such a greenhouse will be 32°F (0°C)! It will not break like glass, nor tear like plastic. There is just one problem: all the available designs for carbonate greenhouses do not have top vents. It is very difficult to ventilate them, and they cannot be automated. This is of no great

concern, though! We will just have to rack our brains to fig-ure something out!

Some Russian farmers have found ways to quickly spread plastic over 3,000–5,000 square feet (300–500 m²) of ground in one fell swoop. Inexpensive and durable modular struc-tures have been especially made for this purpose and can be set up and taken down easily.

You can also build a permanent frame. Photograph 36 shows the tomato greenhouse of Yuri Tsikov, my neighbor from Adygea (Zone 6). These types of simple designs will withstand wind and even snow. Yuri discovered from expe-rience that warm soil is incomparably more important than warm air. So he buries in his beds ordinary plastic pipe filled with water warmed by a simple gas boiler. Tomatoes grow and ripen very quickly, and there are very few diseases in his organic soil mulched with sawdust.

My friend Vladimir Antropov has designed his green-houses very ingeniously—he sinks them into the ground. Walls—which lose half of total heat—are eliminated completely, leaving just a roof (Photograph 39). The deep layers of soil always maintain stable temperatures. The result is that in the summer his greenhouses are cooler, and in the winter they are much warmer without any supplemental heating.

A farmer from Kharkov (Zone 5), Anatoly Paty, has also taken this direction, patenting his "thermos greenhouse." It is completely sunk into the ground with a roof of double-walled polycarbonate. Decreased solar exposure is compensated by reflective plastic which covers the walls and floor. Stable soil temperatures allow him to raise (and even breed) citrus, bananas, pineapples, guavas, and papayas in his "thermos" with almost no supplemental heating.

As we see, even greenhouses can be made more intelligent!

Finally, I will add a few words about cold frames.

The main issue with small, plastic cold frames is that they quickly overheat in sunny weather. If the gardener is too busy with other matters, the plants will be fried. There are two different ways to mitigate this problem.

For those who visit their cold frames every day, I came up with this design (see illustration, next page). The frame has a central "ridge" made from a taut rope or thin rebar. The plastic is attached to it from two directions with stiff clothespins. During the day, some of the clothespins are removed along the "ridge" creating "top vents." Hot air is effectively removed, drawn upwards and out of the cold frame. Refastening the clothespins in the evening, like unfastening them, only takes about seven seconds.

I saw another possibility demonstrated at our experimental station at the Timiriazev Academy. The plastic covering had a polka dot pattern of holes cut into it. It is best to poke out the holes with a hand punch. They should be 1/4 to 5/16 inches (6–8 mm) in diameter and 8–12 inches (20–30 cm) apart. Such plastic is equivalent to nonwoven materials. It is not as good at protecting plants from freezing, but they will not overheat. The advantage of this covering is that in the spring it does not require daily tending.

Intelligent greenhouses are not only for northern climes. They should be used everywhere. Greenhouses can help northerners extend the vegetable-growing season and can help southerners grow crops successfully year-round!

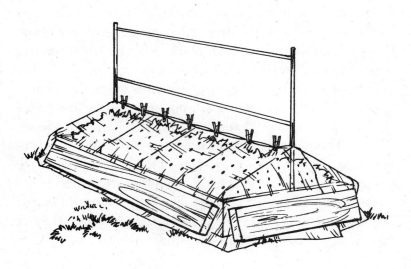

Chapter 11

In Care of Our Young

or

A Tale About Seeds and Seedlings

It was all too easy to give the newborn a first name, but choosing a patronymic took a long time.

Every year we religiously purchase new seeds, intoxicated by a sacred hope that all we need to do is sow these seeds, and the spectacular plants pictured on the packets will magically pop up out of the ground! And each spring we eagerly amass a multitude of transplants from garden stores, marveling at how cheap they are. Yet even in all our excitement, there is this nagging feeling at the back of our minds, a kind of complacency, muttering disconsolately: "Oh, who really cares anyway?"

I don't know how it is in Europe and the US, but in Russia a good third of store-bought seed usually do not germinate. Or something grows from them which has very little resemblance to the picture on the packet. As for the transplants we buy, some of them end up dying immediately, and the rest grow into sickly, stunted plants which usually perish from disease long before yielding any harvest. From my personal experience, I know that this is the way things are in Russia. Yet it just doesn't seem right. You begin to think that some very important instructions were not included, or something relevant was missing from the pictures.

So, as is usually the case, we have to figure out things on our own.

Here is the fundamental law about seedlings and transplants: *the first few days and weeks of development determine the entire life of the plant.* This is a universal and inexorable law for all things living. In fact, seed quality and the seedling stage of the plant determine 80% of the fate of the harvest. Improperly stored seeds can significantly affect plant performance—for instance, by inducing early bolting in root crops, or increasing the amount of "infertile flowers"* on cucumbers and squash. Weak, spindly plants never catch up to normal ones. Such transplants will yield less than half the expected harvest, no matter how much fertilizer you pour on them. For these reasons, the first weeks of a plant's life are the most important. So it is worthwhile to give them careful attention—it always pays off in the end.

A seed is already a plant

"Abracadabra!"
Pinocchio, effervescent with hope

Seeds are actually living plants—bona fide plants with tiny buds, leaves, and roots. They just happen to be very small, often microscopic, hiding inside their seed coats, so we pay very

---

* *Infertile flowers*—the male flowers of cucumbers and other members of the squash family. They give only pollen without setting any fruit.

little attention to them. Actually, though, it is their condition at the moment of sowing which determines how vigorous their initial thrust of life will be, as well as their subsequent development and performance. For this reason, it is sensible to learn more about your seeds before you plant them.

How do you buy good seeds? At the risk of offending our Russian agribusiness industry, I will say quite frankly that there is no possible way to buy good seeds at Russian stores.

Based on my purchases over the past four years, I have calculated that only half of commercial seeds germinate or match the variety advertised on the packet. Why? On the one hand, companies often purchase seeds from a number of private suppliers, and it is virtually impossible to check the quality of every lot. Storing seeds is expensive, and advertising and packaging cost megabucks. They just need to move their products to make a profit!

But there is another side to this: we Slavs are willing to pay double for hope—as long as it is packaged up nice and pretty. I realize that more affluent countries may not be as afflicted by this. Everything is so tediously legitimate and proper there. But our market is really "free." There are no laws which punish substandard products! But then that's what makes our life so exciting. We purchase mystery along with our seeds. We burn with curiosity: will they germinate, or not? And if they do germinate, what exactly will they turn out to be? Every spring becomes a guessing game of what will sprout up. If seeds do not germinate, we aren't that upset—it's just bad luck. And if everything comes out as expected, we are ecstatic!

Russians have two ways for purchasing good seed. 1) Stock up on wholesale high-end seeds for the long-term,

or pool together with friends to buy them collectively each year. These seeds are in packets made of a special kind of foil or in hermetically-sealed jars. They are extremely expensive and only worth it for serious farm production. They germinate fantastically, as if by command! For small gardeners like us, though, turning a profit is not our main motivation. 2) Purchase seeds directly from horticultural experimental stations or seed production farms, since they are usually genuine before they are bought up for packaging in those pretty little packets.

Even better, you can collect your own seeds. In Russia, not everyone has switched to hybrids yet, so there are still enough varieties which yield consistent offspring.

Saved seeds always have maximum viability, so you can sow them with confidence. But to keep a variety from degenerating, you must perform rigorous selection—using only the best, tastiest, earliest, and most fruitful plants for seeds. Some 20 square feet ($2 m^2$) of a bed is all that you need for a good seed crop. In early spring you simply plant a few good carrots, some commendable beets, and maybe onions; you might also throw in a few of your favorite lettuce seeds and radishes, daikon, and other vegetables. By July you will have a handful of seeds from each carrot plant. Sown immediately, they will germinate at nearly 100% and yield an excellent crop of carrots in the fall. As for tomatoes, peppers, cucumbers, and other fruiting vegetables, you simply pick the prime, early fruit and, overcoming your greed, relinquish them for seeds.

It is extremely important to distinguish open-pollinated varieties from hybrids.

Open-pollinated varieties: these plants have the exact same genes. This never occurs in nature, where various parent plants cross-pollinate freely. In order to develop an open-pollinated variety, the offspring of a single plant are isolated and crossed only with themselves. Such "intrafamilial" crossing is repeated over many generations until no outside genes remain, and all offspring are identical to the parents. After that, you can collect these varietal seeds with confidence. Of course, in vegetable gardens insects are constantly carrying in pollen from "outsider" plants, and the purity of the variety may be lost in 3–5 years. Rigorous selection of the best plants which are true to type alleviates this problem of degeneration.

Hybrids: in contrast to open-pollinated varieties, hybrids are the result of one-time cross-pollination between two specific parent plants. From a genetic point of view, you and I are hybrids. Hybrids are obtained by artificial or targeted pollination of plants growing in isolation from the outside environment. That is why hybridized seeds are so expensive. But they are worth it—the offspring of well-matched parents exhibit special powers of growth, vigor, yield, and disease and pest resistance—this effect is called hybrid vigor. Seed quality of hybrids is extremely high, and the harvest always compensates for their higher price. They sometimes exhibit other amazing qualities as well: few or no seeds, more female flowers, and even the ability to set fruit without pollination (parthenocarpy). Nowadays, vegetable farmers in developed countries utilize mostly hybrids. But hybrid vigor is a first-generation phenomenon. If seeds are collected from hybrids, they will at best reproduce their parents, or perhaps their grandparents.

How to store seeds. First of all, they should only be collected from fully ripened fruit. Often because of weather or "operational needs," seeds are gathered while still immature. These seeds will germinate normally, but they will not keep as well as mature seeds and yield less productive plants.

If seeds are stored in humid conditions, they begin to actively breathe, warming up and coming to life, and their viability quickly declines. Mold may even start appearing on seed coats.

Under proper storage conditions, mature seeds retain their vitality for quite some time. Parsnips are the "shortest-lived" seeds—they germinate poorly even in the second year. Dill, celery, parsley, sorrel, bulb onions, and leeks can be sown in the second year, but onions tend to bolt more frequently. Lettuce, peppers, and carrots are good for three years, but their germination energy* declines sharply—they germinate slowly and unevenly. The seeds of garden radishes,

---

* *Germination energy*—simultaneous and vigorous seed germination.

cabbages, beets, turnips, and rhubarb can be stored up to four years, but older seeds produce earlier bolting plants. All these leaf and root vegetables are better sown using fresh seed. Fruiting vegetables, however, are a wholly different matter. The seeds of legumes, cucumbers, pumpkins, melons, peppers, tomatoes, and eggplants can be stored for as many as 7–9 years, and it is actually better to sow 3- to 4-year-old "cured seeds." More compact and fruitful plants are obtained from older seeds.

Warming seeds also produces the same effect. In large greenhouse complexes, cucumber and tomato seeds are warmed in a drying oven for three days at 160°F (70°C). At home you can spread seeds out on a heating radiator for a couple of weeks.

From this we can conclude that cabbage, root crops, lettuce, and onion seeds should be collected from your garden or purchased fresh, but seeds of fruiting vegetables are better stored for several years and used as needed.

Is it necessary to test seed germination? Yes, so that you know their germination rate—sowing a "pig in a poke" is just too extravagant! Yet for some inexplicable reason people are reluctant to bother with this. After all, it takes time, perhaps an entire evening to set up a notebook, prepare waterproof labels and germinating dishes, etc. But to re-sow a bed is by far worse!

Often this is the scenario: you open a packet and pour out the entire contents into your palm. All you see is a few, tiny seeds. So what's there to test with?! You will have to sacrifice a dozen seeds, but there are hardly that many in the first place. If you can already see that they vary both in size and color, this means that the quality is questionable. There is only one thing you can do: germinate them immediately in a cup filled with soil set out in the light and covered with plastic. This will reveal everything. You can then prick out the good seedlings to plant into pots.

During germination, it is vital that seeds receive sufficient air. Otherwise, they will swell up, suffocate, and die. I use damp white rags. Write the name on the rags with a ballpoint pen, drop in the seeds, and fold them over four times. These are piled up in a bowl and occasionally sprinkled with warm water. Be sure to squeeze out any excess water from the rags. It is most important that seeds are not suffocated. Covering the bowl, set it in a warm place. You must also take care not to leave them for too long. Usually they will sprout in 1–3 days; legume seeds—beans and peas—rot especially quickly.

Segregate out Umbelliferae seeds—carrots, parsley, celery, dill, and parsnips. Their shells contain inhibitors which suppress germination. These inhibitors are protective mechanisms for desert plants—until dependable rains manage to soak through the seed coats, they are prevented from germinating. In order to hasten sprouting, change the water three times a day, pouring in clean, warm water and wringing out any excess.

How to speed up germination. The most important consideration is that it is easier to germinate seeds in slightly acidic water. For example, rain water is slightly acidic due to the carbon dioxide dissolved in it. Generally, rain water is the best stimulator for seeds.

A very good way to get quick and simultaneous germination is by setting up a hot water "sauna" for seeds. This is the most effective method I know. Seeds are sprinkled into a bowl, and hot water—up to 140°F! (60°C)—is poured over them. Cover the bowl and leave them to cool. Those that float to the top are not viable while the rest will sprout up twice as quickly.

A "sauna" is the best method for germinating carrots or parsley. Over the course of a day, you should cover seed with hot water 4–5 times, pouring off the resulting brown infusion after an hour of soaking. Following this treatment, they will sprout without problem in 3–5 days—with ample daily watering, of course.

Hard seeds "steam" especially well: Canna seeds, spinach, artichoke, dog rose, milk thistles, etc. They can be covered with nearly boiling water. As the famous Russian gardener Rikhard Shreder wrote, Canna seeds will begin "to leap about, as if in fear, and crackle loudly as the bony platelets which protect the embryo fall off the seeds. If they are planted soon afterwards, these seeds germinate exceptionally well."

It is better to soak hard nuts and the pits of stone fruit, and then carefully split them to remove the kernel. I also grind down the edges of pits with an emery disc grinder. This is the best way to germinate peaches, plums, almonds, filberts, and so on. Also, watermelons and pumpkins sprout a week earlier if seeds are carefully nicked.

Should seeds be stimulated? The fact is that good seeds have everything they need to get off to a good start. They do not require any kind of stimulation or fertilizer in order to germinate. Rather, it is the soil itself which needs these supplements if it is not fertile enough. Stimulators and fertilizers are best used as auxiliary tactics if the soil and seeds themselves do not produce good seedlings.

Principles of sowing

As you sow, so shall you reap!

A pipe dream

Usually, we very carefully loosen the soil before sowing. We believe that small, young rootlets, rejoicing in their freedom, will then be able to push downward without interference. But this fantasy only exists in our imagination! We forget about the most important features—capillarity and root channels. It is precisely in this kind of environment that seeds have germinated for millions of years. Tilled soil draws up very little water from below—there are no guiding channels. So we have to water from above. The young roots are supposed to grow downward, but there is more water above—it's absurd! They have no impetus to seek out water in the depths! The rootlets "go nuts" and alter their genetic programming, remaining as surface roots. Thereafter, these plants depend wholly upon us for watering.

In order for roots to grow downward, **seeds should lie on a hard capillary layer**. Ovsinsky strongly emphasized this. Yuri Slashchinin describes the sowing method which his grandfather used: "He beat down the soil with a 'mallet,' placed seeds in the smooth depressions, and covered them with loose soil. The harvest always yielded more than anyone else's, although he hardly ever tended his garden." Vladimir Fokin recommended planting potatoes in the same way using a planting peg. A "mallet" is now a common tool among Russian intelligent gardeners.

Edward Faulkner designed an ingenious contraption to poke holes for a seedbed: two large, heavy wheels with cone-shaped spikes. He only had to insert the roots of seedlings into the holes and sprinkle soil over them—the plants would be standing tall by the second day, and the harvest was excellent. A farmer from Novosibirsk (Zone 2), Yuri Salnik, increased his wheat harvest three-fold by pushing seeds into a compacted field with a roller. Many modern seeders have a special indenting disk. The effect is remarkable: seeds sprout almost in a single day.

Sometimes I imagine a simple implement, like a row marker, for making seed furrows by pressing down on it with my full body weight. Currently, I make furrows with a smooth slat planed down into a wedge.

Sowing depth. All masters of backyard vegetable gardening agree that optimal planting depth equals the length of the seed. It is best to cover seeds with sand or fine rotted manure, and to water very gently from a watering can.

It is a wholly different matter in the field where it is more important to place seeds in a layer of moist soil, so that they don't dry out. For this reason they are sown deeper. Large seeds are sown especially deep—for instance, watermelons and pumpkins at a depth of 2–3 inches (6–7 cm).

If moisture is not a problem—for instance, in a greenhouse or in flats—then seeds do not need to be buried at all. They will sprout splendidly on the surface—if there is water. Moreover, tiny seeds—such as lettuce, cabbage, and even radishes, as well as small flower seeds—as a rule only germinate well in the presence of light. This is exactly how I sow radishes and lettuce in the spring: I broadcast them onto the ground, water them with "rain," and cover them over with plastic.

Sowing tiny seeds. Some flowers—calceolaria, petunias, snapdragons, lobelia, poppies, etc.—have seeds which are nearly microscopic. They normally germinate only on the surface. It is often recommended to press them down with glass, but there is a better method.

A disposable, rectangular dish makes a convenient container for sowing. It is filled with moist peaty soil which has been well tamped down. Seeds are spread over the surface and sprinkled with water. This "seedbed" is then placed in a transparent plastic bag. The bag is inflated, twisted closed, and fastened with a clothespin. If it leaks, you can put a small stick in the center—this "cold frame" should never be allowed to cave in. The plastic bag will steam up inside, so watering is not necessary, and you can easily oversee the process through the plastic. The hardest part is pricking out the tiny seedlings, so it is better to let them grow up a bit. If you sow them sparsely in the beginning, when they sprout you can space plants at 1–2 inches (3–4 cm) by simply thinning out excess plants.

Achieving simultaneous germination. Spring plantings are easier than summer—the ground is moist, and the days are not scorching hot. On the other hand, in the spring the soil is cooler, so seeds germinate more slowly. These issues can be resolved in different ways.

In the spring, buried and watered seeds should be covered with plastic—simply spread it over the soil and heel in the edges. Under the plastic the soil warms up, and seedlings emerge more quickly. When the seeds have sprouted, raise the plastic onto a frame, or if the crop is cold-tolerant, remove it completely.

While dry seeds are suitable for spring plantings, only soaked ones should be planted in the summer. Frequent watering is also very important—the bed should stay constantly moist. If this is not possible, summer sowings may be covered by a "blanket"—a heavy, opaque mulch. Thick cloth works well—old mats, carpets, throw rugs, or blankets. Black plastic is also suitable. Before sowing, the bed is liberally watered. Seeds are worked in shallowly, the bed is watered again, and then covered with the "blanket."

If conditions become dry, swollen seeds will not die off for a long time; they will simply stop growing while awaiting more water. Under such conditions, seeds begin to develop but will not sprout. This is useful to know for hastening development of flowering plants. But if the seed has already germinated and then dries out, the sprout will quickly die from dehydration.

Therefore, until the appearance of sprouts, summer plantings should be watered 2–3 times per day or tightly covered. It's no big deal if seedlings appear in the dark—they will be fine for a day or two. After the cover is removed, the pale shoots will turn green in two days and start growing vigorously.

If the bed is covered with a loose mulch—sawdust, seed hulls, etc.—do not sow directly onto the mulch! Seeds will simply fall through it, making insufficient contact with the moist earth. Instead, rake off the row, lay seed onto the compacted soil, and cover with sand or compost. Once they have sprouted, you can rake the mulch back on.

For late fall plantings in temperate zones, according to the evidence of Bryzgalov, I would recommend carrots, parsley, parsnips, dill, lettuce, onions from seed, and garlic. Other crops tend to bolt (flower) early the following spring or die back from frost after a thaw. It is warmer where we live in the south (Zone 6), so we can sow many kinds of vegetables before the onset of winter. This is evident from natural self-seeding. Very often tomatoes, beans, squash, and pumpkins—and sometimes even cucumbers—will germinate in the spring and grow up as volunteers. Many crops will even overwinter as young plants: leeks, chicory, parsnips, turnips, rutabagas, kohlrabi, parsley, lettuce, and spinach. You can also sow them in the fall. In a warm winter, carrots, cabbage, and onions will overwinter as seedlings. Frankly speaking, I have very little experience with late fall plantings, so this is all I can share.

How to make planting easier. A very challenging question! Sowing is the most tedious of springtime work, but here are a few ideas.

A very handy seeder can be made from a plastic saltshaker with three holes of different diameters: for parsley-celery, carrots-lettuce, and radishes-beets. When you are sowing one crop, you cover the other two holes with your fingers or tape over them (see illustration).

"Wet seeding" is surprisingly easy and effective. Seeds are poured out with water through an opening in the lid of a plastic bottle. In order to sow evenly, the bottle should be gently agitated.

In general, though, we use a very small handheld seeder for beds. Modern-day models are either too heavy and complicated, or ineffectual. So once again gardeners have had to invent their own solutions!

For instance, a do-it-yourselfer from the Ukrainian city of Cherkassy, Alexander Boldarev, put together a very simple

seeder from improvised materials (see illustration). He calls it the "cuttlefish." He also designed a single-row vari- ant—the "Elf." Now planting is fun for him and his neigh- bors. The main challenge is the seed timing shaft. It must have precisely bored holes, so that various types of seeds can be sown. If done properly, the rest is easy. You can use any kind of wheel, even one made from a tin can lid. The main thing is to make cogs in it for better contact with the soil. The seed "hopper" is a regular shampoo bottle. Pieces of foam are glued inside the neck, flush against the shaft, to keep seeds from falling through. This "hopper" is attached to the handle for stability.

No one has offered to mass produce these yet. But who cares? We can simply make them ourselves! My own proto- type, assembled in a single evening, yields excellent results. I am able to sow an even bed of radishes in just three minutes!

Transplanting subtleties

"Oh, how I love raising seedlings! I get to worry over them so much!"

It is easy to understand what constitutes a superior seed- ling. Imagine a plant growing up from seed right where it will remain in good, fertile soil until maturity, without com- petition, in a warm, sunny location. This would truly be an excellent seedling!

Our process of growing seedlings should approach this ideal as closely as possible. Any limitation, slowdown, or physiological damage during the sprouting phase makes plants two, even three times less productive. However much you subsequently water them, however often you fertilize them, poor seedlings can never catch up to strong ones. This means that there is good sense in raising only the very best seedlings, but this presents our main difficulty. Realistically speaking, most of us do not have the proper conditions to do this. If your seedlings fall behind self-seeded volunteers on open ground, it is definitely worth thinking about whether you should be raising them at all!

Do you need to transplant? The better the conditions and potential for raising transplants, the larger the number of plants which can be sown in a germination bed rather than directly in regular beds. But whether you *need* to do this is really a matter of taste. Tatiana Ugarova is a master of transplanting. She believes that—with the exception of carrots, parsley, radishes, turnips, cress, and dill—it is worthwhile to transplant everything else. The harvest is earlier and greater, but mainly transplants compress time: before the first crop is harvested, the second is already growing in flats. And what's more, flats take up far less space—40–200 times less than beds.

There are also other advantages to transplanting. It saves on seed. If you are using expensive hybrids, this is definitely a plus. Seed quality is easily observed in flats, so you can select out only the best plants. With transplanting, you can confidently grow late varieties, which are often more productive than early ones. For northerners, transplants are the only way to raise heat-loving crops and to extend the summer growing season; and for southerners they make it possible to harvest earlier.

All this is very valuable to the master of intensive gardening, but for the weekend gardener it is highly questionable! For truly good transplants, you need either a greenhouse with supplementary heat (a closed-in balcony facing the sun), or indoor shelving with strong artificial lighting. Without

artificial lights transplants inside your home are highly unlikely to be worth the effort. In Russia, small greenhouses
for growing transplants are few and far between. This means
that transplants have to be raised at home, transported to
the countryside, and immediately planted—not exactly easy
work! As for achieving an early and more bounteous harvest,
I repeat: this only occurs with ideal transplants. And finally,
you must guarantee that transplants will not suffer in the
process—you have to harden them off and then plant them
in warm soil, providing supplementary shading for the first
few days. In reality we plant when we are able to and have
time! It is a sad fact that our transplants are planted only to
survive, and because of this they could care less about providing us with a good harvest.

In the following pages, we will look at best practices for
raising vigorous transplants successfully.

1. LIGHT is the main element which transplants usually
lack. As a rule, transplants for sale are sown very densely
and held in flats for too long, so the plants become spindly. The lower leaves quickly die in the shade, and the upper
buds are what mainly grow. Young plants get the message
that good conditions for development are not in the cards
for them! Therefore, they begin forming flowering heads in
expectation of a brief, cursed life—they will yield little fruit
and what does set will be very seedy.

A germination bed or south-facing balcony can provide
sufficient light, but the main concern here is not to over-
crowd plants. Lighting on a window sill inside a room is
wholly insufficient. For normal development, transplants
require a light intensity of 8,000 lux.* On a clear day in early
March, there are 5,000 lux in Moscow (55th parallel)—6,500
lux where we live in the south (45th parallel). In February,

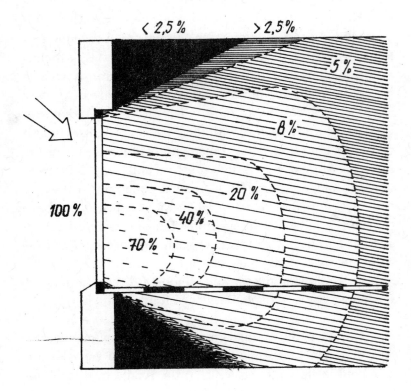

there is even less light, and the days are shorter. Under plastic and glass this is lowered by yet another 15%.

A southern windowsill receives about 3,000 lux during the day, but only half that for every 8 inches (20 cm) which plants are moved away from the window (see illustration). And this is on a sunny day! On cloudy days, light intensity falls by as much as 10–15 times. If you take into account that in the spring where we live a third of all days are cloudy, then

---

* *Lux*—a unit of measurement of surface illumination. Difference in illumination is easy to see by putting the same surface in various places and observing it through a camera at the same distance.

on average the light intensity on our windowsill is *about ten times below* the required amount.

But this doesn't even show the entire picture. Good transplants need 15–16 hours of light per day. Spring days are only half that long, which further reduces the amount of available light. So much for a southern window! *Plants grown inside receive about 20 times less light than they require.* And light is their primary source of energy! How would *you* have turned out if you had been given twenty times less food starting at birth? How productive would you have become?

Spindly transplants. Imagine that there is little light available to seedlings but an abundance of heat. Plants are compelled to breathe and divide cells at an accelerated rate, producing little organic matter. They consume nearly all their supply of glucose produced through photosynthesis. Becoming pale, they elongate like potato sprouts in a dark cupboard. Warmth without light is a veritable torture chamber for plants!

Hence arises the artificially-created problem of "holding back growth": having compelled transplants to elongate, we then try to force them to "stop elongating"!

The easiest way to slow growth is with cold. But it is always warm, even hot, in an apartment. In an outdoor germination bed, temperatures fluctuate wildly and there is also risk of freezing. You can haul transplants out onto a balcony every day and then back inside at night, but if you have lots of them, only body builders would find this task enjoyable.

So another method to slow growth can be employed: pinching off the upper buds. This only works for a while—in warm conditions growth is quickly resumed, and plants begin developing side shoots, becoming both bushy and spindly at the same time.

Mittleider found what may be the most successful method for holding back transplants. He regularly removed the lowest, biggest leaves, leaving only the young, upper rosettes. As soon as leaves pushed up against their neighbors, it was time to pinch them off. Finding themselves shaded, lower leaves communicate to plants that they should elongate their stems between nodes. Losing these lower leaves, plants freeze in their footsteps, not elongating but rather thickening their stems. The result is sturdy transplants. They are planted in beds "up to their necks," where they form secondary roots along the buried stems, and quickly start growing. Of course, this depends on the condition that plants were grown in individual cups and their roots were not damaged.

This brings us to the real question: why should we slow plants down at all? As many Russian gardeners write to me: "What sense is there in starting transplants early, and then, using various gimmicks, to discourage them from growing?" The urge to plant early—even in January—comes to us from commercial greenhouse growers. These large operations have a special section for transplants with strong supplementary lighting, and the ground is warm and ready to receive plants even in the depths of winter. In greenhouses you have to plant early for commercial reasons. But for our garden beds, what possible sense is there in this?

Compare these alternatives: either all conditions for proper growth are provided for plants, and they can grow rapidly, maturing in 2–3 months; or we torture them by retarding their growth, so that they lag behind even self-seeded volunteers growing outside. Why do we persist in planting so early?

Konstantin Malyshevsky came up with an excellent explanation. "We attempt to reconcile the irreconcilable:

both a little earlier and a little bigger! But you can't sit on two chairs at once." So he apportions transplants for *early* and *regular* plantings. Only 8–10 plants are grown for early transplanting. No more are needed! They are sown early but under proper conditions with sufficient light and space. As they grow taller, they are periodically transplanted into larger and wider containers: first in 6-ounce (0.2-L), then 12-ounce (0.5-L), and finally in 1-quart (1-L) bags. When they are ready, the bottom of the bag is cut off, and the plants are moved to a forcing bed in plastic fruit boxes with two plants per box. Finally, once moved to their permanent spot in the greenhouse, the boxes are simply placed on the ground and buried in mounds of rotted sawdust or soil. In this way, plants keep growing without a single day's delay! And there are enough early vegetables for everyone.

Main-crop transplants are sown at the end of March. By then there is plenty of light and warmth, days are longer, and the early plants have gone out to the cold frame, so there is plenty of space. Transplants grow up perfectly well without any stress at all.

If you decide to provide all conditions necessary for quick growth, the most important issue is to provide adequate supplementary lighting. Incandescent lights are not suitable—they give off more heat than light. At a distance they are useless, and up close they will scorch the plants. Only fluorescent or halogen lights (daylight) are suitable. But the most beneficial for plants are specialized plant lights which emit red or orange light. They are also better on the eyes.

Lights should be kept on for 15 hours per day, except for the 3–4 hours of the sunniest part of the day when the sun is emitting around 8,000 lux—30–40 watt daylight lamps provide the required luminescence at a distance of 10–12 inches

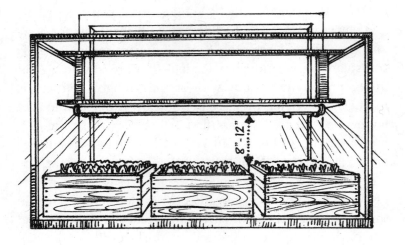

(25–30 cm). Two lamps are required for wide boxes (see illustration), and they should definitely have top reflection shields! Without shields, up to 60% of light is lost. It is even better to attach reflective plastic to the inside of the entire germination bed. In a mirrored box, there is so much reflected light that the wattage of lamps can be decreased by one third.

2. **SPACE** is the second factor required for good transplants. In observing the development of trees, I have seen for myself that even in direct sunlight trees "shy away" from any object which blocks the light. Young plants behave in exactly the same way. They want to feel freedom from any possible competition and interference. Everything which steals away light is hostile to them. In commercial greenhouses, transplants in peat-compost blocks are spaced far apart from each other—about 6–8 inches (15–20 cm). Healthy transplants tend to grow wider rather than taller. It is in the first two months of their lives that plants "evaluate"

the conditions they find themselves in and establish a program for subsequent development—above all, the vigor and quality of flowering clusters.

The exact same thing happens with roots. If roots find themselves in a very confined amount of soil, they intertwine and become crumpled up. When this happens, plants become convinced that there is nowhere to grow, and that they are destined to live a bleak, horrible life. Most of the matted roots die when transplanted into the ground, and the plant resolutely refuses to grow well. What can they do? Flower quickly and put out a few scrawny seeds! So we end up with stunted plants bearing miniscule fruit. Do you know why flowerpots taper downwards? So that flowering plants grow less vigorously and blossom sooner due to close quarters!

Following is the minimal area and volume for transplants grown for 4–7 weeks. After the 8th week, this area should be doubled. Also, double the planting area if there is no supplemental lighting or insufficient natural sunlight.

Celery and **onions**: with good supplemental lighting—1 square inch (5 cm²) per plant: 3/8 inch (1 cm) apart in the row with 2 inches (5 cm) between rows, without thinning. Up to 200 plants can be grown on 1 square foot (0.1 m²). Transplant trays with cells measuring about 1 x 1 inch (2.5 x 2.5 cm) are also suitable.

Beets, **lettuce**, and all **cabbage family**: with supplemental lighting—on average 5 square inches (30 cm²) per plant, or approximately 2 x 2 3/8 inches (5 x 6 cm) after thinning.

Peppers, eggplant, tomatoes, cucumbers, and **squash family**: with supplementary lighting—on average 12 square inches (80 cm²) per plant, or in a 3 1/2 x 3 1/2 inches (9 x 9 cm) pattern after thinning.

Flat depth should be no less than 3 inches (8 cm) but no more than 4 inches (10 cm). It is difficult to transplant seedlings with long roots since planting holes will have to be that much deeper.

3. WARMTH is the primary factor which determines *growth rate*. Vegetable transplants develop best of all at 68–75°F (20–24°C). They must not overheat as this will cause them to become spindly and diseased! They also should be protected from becoming too cold. This will arrest development which will affect their growth for a long time to come.

As has already been mentioned, *soil temperature is much more important than air temperature*. Do you want your transplants to develop quickly? Provide supplementary heating to the flat. Soil temperature can be 78–82°F (26–28°C) while air temperature is only 68–72°F (20–22°C). Under these conditions, not only transplants but any kind of cutting will instantly strike root. But transplants accustomed to warm soil must be slowly and painstakingly hardened off. If you transplant them directly into open ground, they may die from stress.

4. AIR HUMIDITY is the fourth factor for good transplants. Unfortunately, our houses and apartments have dreadfully dry air. In our heated living rooms, the humidity is usually no greater than 25–35%—that's like a desert!—but average humidity outside is 70–80%. Remember Timiriazev's work which we cited earlier: under dry conditions plants are forced to circulate huge amounts of extra water. This is especially harmful to young plants. Even if the ground is moist, small roots can hardly cope with it all! And in the process, surplus salts quickly accumulate in cells. All this causes increased stress on plants.

Ugarova recommends a simple home-made "device" for maintaining high humidity in her home. She spreads a thick cloth over a heating radiator, with the lower part submerged in a large container of water placed under a window. If the cloth dries out, it means that it is not heavy enough. In a single day, this "device" will vaporize up to 3 gallons (10 L) of water. Now do you understand why it is so difficult to raise transplants in your apartment?

5. SOIL MIXTURES, FERTILIZERS, AND WATERING. The main principle here is that it is better to underfeed than overfeed, and better to underwater than overwater.

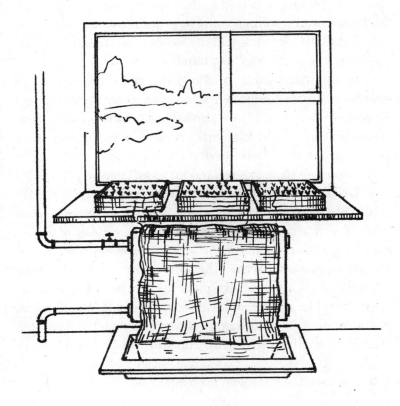

I believe that potting soil should contain no more than 1/3 garden soil, and I do not recommend adding sand. Growing blocks can weigh up to half a kilogram. If you have ever hauled around transplant flats, you understand what this means! The main thing for seedling roots is air. You do not need much water—for young plants an overabundance of moisture is just as devastating as severe drying.

A good soil mixture should be lightweight, containing rotted sawdust, perlite, vermiculite, or clay pellet residue (fines) for up to half the volume. You can even go without garden soil completely—for example, 1/3 mature compost or purchased peat moss, 1/3 clay pellet residue or perlite, and 1/3 sawdust or rotted hulls. This provides plentiful air and good water storage capacity—the most important requirements for potting soil. By no means should you add manure; it is acidic and very harsh.

The important thing is to mix the soil correctly. If you combine the dry components and then water them, the soil becomes compacted into a solid mass with no structure. There is little air, and nutrients become bound up anaerobically.* This is often exactly what we find in potted plants. *In order to create structure, soil should be mixed when optimally moist.* It is easy to do this. Spread out a large piece of plastic and place everything to be mixed in layers along one edge. Make a depression in the middle of the pile, pour in water, allowing it to soak in. Turn it with a trowel and then move the entire pile over to the other side of the plastic by raking it a little bit at a time. Next, push the pile back in the same way. Do not knead the soil with your hands! If some dry soil remains, pour on a little more water, and rake the soil back and forth again to mix it in. The soil will form into *small*

---

* *Anaerobic*—without oxygen; see Chapter 3.

clumps right before your eyes. Turn it over another couple of times until it is completely homogenous. Now you can handle it—it is living, porous. Clumping ensures a stable structure in the potting soil.

The proper moisture level of a structured soil can be determined in this way: soil clenched in your fist stays in a clump, does not drip water, and does not muddy your palm. If you do overwater, the soil starts feeling doughy. At that point, you will have to add more dry components and mix everything again—this time more evenly and for a much longer period.

As for fertilizing, I will cover only the main points.

To think that transplants need to be "fattened for slaughter" is a huge mistake! What is worse than becoming "obese" in childhood? Gorged with nitrogen, plants become flaccid, semi-transparent, and die off at the slightest stress. Finding themselves in a high-nutrient environment, the roots become "lazy" and "pampered." They do not elongate or bother seeking out nutrients; they hardly even develop. The immunity of these early starts "plunges through the floor." For them, outside beds do not represent the freedom they desire but rather a source of intense stress. Programmed for opulence, plants will begin suffering at the slightest lack of expected "luxury." An intelligent deficiency of nutrients is much more beneficial to young plants! Having become accustomed to forming roots and fighting for life, they will thrive in outdoor beds as well.

In contrast to mature plants, transplants are unable to assimilate very many nutrients—they are simply too young. Yet it is when they are young that seedlings are still "actively seeking"—in poor soil their roots develop much more vigorously. Rich soil, on the other hand, slows the growth of roots. It can even impair seed germination! As a university student, I observed this phenomenon myself in laboratory experiments. For this reason, keep both organic matter and mineral fertilizers to a minimum. For example, for every bucket of poor sandy-peat soil, you should add no more than 3–4 spoonfuls of ash and a spoonful of a compound fertilizer like Kristalon. If the mix contains a third garden soil, then I would wait on the initial feeding until the fourth true leaf develops, and even then only if there are signs of nitrogen deficiency—i.e., the young upper leaves become pale and light.

Watering transplants is usually done from below with a tray. It is very harmful to water from above with a strong stream of water or by pouring water over the leaves. You also should not overdo it—overwatering is the main cause of a root and stem rot called "damping off." All cabbage family, squash, and melons are particularly susceptible to it. To prevent stem rot, fill the upper third of pots with sawdust, sand, or perlite. This will not harm any kind of seedling.

Slight drying can be very beneficial for squash family seedlings—especially cucumbers beginning to flower. If watering is limited once for as long as it takes them to "droop their ears," then plants will start bearing early and abundantly.

6. HARDENING OFF is the most important factor which determines a plant's hardiness after transplanting. Many of my readers have observed a huge difference: greenhouse-grown transplants grow into seemingly "normal" plants which are quickly decimated by disease, while *plants from hardened-off seedlings stay green and bear fruit all the way up to the first frost.*

The most reliable way to harden off plants is to grow seedlings outside in a cold frame. This process may be initiated at their very birth—soaked seeds are "chilled" on the upper shelf of the refrigerator at 32–37°F (0–3°C) for three days. Such seedlings are notably more resistant to frost.

Their Spartan upbringing continues in the cold frame. Plants always on the edge of survival—at 34–36°F (1–2°C), or even touched by frosts—become especially hardy. At this time, watering should be sharply curtailed: let the roots "dig down into the earth"! Victimized in this way, tomato plants will sometimes turn blue or red, and even lose their tops to the frost. Sometimes they have to be transplanted with everything trimmed off except a few lateral shoots from a lower bud. And cucumbers may end up completely without leaves, with only a single, living growing tip. But as they say, "difficult in learning—easy in battle!" While becoming accustomed to the nighttime cold, direct sunlight, and wide temperature fluctuations, plants will at first hold back growth, but in time this activates defense mechanisms, powerfully programming them for survival. These are the plants which yield the best harvests. This brings us to yet another law of intelligent transplanting: *beds should not be stressful for transplants!*

Of course, there is no sense in hardening off seeds if seedlings will be grown in a heated greenhouse. But then you will have to bother with hardening off the highly pampered seedlings. Generally, this means "walking" plants in the open air as much as possible. They should be brought outside (or uncovered) as early in the day as possible and brought in (or covered) as late in the day as possible. The main thing is to keep them from freezing. It's also good if they get used to the sun at an early age. Seedlings raised in an apartment but then transplanted into bright sunlight usually burn severely and lose their leaves. They must be trained gradually: at first set them in the shade, then in partial shade. Can you really expect good results from plants which require such pampering?

Here arise my two main conclusions: first, heating and feeding transplants generally means weakening them just to please your desire to admire lush growth; and second, conditions for seedlings should reflect the conditions they will live in as mature plants. If your tomatoes will end up in a greenhouse with regulated temperatures, you can spoil seedlings as much as you like. If they are destined to grow in an outside bed, then it is better to prepare them for this early on, arranging a "Spartan childhood" for them.

I suppose that the most optimal regime is to grow transplants in a cold frame outside. You should wait until after the last strong frost and keep a second piece of plastic handy for covering the cold frame in emergencies. In Rostov and Kharkov in the south (Zones 6 and 5), you can sow a cold frame as early as the middle of April. It is especially good if the cold frame subsequently becomes an outside bed— some of the plants can be left there to grow without transplanting. These plants will develop more quickly than even the very best transplants.

There are still a couple more points we should address.

Pricking out,* according to many studies, does not strengthen the development of plants. In my view, it is not worth it. Sowing in flats is inadvisable in the first place. Emerging in a dense "thicket," seedlings begin to elongate

---

* *Pricking out*—transplanting very young seedlings (at the time of their first true leaves) from flats into pots. In the process the tap root is shortened "in an effort to develop lateral roots."

as soon as the third day! We only regard this as normal because the transplants we customarily grow on windowsills
are so crammed together. It is more reasonable to test the
viability of seeds in advance, and then plant them in cellular
transplant trays or pots. If viability is less than 90%, sow two
seeds. When they emerge, nip off the weaker seedling.

Containers for transplants should be easy to work with,
sufficiently insulated, opaque, durable, and have good drainage. The very best options are seed-starting trays or com-
pressed peat pellets.

The main point of peat pellets is that they can be easily
transplanted without damaging roots at all. Russian gardeners, not waiting for favors from business, simply pack a light
soil mix into small polyethylene containers or non-reusable
cups with the bottoms cut off. These are placed into flats on

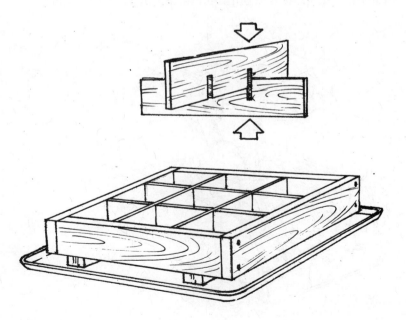

a layer of rotted sawdust spread over plastic. When setting out transplants, the containers are cut away and discarded.

Transplanting any plant can be done without serious consequence if you immediately *dip the roots in a slurry of clay*. In the open air, root hairs may dry out in just half a minute. The slurry is an amazing "preparation"! The clay coats rootlets without damaging them. It also increases their absorbing surface area many times over and improves contact of rootlets with the soil. In the planting hole, this stimulates growth and creates a beneficial, temporary protective layer.

Raising transplants occupies about the same cycle of work as caring for outside beds. And the more detailed and intelligent everything is arranged for transplants—from location to growing containers—the better the results. For

instance, we still don't have enough space in our home for transplants, and a permanent greenhouse is not likely to happen in the near future. Therefore, I use a simple plastic cold frame for transplants. I believe that southerners should utilize the benefits of their climate and master non-transplanting methods—direct seeding and covering. I am, in fact, moving more and more in this direction. I would appreciate hearing about your own experiences with transplanting which you are willing to share.

Just say "no" to digging, and I will do
the rest for you!

Chapter 12

Meeting Pests With a Smile

or

A Tale About How We Abuse Our Plants

Humans are the primary enemy of the harvest.
Yuri Slashchinin

For almost a hundred years now, humans have been happily buying sprayers to apply every possible kind of poison to annihilate any and all living creatures which are lusting for our plants with their fangs out. The chemicals keep multiplying, the labels become more garish, and we continue to diligently spray—according to the dictates of science—maybe ten or fifteen times through the season! And with what results? Have pests and diseases gone away? Not at all! On the contrary, since humans started using these chemicals, pest populations, diversity, and resistance to pesticides have increased many times over!

Yet in nature everything is still in balance. In natural ecosystems, as yet untouched by "human genius," processes of self-organization and self-regulation operate as well as ever. Organic matter falls onto the ground, microbes and worms create soil, and plants receive all they need for harmonious development. Various diseases and insect populations* exist there, but predators aggressively hold their numbers in check. As a result, everything co-exists harmoniously without inflicting significant damage on each other, without large-scale catastrophes or rampant devastation, but rather quite the opposite—all mutually attending to the prosperity of the food supply system for everyone.

Only we *"sapiens"* believe that indiscriminate killing is helpful.

Whenever we stop in at the local pesticide dealer, like at a pharmacy, we pay for fleeting hope—if only we could feel relief right now; we don't care about tomorrow. Pesticides are like taking aspirin. We naively expect that pests will die off instantly, and those which are still alive will be so frightened that they will swear never to do any damage again. We underestimate them in vain!

The goal of any living creature is to adapt to its environment. Our poisons and other "acts of war" are merely the next onerous factor in their lives. The potential of a population to multiply as well as the genetic flexibility of insects is so well-developed that they easily anticipate our every technological fantasy. It only takes them 2–3 years to adapt to any new poison. For fungi, one year is often enough.

Science has already identified hundreds of insect species which are resistant to every chemical poison known to man. First and foremost are common houseflies—they responded to full-scale applications of DDT with the appearance of several populations which were immediately resistant to entire classes of poisons. As for the Colorado beetle, you can almost hear them sneeringly taking stock of the previous season: "So what? Malathion and Chlorophos are old hat! And Decis, Cypermethrin, and Coloracide are no big deal, we just learned to digest them. As for Karate, Topaz, Thunder,

* *Population*—representatives of a single species which reside in a specific place under specific conditions and selective factors.

and Regent (the names alone are enough to make us laugh!), they may have made our tummies ache a bit, but even that's history now. So what's left? Actara? Confidor? Just give us a couple more years, and we'll figure them out, too!" In every garden, even after applications of Actara, a few surviving heroes who could care less about Actara always manage to make it into winter. The following growing season they will become several hundred strong, and after only one year a full-fledged breeding population will exist.

I recently trekked through the Caucasus Mountains and came upon masses of Colorado beetles at an elevation of more than 6,500 feet (2,000 m). They were crawling around all over the place—on plants, over snowfields, even clinging to blades of grass in icy streams! Currently they are successfully assaulting the central ridge of the Caucasus and will soon march into Sochi on the Black Sea. Of course, these are the very same heroes who already passed victoriously through all the chemicals of the Kuban Region, which is the breadbasket of Russia.

The overriding effect of chemical pesticides is to create resistant pests. But this is only one side of the issue. The other is the technology itself. Chemical preparations are only effective when properly applied! This is not generally understood by gardeners. The exact time, appropriate developmental phase of the pest, weather, air temperature, pesticide quality, dilution rate, and degree of atomization—all of these must be optimal; otherwise, the effect is the opposite. They will only strengthen the resistance of pest populations. It is extremely difficult to accurately observe all these subtleties. This brings us to the third aspect of chemicals: even applied precisely, pesticides do not reduce pest populations! They only kill one portion of a single generation. Towards autumn the number of pests rebounds, and populations head into winter strengthened and fortified.

We now arrive at the saddest part of chemical crop protection: poisons are, after all, poisonous! But we seemingly have little regard for preserving our health, let alone our environment—the biosphere!

Finally, there is the quality of the chemical preparation itself. According to the law of Russia's "very free" market, this is not always predictable. A manufacturer may worry about its good name, but the intermediaries who do the packaging could care less—they ride on the backs of brand names. And very few are above exploiting sudden high demand for a product. If a preparation demonstrates good effects, output is doubled, reducing quality by half. In this way, new preparations quickly "lose effectiveness." Then conditions may turn into a veritable resort for pests. Only the gardener, dragging around his sprayer, is traumatized. Seeing flourishing, healthy "vacationers" crawling all over his plants, he becomes completely overwhelmed.

To sum up, harsh chemicals are not the proper way to protect and promote the health of plants, nor a good method for getting rid of disease pathogens. *Like a silver-tongued spy, chemical preparations may speak with sweet and beautiful words, but ultimately they are on the side of pests*—or more exactly, they exist only for their own profit.

"So you're saying that pesticides shouldn't be applied at all?!" Unfortunately, it seldom works nowadays to go completely without pesticides; you can become stuck. But poisons should be kept in their place. This means that only in the most extreme circumstances—if there is no other way to save the harvest—should the safest and most effective pesticides be used, very carefully over a limited area, and applied correctly at the proper time.

There are alternatives to chemical pesticides—biopesticides. These may be fungal toxins and microbes, insect hormones, or living bacteria. They work just as well as chemicals but are much safer, and pathogens do not become resistant to living preparations. For many years now, I have used exclusively biopesticides; I would consider synthetic preparations only in very particular times of need.

"Folk" control methods—concoctions and infusions of plants, homemade decoys, and traps—can be an alternative to pesticides. There are a jillion of them, and many have been extensively publicized. Generally, I have observed that their effect depends on specific conditions. And more often than not, what works for one person will not work for another! In some places mole crickets can be trapped in beer, but in my garden they have no interest in beer at all. In other people's gardens, fruit is decimated by bud weevils, but in ours there are very few of these pests. In Kiev, aphids are annihilated with a tobacco concoction, but where we live they hardly wince at it. And so on and on.

The only conclusion we can reach is that *each of us must find the means best suited to our own garden plot*—just like with the particular herbs used in herbal medicines. Evidently, both specific conditions and the genes of pests are simply too multifarious! Once again this demonstrates that struggle is the wrong path to take. Generally, the aim of plant protection should be to eliminate any necessity for using preparations in the first place!

We do not need cures—*what we need is that our plants do not become diseased.* We do not need to annihilate pests— *what we need is that their populations do not explode.* We do not need better battle tactics—*what we need is for struggle to no longer be necessary.* Rather than wracking our brains over the next poison to attack with, it would be better to quietly ponder: what is the real reason behind this outbreak of pests? Why are my plants so vulnerable? And if poisons do not resolve the problem, then how can it be better dealt with?

Various answers to these questions have long been known, and they have absolutely no relation to chemical protection.

Plants which become diseased are mainly those which are weak, overly pampered, over-fertilized, or not adapted well to a specific environment. Pest populations explode for two principal reasons: a) monoculture instead of natural diversity; and b) in a monoculture the natural enemies of pests have been annihilated by previous applications of poisons. So what destroys our harvests? Weak plants, monoculture, and poisons which kill everything without discrimination—and we do all this with our very own hands. We ourselves have caused the problem, which means that it is in our power to change everything!

My goal is to forget about pesticides—well, almost forget. The best and safest of them sit on my shelves just in case. But I am constantly searching for means which will make them unnecessary. I am developing a method of *meeting pests with a smile*—something like "garden aikido."*

This is the most practical line of defense. It has been highly developed by biodynamic gardeners, permaculturists, and organic gardeners throughout the world. But in Russia, this has been little researched, and what has been done is mainly by amateur gardeners. Moreover, each of us must devise our own methods for our unique situation—along with the various nuances of our personal gardening style.

---

* *Aikido* is a Japanese school of philosophy and martial arts based on love for everything living, including the attacking enemy. The essence of this technique is to be absolutely invulnerable, not attacking and not inflicting blows. You are completely relaxed, and your enemy's own strength is used against him.

I see three ways to approach this issue:

1. By strengthening the vigor and immunity of our plantings with the help of resistant varieties and well-structured soil rich in organic matter, and when necessary, utilizing foliar sprays, natural stimulators, and microbial cultures.

2. By creating a diverse and resilient ecosystem over the entire landscape where we live, and by utilizing plant diversity on garden plots and intercropping in individual beds. In other words, by utilizing the mutual protection systems of various plants in full measure, and by creating conditions which are beneficial to our allies, including protective microbes and insect predators.

3. By understanding the habits and life cycles of parasites and, using this knowledge, setting up every kind of impediment against them: luring them with bait, frightening them off, blockading them with barriers and covers, preventing propagation, beguiling them in any possible way, "tweaking their brains," "leading them by their noses," etc.

In order to keep struggle to a minimum, all these methods should be: a) inexpensive and not labor-intensive, b) safe for us and the environment, and c) should give the same reliable result in various places and in different years. For example, covering soils with black plastic reliably blocks out weeds under any conditions, and light traps reliably catch harmful evening and night-flying moths—techniques in this vein.

I have begun moving in this direction in recent years and have tested for myself most of the methods cited in the coming pages. I certainly did not take any of them from garden magazines. I have a much greater trust in the veracity of experienced gardeners. Now I have accumulated so much information that I wrote a book on how to protect plants safely. Its title reflects exactly what we have been covering in this section: *Meeting Pests with a Smile.*

Intelligent tank mixtures

"Look! My cucumbers hardly have any diseases at all!"
"Then why are you spraying?!"

Synergy is the interaction and mutual strengthening of elements in a given system. In nature a plant interacts with the entire ecosystem. All beneficial factors—light, nutrients, moisture, stimulators, and protection—influence it *simultaneously*.

Science does the opposite: it discovers beneficial factors in isolation and at different times. Peering into microscopes, scientists see specific details separated off from each other—like the blind men of the ancient tale who, each touching a different part of an elephant—the trunk, an ear, the tail—described it completely differently. This is why we attend to our plants the way we do: today we fertilize a bit, a week later we spray them, and then another time we might give them stimulators. But this all works much worse in separation! In fact, if you stimulate growth, plants instantly want more to eat and drink, and consequently they require added protection—otherwise, why would you stimulate them? Likewise, if you adopt measures for their protection, you will also want to encourage momentum: to provide nutrients and stimulation; otherwise, there is not much sense in protecting them. Finally, if you give them a little fertilizer, you are stimulating them—so you should give protection as well, or else you will just be feeding the pests.

Beneficial elements provided simultaneously enhance the work of each individual element. This is called a *synergetic effect*. To ignore it is a sin against nature!

The best way to protect plants is to increase the vigor of the plant itself. This is what all leading specialists in plant protection now believe. But what means for strengthening plants are available to us?

1. Growth stimulators and immunity boosters: humates and their compounds, gibberellin preparations, complex extracts of biohumus or specialized fungi, and various microbial extracts.
2. Compound chelate fertilizer containing trace minerals, as well as their various mixtures with complex organic matter.
3. Microbial preparations for improving soils: effective microorganisms products (EM), cultures of various types of microbes—Trichodermin, Rhizoplan, Subtillin—and many other biopreparations.
4. Biological pesticides—preparations derived from biological sources to protect plants both from insect pests and from fungal diseases.
5. Homemade microbial cultures: yeast, hay bacillus, one-celled algae, lactobacillus, as well as natural mixtures of these cultures with extracts of organic matter.

All these components which contain no harsh chemicals can be mixed together in the same sprayer tank. In so doing, their dosage rate can be lowered by a third, although the effect will actually increase. There is no sense in using preparations separately. It is much better to kill two birds with one stone—a single spraying is more effective, and much less work is required!

I would remind those who love to spray of a simple truth, so difficult for the "chemical" mind to comprehend: *no preparation will replace the natural fertility of soil.* The required conditions—without which no type of protection makes any sense at all—are soil moisture, organic matter, and mulch.

Stimulators work well only in conjunction with good gardening practices. If there is nothing for plants to grow on, what sense is there to energize them to grow?! But naïve gardeners are always hoping for some kind of panacea: they read the advertising, apply a product once or twice, forget about proper gardening practices, and expect a miracle—mountains of tomatoes! Such endearing simple-heartedness is fraught with losses of both money and harvest. You will never find a product that will make your plants thrive on infertile land. And no product can improve the state of your plants in one fell swoop. What really works is to provide *consistently good conditions*.

The use of *tank mixtures* has long been practiced and proven to be very effective. In the past, it was even utilized in chemical plant protection: if a certain poison no longer worked on a pest, then mixtures of poisons, it was believed, would certainly kill it. But massive application of poisons is a slippery slope which leads only to more complex entanglements, whereas actually benefiting plants is a completely different matter. Mixtures of protective biopreparations

have already become common practice in Russian vegetable gardens.

The concept behind "intelligent tank mixtures" is simple: always maintain a broad mix of beneficial components as background material in the tank, and then introduce various protective biopreparations when necessary.

What is the best way to apply these mixtures?

The most important thing to understand is that *cures do not exist in crop production*. You cannot rescue what has become diseased or damaged. Only preventive measures save plants—i.e., not allowing damage to occur in the first place. Prevention is a way of life. Beneficial mixtures should be applied *in stages*—that is, regularly at every phase of development: germination, transplanting, first blossom, full blossom, the beginning of fruiting, and peak of fruiting. Each new phase requires new expenditures of energy from plants—they have to be helped along.

Put simply, it is best to reach for the sprayer every ten days. Protecting plants only makes sense when they are not yet diseased. Then they will not become diseased! For Russians, accustomed to undergoing "treatment" only when it is time for the intensive care ward, this simple idea is extremely difficult to assimilate!

So we have here a positive gardening trend: different means of protection and support are being combined into cocktails. Nowadays store shelves are packed with various dark elixirs. This is only natural. It is as if with these sprays we are striving to return to plants everything which we robbed from them by our gardening practices.

But the question remains: was it necessary to rob plants of these in the first place?

The mishmosh effect

"So, how are you feeling?"
"Oh, don't even ask!"

For over half a century, organic farmers have consistently been raising impressive harvests of vegetables and grains without using any kind of poisonous substances at all. An important part of their success has been by identifying causes of outbreaks of pests and disease, and studying the consequences of a surplus or deficit of various weeds, insects, and microbes. Their aim—to create a stable ecosystem—may be unfamiliar to us. The practical implications are quite astonishing.

This is their main conclusion: a stable ecosystem should include everything.

Weeds. *The best harvest requires the presence of an optimal amount of various types of weeds.* Having too many weeds is harmful, but their complete absence can also cause huge problems! Specialists from the European Agricultural Association Bioland have made similar observations. For instance, in the complete absence of weeds of the goosefoot and sunflower families (lamb's quarters, various thistles, salsify), plants are attacked much more severely by insects— these weeds are a delicacy for polyphagous pests.* Weeds of the Umbelliferous family (wild carrots, hemlock, elderberry, hogweed) offer food and safe haven to beneficial predators. Without their nectar, predator populations sharply decline, and pest populations subsequently increase.

John Jeavons, proponent of biointensive mini-farming, cites a wide range of *beneficial weeds* in his book *How to*

* *Polyphagous insects* feed on many different types of food. [trans]

Grow More Vegetables: various species of white deadnettle (*Lamium album*), goosefoot, lamb's quarters, milkweed, field mint, sow thistle, tansy, wormwood, chamomile, and yarrow. These fragrant plants, grown in small numbers around the garden, frighten away pests, stimulate growth of vegetables, and improve the taste of crops. On the whole, such a "botanical garden" is extremely repulsive to insects, so they skedaddle off to other plots—those of gardeners who love cleanliness and order.

Pests *should also always be present in optimal numbers.* "We have to get used to the fact that pests are food for their enemies. In order for predators to be constantly present, their food must be present as well," writes Susanne Padel, a specialist at Bioland. The presence of pests is not by any means cause for panic! According to the research of Jeavons, losing even 30% of leaves does not affect the yields of most crops. Jeavons simply plants 10% more vegetables—in mixed plantings pests rarely consume more than that. Why don't we do this? Is it greed? I guess that means I'm not very greedy. In fact, until pests become especially brazen, I pay no attention to them at all, and I always get a harvest. My neighbors plant much more and, good heavens, how many pest problems they have!

Experiments have shown that applications of harsh chemicals prove to be much more deadly for our predator friends than for the pests themselves. This is precisely why "extermination" treatments are always followed by renewed outbreaks. Plots owned by "chemical gladiators" are particularly unstable. If they let up just a little, their gardens become overwhelmed by pests.

"Plants remain healthy when the enemies of pests and diseases have time to do their part," Padel concludes. *The most intelligent strategy is not the annihilation of pests but support for their enemies.* Otherwise, we become caught in a vicious circle. It took Europe half a century to realize that their enemies were actually their friends. How much time will it take us before we stop grabbing the sprayer as if it's a submachine gun?

Diseases. We should not strive to completely eliminate all microbes—that is, of course, impossible. *What is most important is to have an abundance of beneficial microbes.* A truism of organic gardeners is that good compost invigorates the soil and reduces incidence of plant disease. Compost is essentially a concentration of beneficial microbes. Dead organic matter is food for these predators. Entering the soil in large numbers, they crowd out and suppress pathogens.* On the other hand, where there is little organic matter and lots of fertilizer, beneficial microbes cannot survive; there is nothing for them to feed on. At the same time, pathogens are provided with massive quantities of food: the dense stand of weakened plants growing there!

We can now imagine the ideal "sustainable garden": variegated, fragrant, full of flowers, a mix of interplanted beds with wide belts of corn and sunflowers, all surrounded by thickets of wild brush; and with open ground permanently covered by a diversified mix of wild grasses. This is not unlike my own plot—half-wild, in fact, almost completely wild. And there are very few pests. Colorado beetles can be somewhat worrisome; ants herd aphids into certain trees, and mole crickets sometimes crawl into my beds. But there has been no significant damage for a long time. Even potato blight and peronospora (downy mildew) behave themselves pretty well, even though I never bother to burn diseased leaves, composting them instead.

But how can we actively help our friends, the predators?

---

* *Pathogens* are organisms which cause diseases.

The enemy of my enemy is my friend!

Tell me who my friend is, and then I'll under-
stand who I am.

For fear of overdoing it, I will desist from writing more about soil and mulch.

Instead, we will take a look at plants, where things are even more interesting. In spite of all our follies, there are some very cool fellows—bloodthirsty, impetuous, and fierce predators—who help us out in our gardens. Day and night, they tirelessly hunt, attack, and kill mercilessly. If there are enough of them, pest populations are effectively suppressed; predators will destroy up to 70% of them. However, in contrast to pests, which are the offspring of our agriculture, predators occur naturally. They are not resistant to poisons, nor can they survive on bare ground! But we can easily provide them with both food and shelter to survive. I cover this in detail in my book *Meeting Pests with a Smile*, so here I will mention only a few of the most salient points.

Ichneumons are small, nimble wasps—a huge order of insects which annihilate around three fourths of all plant-eating pests. Ichneumons are parasites. They lay their eggs in the eggs of other insects, in the bodies of various caterpillars and larva, and in aphids. One elusive thrust of their ovipositor, and the pest becomes food for their young! These born hunters find their victims everywhere, even inside vegetables and stalks. In order to implant their egg into the larva of woodborers, they can drill as deep as five millimeters into wood with their ovipositor. Mature ichneumons overwinter *in fallen leaves, in grasses*, and under bark. They feed on *nectar and pollen of meadow plants*, primarily those of the Umbelliferae and Compositae families.

Ladybugs (ladybirds) are the symbol of ecological agriculture. Both the beetle and its larva consume 60–70 aphids per day. They also overwinter *in fallen leaves*.

Lacewings look like gigantic gnats. In their brief life, lacewings can annihilate up to 500 aphids, scale insects, and mites. They overwinter *under layers of leaves, in compost*, and in ice-free cracks and crevices. In the spring, they require *pollen, nectar*, and *aphids* for regeneration of their population following winter.

Ground beetles are nimble and quick, fierce hunters in the night. Their victims are slugs, wireworms, caterpillars, juvenile mole crickets, and Colorado beetle larva. They dig their burrows *in leaf litter*, in dense brush, and in perennial grasses.

As we see, wild meadows, early flowering weeds, leaf litter, mulch on beds and pathways, and piles of plant residues provide vital protection for predators in orchards and vegetable gardens.

No less important partners are the natural pollinators of our fruiting plants. After all, apiaries are by no means common in every community, but gardens are everywhere.

Basically, these are **bumblebees**, wild **honeybees**, and various **wasps**. They only live in natural environments—in forest groves, shrubbery, and meadows where the soil has not been disturbed. You cannot overestimate their role. Why has seed production of legume grasses become so unprofitable in Russia? Because plowing the land has caused wild honeybees and bumblebees to virtually disappear. Experiments by the Russian beekeeper Valery Shcherbak have demonstrated that the seed producing capacity of alfalfa pollinated by large bee colonies increases by 18–110 times; yields of sunflower and coriander seeds are doubled; and the same is true in orchards. Apple harvests are doubled, and cherry harvests tripled.

Many types of pollinators have been well researched. For instance, our scientists have long known how to propagate bumblebees. Small, busy mason bees (*Osmia*) have also been studied. They are solitary and exceptionally peace loving—the solitary female cannot allow itself to fight and be killed. They nest in wood crevices, corn stalks, blackberries, raspberries, rushes, and reeds, reproducing very quickly. They feed pollen saturated with nectar to their larvae. Hence their unrivaled talent as pollinators—each little bee circles up to 5,000 blossoms per day! Mason bees also superbly pollinate various grasses and herbs.

I am glad that my plot is surrounded by belts of natural forest, that my lawn consists of wild grasses, that tufts of dried grass clippings are scattered about my yard, and that my beds are always mulched. More and more often I encounter ground beetles scurrying under my feet. In my vegetable garden there are almost no pests, only the ever-present ants herding aphids into trees each year. But I have finally got the better of them as well. If I could only figure out how to outwit the mole crickets and Colorado beetles, then I could live in perfect peace!

However, I have not managed to outfox them yet.

The despicable duo

Walking out into the garden felt like going to Colorado—there were so many beetles!

In our area two competitors for our crops bring the most misfortune: mole crickets and Colorado beetles. If it were not for these "dear friends," my vegetable garden would bring me only joy!

Mole crickets. For ten years now, I have composted manure and everything I could find, so my beds are packed with organic matter. You would expect them to be a veritable paradise for mole crickets, but, in fact, I find the "little monsters" crawling around my beds less and less often, usually only two or three at a time in any one bed. Strange as it sounds, even in the compost pile there are fewer of them. In the first couple years of establishing my beds, there were masses of them, but we didn't beat around the bush: after losing the first batch of transplants, we immediately applied poisonous granules of Bazudin. We still apply them when absolutely necessary. The effect is superb: within half an hour several mole crickets, "dying hard," stumble onto the surface. However, they crawl out by the hundreds from my neighbor's beds, who digs in manure and tills his soil. This is why I am not against poison baits. Some of the preparations now on the market aren't so bad. But it would be much better if they did not have to be applied at all! Or at least very seldom.

Having watched how mole crickets, frolicking playfully about, have brought even the hardest-working gardeners to a state of raving hysteria, I finally saw the light—and started respecting them instead. I began viewing these beautiful, powerful, and intelligent creatures as truly worthy opponents! It is naïve folly to fight against them. Only by knowing and understanding them can they be vanquished. I suggest that you, too, make the effort to learn more about mole crickets.

It makes sense to start the battle in May, before they lay their eggs. Evidently, these beasts are domesticated—they love dug-up, bare ground, heated thoroughly by the sun. It is easier for them to dig their burrows there, and most importantly, it makes their nests warm and cozy. They prepare their nests in the beginning and middle of June at a depth of 4–6 inches (10–15 cm). And just off to the side, 20 inches (50 cm) or more deep, they dig out a cubbyhole for their daytime lair. Often it is easy to determine where their nests are located: mole crickets will usually chew down all mature plants 12–16 inches (30–40 cm) to the south of their nest so that it will not be shaded. Wherever you notice such impudence, you can dig up the nest purely out of spite! But not all mole cricket nests are so easily found, and towards the middle of July "baby cricketlings" will be seen scurrying about everywhere.

Mole crickets sink like a rock in water and will not survive. So they are very afraid of water. Many people advise flooding their burrows with water. But in my clay soil, pitted with burrows and permeated by cracks, you could pour in an entire swimming pool—with zero result.

In most cases, mole crickets can be caught with honey, kvas,* or beer. You take a plastic bottle, cover the inside below the neck with honey—or pour in a little beer—and bury it into the ground at a slant with the mouth level to the soil. Cover the top with a piece of metal or cardboard.

However, mole crickets do not have such a sweet tooth everywhere, and much depends on how the trap itself is positioned. But I am certain that there is always some way to adapt such a trap to work; you just have to keep trying. For instance, gardeners from Samara ridiculed my "kvas and honey" solution—their mole crickets can only be caught

---

* *Kvas*—a fermented beverage traditionally made from rye bread, sometimes with addition of other cereals and flavorings. [trans]

with beer. The crickets become so drunk that they forget where they are and simply march willingly into bottles en masse, practically in columns. Kudos to the mastery of our Samara brewers! But on the other hand, mole crickets in Taganrog disdain beer but are easily lured with wheat porridge.

Apparently, there does exist a universal bait for all mole crickets: sprouted corn, peas, and wheat. Soak them in a solution of a systemic insecticide like Actara and "sow" into beds about two weeks before transplanting. Mole crickets will definitely not get past these. Later, you can remove unnecessary sprouts.

There is a completely different method as well: protecting the transplant itself. We have tried planting them along with

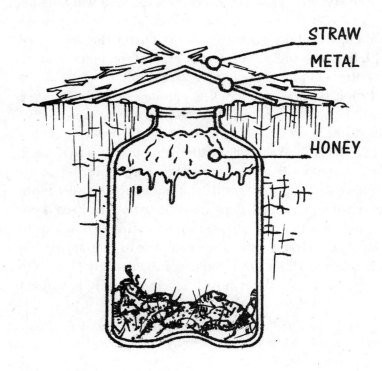

STRAW

METAL

HONEY

their pots—in cartons with the bottom cut off. It worked at first, but the following year the mole crickets figured it out and started crawling over the top into the carton. What clever little fellows! Then we began wrapping transplants in narrow cylinders—for instance, a section of thin-walled hose about 4–6 inches (10–15 cm) long. It does help, but the work is far too tedious.

Here is an acceptable variant for those who raise their own transplants. Make seeding pots by cutting the tops off plastic bottles and, with a large fork heated to red-hot, densely perforate the bottom half with half-centimeter holes. This "cage" only has to be made once since it will last for many years. Plant the entire pot with its seedling directly into the bed with 2–4 inches (5–10 cm) of the neck protruding above the ground. Roots penetrate through the holes and develop superbly.

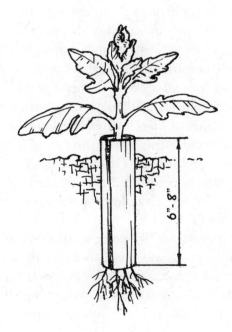

But the most effective protection from mole crickets is strategy.

Mole crickets, like the rest of us, are always searching for a better place to live. They overwinter in warm spots with plentiful food, usually in manure piles or compost. It is there that they most love to establish their nests—dead organic matter is the first food for their babies. Now imagine this: if manure suddenly appears in the cultivated soil of your beds (you decided to scientifically improve your soil!), where are conditions better? Obviously, in the beds with manure! Here is an alternative scenario: a pile of fresh manure or compost appears next to your freezing cold beds filled with humus. Where are conditions better? In the pile!

Therefore, the first line of strategy is a **diversion pile**.

This pile should be made available to mole crickets no later than the end of July: by August or September, they are already searching for a place to overwinter. If you do not manage to get a pile made, they will go into your beds to overwinter. Even better is to have a couple of permanent piles next to the garden; that is what I do.

It is not so difficult a chore to turn the pile twice a year, at the same time destroying all the mole crickets—the first time in November or March when the adult "mommies" are found. The second turning is at the end of May or in June, when the baby mole crickets have hatched. My cat Fenya especially loves this operation. The mole crickets are like beer and chips to her. She completely gorges herself, munching and crunching away!

Actually, they do not like permanent, compost-filled beds that much. My observations cause me to speculate that mole crickets are not comfortable under a thick mulch in moist ground: it is too cold and damp. And if watering is done under the mulch, it is downright miserable for them!

So the mole crickets wisely set out to find a dug-up plot. This is the second line of my anti-mole cricket strategy and yet another argument in favor of permanent beds.

The third line of strategy is vigilance: a little poison placed in the transplant holes. You can prepare it yourself: 0.3–0.5 ounce of any good insecticide is enough for a pound of cooked wheat kernels (20–30 g per kg). Stored in a cool place, this bait will keep for at least two weeks.

As we see, you can find a way to deal with these pesky little creatures! The main thing is to approach them attentively, and with love.

Colorado potato beetles. Finding a way to deal with Colorado beetles is much more difficult—there are simply too many of them! The good thing is that they just sit out in plain view. Therefore, we usually approach them with a sprayer over our shoulders. There are excellent biopreparations for this—toxins extracted from the living culture of a certain fungus. They are harmless to humans and animals but kill beetles and other pests outright—both larva and adults. And they do not induce tolerance, since their composition is always slightly changing. It is better to spray in hot weather because the effect is much greater. These preparations work by contact with the digestive system—they should land either onto pests, or onto the leaves which they eat. Normally, we only need to treat individual plants where their larva is hatching.*

Inasmuch as "Colorados" are chewing pests, a solution may also be a concoction which is horribly distasteful to them. I know gardeners who for several years have rescued

* In the US, one of the many organic biopesticides used to control Colorado potato beetles is Spinosad. [trans]

their potatoes with an infusion of celandine: a bucketful of these plants is covered with boiling water, allowed to cool, and sprayed onto potatoes once a week. However, I am not sure that this will work everywhere: "Colorados" are way too unpretentious and not at all finicky!

Here as well there is a time and place for strategy.

Potatoes mulched with straw definitely have less beetles. It is cooler under the straw, and so beetles are aroused later in the season. By then the plants have coarsened and are not so appetizing. Also, it is much more difficult for beetles to emerge and crawl around under the straw.

This brings up a valuable observation: beetles prefer younger plants. If your potatoes come up earlier and are already bushing out while your neighbor's are just sprouting, the beetles will move over to your neighbor. We plant potatoes early and in this way use neighboring gardens as catch crops. Just don't tell your neighbors about this! There is only one danger to early plantings—frost. But experiments in Kuban (Zone 6) have shown that February plantings only suffer severe damage once every five years. Also, straw is excellent protection from frost.

In the case of "Colorados," folk methods seem especially naïve. Plantings of night-scented stock flowers (*Matthiola bicornis*), spraying with chili peppers, even steeping tubers in vodka have had no effect for me whatsoever. So what we really should concentrate on is proper cultivation methods of the potatoes themselves. In the end, beetles may steal a third of the harvest. Without good gardening techniques, we could lose much more than this!

Incidentally, I can say the same thing about aphids on squash family crops: the stronger and coarser the plants, the less brazen aphids become. Tender young aphids can be killed with an infusion of chili peppers and garlic, but it has to come in physical contact with them—and they hide under leaves. Try to spray cucumber leaves from below! Infusions of tobacco are dangerous since they can infect plants with tobacco mosaic virus. It is only safe when made into a tea. But the main thing is to keep your eyes wide open! When the first folded leaves appear, tear them off immediately. If there is already a full-fledged outbreak, treat plants with a systemic insecticide one time. But first pick off the harvest, all the way down to the youngest fruit—a systemic poison will even get into the fruit.

Reflections on genetic engineering

A veritable dream of agricultural scientists is a potato which is resistant to beetles. In America such a variety appeared about twenty years ago. It had so many small hairs covering it that beetles had nowhere to deposit their eggs, and they showed no interest in eating it either. However, the productivity of this variety left much to be desired. Also, there are now genetically engineered varieties which are poisonous to beetles—this is serious business! They are already growing these potatoes all over the world. Meanwhile, in Russia they are still being researched. The potato itself produces a toxin derived from a certain bacteria. Beetles eat it and die right before your eyes! But personally I am very cautious with GMO plants: their effects have not been sufficiently studied.

At this point I cannot help but say a few words about GMO plants in general.

Once I had the occasion to be in Krasnodar at an international conference on GMOs conducted by the Russian Research Institute of Biological Plant Protection. They debated the issue of genetic engineering for a whole two days! Among the many papers presented was one by a leading specialist at a nutrition institute responsible for monitoring the safety of food products. All GMO products have passed through such rigorous testing that, as one prominent professor put it, "if what we eat every day was tested even a quarter as much, we would be the healthiest people in the world." Everything from biochemistry to genetics has been investigated. After testing on ten generations of various animals, and then studying the condition of human volunteers for an entire year, nutritionists found no harmful effects at all. As for the potato mentioned above, the toxin itself was broken down both by cooking and by stomach gastric juices. And these bacteria exist everywhere in the environment; since birth we have been breathing them and eating them in fruit and berries.

At first glance, it all seems perfect! However, you should bear in mind that the published research was primarily funded by the same firms which produce GMO varieties— that is to say, under their supervision. Administrators and scientists at the various institutes and universities subsist off these companies. Thank goodness, we have the Internet. There you can find real independent research.

In Russia, Doctor of Neurobiology Irina Ermakova has conducted some of this alternative research. Actually, she repeated the experiments of Professor Arpad Pusztai, who was dismissed from the university for his findings. She fed rats GMO potatoes and discovered the same effect that Pusztai did: an evident degradation of organs and, most important, damage to the reproductive functions of offspring. The rats simply degenerated.

Unfortunately, inserted GMO genes are showing signs of getting out of control. Sometimes they do not function properly, stop working altogether, or, in the worse cases, start synthesizing toxic substances. In America, there were several such scandals, but they were not made public. Moreover, these new genes can penetrate into the genomes of intestinal bacteria and eventually into our own genome. No one knows how they behave in these or any other circumstances. But most significant is that genes know how to wander. In nature, there are more than a hundred means of asexual transfer of genes—for example, everything eats everything else, pollen floats through the air, and bacteria and protozoa come in contact with each other. In these ways, any unnatural gene can begin changing the biosphere irreversibly—in the same way that plants, fungi, and insects imported from other continents change their new ecosystem forever.

Nowadays, already more than half of all cropped acreage in the world has been planted in GMO varieties of soybeans, corn, sugar beets, potatoes, rice, and cotton. They make plants poisonous for their principal pests and give tolerance to herbicides. This allows for a significant reduction in the use of farm chemicals, thereby reducing pollution in the environment. Production of pesticides has fallen by 7% per year, and field crops have become cleaner. But I'm not sure that this makes them any more edible, more healthful, or safer! In the US, a law requiring special labeling of GMO products failed. We know that Americans are extremely scrupulous but evidently very naïve as well. Europe continues its battle against GMO products, as does Russia. As long as this is the case, I feel safe and out of harm's way.

But insect pests are only one segment of competitors for our food. Another third, or perhaps even half, the harvest is lost to disease. My "favorite" garden diseases are potato blight and peronospora (downy mildew).

Mushrooms popping up
in a summer shower

"Unfortunately, we do not see blight on these to-matoes. But over here—it's better: the cucumbers are literally decimated by downy mildew!"
From the television program "Our Garden"

If it were not for blight and peronospora (downy mildew), we would not even bother with diseases! What I definitely know about these fungi is the following:

1. Their spores fall down onto leaves from above. They germinate in droplets of water, and the hotter it is, the quicker the germination—at 59°F (15°C) in 1–2 days, but at 86°F (30°C) in 1–2 hours. Hence these conclusions: a) one good solution is to produce an early harvest before hot weather sets in; and b) *if there are no water droplets on the leaves, the disease will not develop.*

It is this last point that I have often observed in gardens. The rainy year of 1997 was especially illustrative. Gardeners literally poured bucketfuls of Bordeaux liquid and other contact fungicides onto their crops, but it hardly helped at all. However, those who protected plants from dew and precipitation by sheltering them with plastic had tomato plants which produced all the way up to autumn frosts! At this same time, grapes in the field were rotting from the fungal disease downy mildew. Their leaves were almost completely destroyed. Only those vines which happened to be under cover remained healthy, ripening their fruit and overwintering superbly!

We can conclude from this that transparent roofs and awnings over beds are not just some frivolous amusement. If at all possible, it is best to construct them permanently when you are first setting beds up. This more than anything will bring fungal diseases down to an acceptable minimum.

2. If vegetables grow vigorously, and beds have an abundance of compost and a thick layer of organic mulch, then even uncovered plants will endure these diseases without suffering significant damage. In this case, an adequate harvest can be obtained without any protective measures at all. How do plants withstand disease? Through rapid and vigorous growth. Plants are saved by growing more quickly than diseased leaves are lost. I have observed this in my own garden. It never hurts to remove all the lower, older leaves in a timely manner anyway—this stimulates growth and makes fruit larger—but the growing tips must be vigorous enough to compensate for the loss of leaves.

3. Other important sources of disease resistance are intercropping and using resistant varieties.

Intermingled with corn or sunflowers, or under the branches of trees, cucumbers feel much happier—they grow robustly and are much less diseased. Probably the cool shade slows down the germination of spores, and among the leaves of other plants less dew precipitates onto them. As yet there are no cucumbers known to be completely immune to downy mildew, but there are a few that are more tolerant of it. The most resistant of our southern cucumbers is the variety Phoenix. It is consistently greener and more vigorous than other cultivars.

Here in the south (Zone 6), blight is not as much of a problem—it appears in July when potatoes and early tomatoes have pretty much already ripened. It develops more slowly than mildew and is not as damaging to vigorous plants. It mainly strikes tomatoes lying on the ground. Even hanging fruit will begin rotting from the bottom where dew collects in the early morning. Dry mulch and plastic thrown over plants at night resolves this problem well. There are some extremely hardy tomato varieties—for example, Debarao. Even after recovering from an attack, they can renew growth and bear fruit until frost.

The best strategy is to mulch without digging the soil. After all, fungi overwinter on the soil, and in the early spring spores float up from the surface. If a layer of compost and mulch is spread out in late autumn, then fungi are held in the compost for a while where saprophytic microbes gobble them up or poison them.

Unfortunately, it is impossible to destroy the spores of pathogenic fungi. You can only kill the fungus by spraying a *systemic* fungicide. Systemic preparations are absorbed into tissues, killing the fungus from within. But even the best of them, Strobilurin, should not be applied on fruiting plants—it requires three weeks to break down.

I prefer to *prevent and contain* diseases by applying biologically active tank mixtures. Here are some of the qualities of this kind of mixture which make them effective: 1) Unlike bacteria, fungi love an acidic environment. This means that any protective solution should be alkaline. Two tablespoons of baking soda (sodium carbonate) plus a tablespoon of liquid detergent poured into a bucket of water makes a good contact fungicide. An ash infusion also works well—about half a liter of ashes per bucket. These solutions should be the primary component of tank mixtures. 2) Cultures of beneficial microbes—EM, trichoderma, and hay bacillus. These are easy to prepare by making a one-day-old infusion of rotted hay or straw and straining it through cheesecloth. 3) Whey. Russian scientists have demonstrated that whey protein is a powerful stimulator of immunity. Moreover, it forms a membrane over plants which creates a good environment for propagation of various protective microbes.

It should be reiterated that the effect of tank mixtures is determined by how regularly they are applied. At the first signs of disease, they should be applied every week.

Plants protect each other

In the winter caterpillars masquerade as chrys- alises, and in summer—as butterflies. You see what tricky creatures they are!

It is undeniable that natural communities are very stable. There are never severe outbreaks of pests or rampant dis- ease in them. Over millions of years, plants have learned to interact intimately with each other as well as with animals, insects, and microbes. Research on this phenomenon has been conducted for decades, but our agriculture has not yet begun to practice it.

No plant remains passive when it is threatened by danger. Any threat instantly activates various mechanisms of com- munication! Plants interact chemically with their brethren growing far away, with close competitors, and even with in- sects. When they feel injured, they excrete signal substanc- es. Here is a well-known example: a giraffe begins browsing on an acacia. In response to losing its leaves, the tree synthe- sizes a compound which is poisonous to giraffes. Emitted into the air, this substance signals to neighboring trees the presence of the giraffe, and those trees also become tempo- rarily indigestible. So giraffes are forced to constantly move on to new areas to feed.

In the same way, plants react to attacks by pests and disease, having various ways of responding to every threat. Many even attract defenders; for instance, they chemically signal predatory wasps, literally "calling 911"! Predators then fly up in response to their "call for help" to investigate the attacking caterpillars. Many plants utilize gas attacks—they exude pungent substances into the air, or even poisonous compounds called phytoncides. Neighboring plants will then also emit them for protection. In general, the world of plants, microbes, and insects is a huge, bustling city with constant cellular communication, well-developed corporate partnerships, and ongoing mutually beneficial transactions.

Plants also battle with each other for a place under the sun. Many secrete poisonous substances which suppress the young shoots of other plants, even causing their death—for example, rye and barley excrete gramine, a natural herbicide to many weeds. This has long been utilized in crop rotation and green manuring. Wormwood kills almost all its neighbors. In monocultures such aggressiveness is dangerous, but in complex communities it is restrained by the response reactions of a plant's neighbors. The more diverse the environment, the greater the possibility for partnerships, and the more effectively competition is evened out.

With close contact, plants intercommunicate by means of electromagnetic signals. The same mechanism is used to regulate their bodies. After intensely studying this process, the Moldovan Academician Sergey Nikitovich Maslobrod has demonstrated that these signals are encrypted and carry various kinds of information. Plants have an extracellular nervous system with their own unique signaling language. With its help, they accurately and precisely react to external stimuli.

We have now come to the final piece of this intricate web of complex interactions between plants. The experiments of Sergey Maslobrod have demonstrated that plants are also

connected psychically with all other living beings. They clearly react not only to our moods but even to mental messages. Also, seeds sprouting up together form, as it were, a "common aura." Through their entire life, these plants are intimately connected to each other. If one is damaged, the others will react at the same time irrespective of separation in space.

This is how, after adapting to each other through cohabitation, plants create a stable commonwealth. And what do we do? Our plantings are uniform which makes them wholly defenseless! Realizing this, many gardeners observe the relationships between plants in order to uncover various beneficial options. Many authors are currently writing about this, but, as has already been noted, their conclusions are often extremely varied. Evidently, plants do not behave the same in different places.

For instance, Sergey Dubinin reports that no sooner had he planted lettuce next to cabbage family plants than flea beetles lost their way to the beds. Planting onions, garlic, mint, hyssop, savory, marigolds, and nasturtiums drove aphids away. Celery and lovage also frightened away insects.

I have often heard about the benefits of chrysanthemums. They say that, planted around berries, they protect currents and gooseberries from powdery mildew. In my garden, all weeds have disappeared beneath a stand of chrysanthemums.

Many authors have pointed out the potency of various aromatic plants. It is definitely beneficial to plant herbs around the garden—basil, marjoram, hyssop, catnip, creeping thyme, savory, and thyme. Nasturtiums (incidentally, they are edible, their flowers are even tastier than cress), marigolds (*Tagetes*), pot marigolds (*Calendula*), tansy, yarrow, and bee balm are both beautiful and beneficial to plants. Lemon balm, celery, lovage, valerian, common borage, chives and scallions, various types of mint, petunias (they attract aphids to themselves), tarragon, sage, German chamomile, and pineapple weed are also considered therapeutic, aromatic plants.

Of course, you can attempt to select specific pairs or determine the most effectual plants. But I have a simpler approach: *the more diverse the plant community, the healthier it will be*—a healthy garden is fragrant and flowery over its entire area!

Chapter 13

Vegetable Miscellanea

or

Notes on the Potential of Plants And The Ingenuity of Gardeners

Does watering down a book make it deeper?

This chapter is more for entertainment than anything else. I have gathered here a collection of gardening experiences in the hope that "something may someday be useful to someone." Much of the cited material is not even that practical, yet nonetheless interesting "for our edification." First off, though, I must qualify myself: this is not a general reference guide. If I do not describe some particular vegetable, it simply means that I don't know that much about it. And why should I rewrite another author's words?

Once again about desire and ability

Well, you could at least grant me a few paltry desires!

Let's look back to Ovsinsky: "Above all, you must determine exactly where conflict occurs between the self-identity of plants and the goals of the farmer."

In the seventies, the journal *Nauka i Zhizn** published a report about the work of the Academician Nikolay Kholodny of Kiev, who constructed a greenhouse literally crammed with every imaginable type of electronic device and automated equipment. Plants were wired with sensors to collect information about nutrient uptake, moisture, temperature, and other factors. Monitoring the dynamics of growth and development, the electronic devices determined the most optimal conditions for plants, so that the automated equipment could provide them with whatever they required at any particular moment. The results were astounding. Tomatoes grew to an enormous size and yielded three harvests per year. Wheat plants and other grains grew twice as fast and formed 120–150 heads. Other plants behaved just as spectacularly. Since then, I have not heard of any similar experiments in Russia or the other nations of the former Soviet Union.

But then, in the mystery novel *Private Investigation* by Friedrich Neznansky, I found something like Kholodny's growing room described fantastically, as would be expected, but essentially accurately.

"You have no doubt heard that there are various electric processes which occur in every living creature. And maybe you know about bioelectricity, too. This means that, if you attach electronic sensors to your forehead, a chicken's leg, or a plant's leaves, you can detect a very weak yet measurable voltage.

"One day Doctor Gramov attached sensors to a tomato leaf and recorded its pattern—its specific electronic curlicue. He watered the tomato with pure spring water,

* *Science and Life*. [trans]

provided it with natural fertilizers, and placed it in the sunlight. The tomato was so happy! And the curlicue also changed. Gramov labeled it the 'tomato is contented' curlicue. Then he took a scalpel and began cutting into the stem of the tomato. The curlicue changed again, forming a 'tomato is suffering' curlicue.

"Next Gramov transplanted his tomato into a tub with wheels—or, more exactly, in a motorized cart which could roll around freely. And what controlled the cart's motor? *The tomato itself.* A specialized instrument analyzed its curlicues. When the tomato was unhappy, it skedaddled off, and when it felt contented, it stayed put. And so the tomato started rolling around at will. It warmed itself in the sun, or moved into the shade—whatever it wanted. Next it was programmed to roll under a trickle emitter every hour for water. As soon as the tomato felt any hint of discontent, the water stopped. After several days it became clear that the tomato was thirsty twice a day. Basically, it watered itself!

"This was followed by the 'no holds barred' stage of the experiment to identify its preferred moisture level, air temperature, nutrients, light spectrum, hours of light, etc. The tomato itself chose everything, and Dr. Gramov recorded what and how much. Then he transplanted the tomato into a specially adapted greenhouse, and raised it, not according to established specifications, but rather using its own chosen requirements. Let's go in, and I'll show you the result."

There were no tomatoes anywhere. A gigantic tree was growing in the middle of the large greenhouse. It looked similar to a baobab, with a thick, green trunk three arm spans around. The crown of the tree was three stories high spreading out for tens of meters, almost completely blocking out the glass ceiling and devouring every bit of light, which made the greenhouse rather gloomy.

"But where is your tomato?"

"We are standing under it. And the fruit, as you can see, is the size of watermelons! We pick the fruit when it is underripe—otherwise, if it fell down, it could kill you!"

Amazingly enough, this scenario is not entirely fictitious. Other than the trunk being three arm spans wide and the fruit the size of watermelons, everything else is fairly accurate. The Japanese already use similar production methods, known as high-tech hydroponics. Vegetables are fed automatically and grow to gigantic proportions. Recently, a Japanese grower made it into the Guinness Book of World Records with "a tomato tree as high as a three-story house" grown on a special frame. He harvested about three tons of tomatoes from it. These Japanese growers have brought greenhouse gardening to perfection. In comparison, a harvest of 220 pounds (100 kg) from one of our tomato plants looks rather meager.

It is hardly worthwhile for us to grow such plants, but it does show how poorly we understand the potential of plants, and how far we still are from truly cohabitating with them. Plants, apparently, have a much greater capacity than we could ever imagine! To understand and discover their potential is one of the principal tasks of intelligent vegetable gardening.

Tomatoes & Company

What better place to begin than tomatoes—a world-class vegetable second only to potatoes, and in my estimation at the top?

There are three basic types of tomatoes: **vining** (indeterminate) grow indefinitely and have flower clusters every two or three leaves; **tall** (determinate) have flower clusters every one or two leaves and stop growing above the fifth or sixth flower cluster; and **bush** (super-determinate) have flower clusters at every leaf and stop growing above the second, third, or fourth flower cluster.

These differences in growth habit determine how each is trained. Vining tomatoes are usually grown as a single stalk up twine on a trellis. Tall tomatoes are trained to two or three stalks, also on a trellis. Bush tomatoes, with three to five stalks, can sprawl on the ground or be supported by stakes.

There are some varieties which grow rampantly with vigorous, non-fruiting laterals. These lateral shoots should be pinched off as soon as possible. Other varieties have weak lateral shoots which do not have to be removed. And there are varieties whose lateral shoots bear fruit quite well. Some of the tiny, excess fruit buds should be pinched off, so that the remaining fruit will be larger. The plant itself reveals its nature. You need only grow the plant to the third flowering head and carefully note its growth habit.

Most important, though, is to regularly remove old, lower leaves from vining and tall varieties. Maturing flower heads do not require these leaves, and there will always be less disease if stalks are bare, well-ventilated, and touched by the sun. My own experience confirms this advice, and now my tomatoes always stand "on bare legs." I even go so far as to cut healthy older leaves in half—this quickens ripening of fruit.

The vigor of a fruiting cluster is usually shared between all set fruit. If there are a dozen, each may weigh in at about 4 ounces (100 g), but if we leave only three, they will grow to

12 ounces (300 g). In this way, it is possible to regulate the amount and size of fruit.

Actually, tomatoes are natural perennials. This is how they grow in the tropics. If plants are pruned for winter and kept at above freezing temperatures, they can live for two, even three years—the tops grow vigorously, the stalks are nearly as thick as your arm, and plants will yield 200–300 tomatoes each.

Tomatoes are very easy to propagate vegetatively. Lateral shoots and growing tips broken off and placed in a glass of water will strike root in 5–7 days. The same is true in moist sand under plastic. This means that you can propagate plants by breaking off the tops of overgrown transplants. This gains you a little time! And an especially expensive hybrid can be kept through winter in a pot, periodically breaking off shoots for rooting. Of course, you will need a well-lit hotbed for this, but you end up with nearly mature plants without having to buy expensive seed.

This technique has been used by Russian growers since before WWII. They overwintered whole plants in cool greenhouses. In the spring, these plants were propagated by cuttings. Branches were laid down onto the soil and covered with earth, producing roots. By May they were nearly mature plants with flowers, when they could be separated off and transplanted for a super-early harvest.

I expect that this technique could be utilized in raising peppers as well. After all, they are also natural perennials.

Tomatoes are plants without rules or limits. Secondary roots are quickly formed on any part of the stalk or branch which comes in contact with moist soil. In greenhouses vines can be rejuvenated by running them down the trellis and heeling them in near the growing tip. Plants start up renewed growth immediately. Tomatoes can also be grown horizontally along the ground, crawling over the bed and periodically "diving" under the surface. All of their branches can be heeled in for secondary rooting with the flower clusters hung on wires stretched above the plants. Yields can reach up to 150 pounds (70 kg). With this method the Japanese push plants to their limit, harvesting as much as 1,500 pounds (700 kg) per plant. I doubt, though, that this is very practical for us but is illustrative of their amazing potential!

Tomato flowers are self-pollinating, but setting fruit is dependent on temperature. In extreme heat and dry winds, the stigmas of pistils dry out. If it is cold, the pollen will not mature. In practice, normal flowering occurs within a temperature range of 55–86°F (13–30°C). Setting fruit is notably improved if: a) plants are shaken or lightly tapped on the flowering clusters with a stick; and b) a 0.5% solution of boric acid is sprayed over them while in full bloom.

Ordinary tomatoes germinate at 59°F (15°C), but our northern varieties can tolerate 48–50°F (9–10°C)—sprouts will withstand frosts even down to 16°F (-9°C). Hardened-off tomato seedlings can survive temperatures as low as 25°F (-4°C) for several hours while those from a greenhouse will die off at 30°F (-1°C). With proper hardening-off, the Siberian varieties developed by Pavel Saraev—Mutant and Spring Frost—can survive frosts down to 14°F (-10°C)! Frost tolerance of transplants increases if you presoak seeds for six hours in a strong solution of double superphosphate, 5 ounces per quart (150 g/L).

Some aficionados graft tomatoes onto potatoes, obtaining a smaller harvest of both fruit and tubers. But there is a simpler way to do this. If you side graft* two young plants, and then nip off one of them, you get a plant with two sets of roots. Its harvest will be one-and-a-half to two times greater than normal. This is good for saving space in beds.

Not watering tomatoes too much is another example of the importance of proper care. Alexey Kazarin from the northern city of Pskov raises excellent tomatoes even from overgrown transplants. His main technique is to not water after planting. He prepares his tomato bed in a large pit. First, half a bucket of water is poured into the bottom. Next, he adds a bucket of rotted manure (tomatoes cannot tolerate raw manure!) and a half cup each of ashes and superphosphate. Then another half-bucket of water. He sets the transplants into the ground horizontally at a depth of 1 inch (2–3 cm), and if they are highly elongated, he will even curl them up into a ring. Finally, he sprinkles a thin layer of dry earth on top.

After that, the plants are not watered at all, yet they still yield an abundance of fruit—even in a drought. Why? Only in the first week is abundant moisture needed by roots to take hold. If you then keep watering every week, as we so often do, the roots have no need to grow deeper—and they don't! When they start setting fruit, their root systems cannot support a large yield. *It is essential to compel plants to work to increase the size of their roots systems.* For this reason, water should be supplied only in the depths, leaving the surface dry. "To plant shallowly is better for any transplant," writes Kazarin. "Many people plant seedlings on a slant but with roots buried 4–6 inches (10–15 cm) deep. This is a mistake! At that depth there are no symbiotic microbes essential for

---

* *Side grafting*—strips of the outer cortex up to 4–6 inches (10–15 cm) long are cut off from two young seedlings, and the exposed portions are pressed tightly against each other and wrapped. After two weeks, when the plants have fused together, begin pinching off one of the seedlings, limiting the nutrients flowing to it. After a month, remove it completely. The remaining plant is left with two root systems.

roots, and the soil is much cooler. After developing secondary roots, deeply buried roots often die off. But if you plant horizontally, why water at all?! Don't be afraid; let the plants build up their roots. When it is dry, the plants may shrivel up a bit and slow their growth, even to the point of wilting. *This is normal!* Tomatoes love living and will put all their energy into growing strong roots. Once roots are well-developed after a couple weeks, these plants will outstrip all others! But if you water them, then you 'slap them on the wrists.' You see, tomato 'psychology' is not as simple as you might have thought!"

Kazarin advises watering tomatoes only during the main flush of fruit bearing, and even then only gingerly. Of course, we southerners must make allowance for our hotter weather and dryer conditions by spreading down a thick layer of mulch, or by occasionally supplying water directly to the roots. But it is even more important for us to skillfully compel plants to develop deep roots.

Kazarin receives *two harvests each summer* in his greenhouse, and we do this in our outdoor beds. "After the main harvest (in Pskov, Zone 5, at the end of July), I pick everything except the fruit buds and tiniest tomatoes. Next, I remove all shoots and laterals except those which are actually blooming. I give each plant a bucket of liquid fertilizer (droppings 1:20, manure 1:10) and treat them for disease. If all this is carried out over a couple of days, in a month plants will bear a second, superb harvest on the upper part of their vines. If you stretch it out over two weeks, you will not get half that."

Recently, I released an edited version of Alexey Kazarin's book, *Diaries of an Intelligent Gardener*. It contains many invaluable practical experiences.

Tomatoes do not like water on their leaves at all, and in the sun this will cause them to wilt. If after drought the soil

is suddenly soaked through, the swollen fruit of some varieties will crack. Incidentally, this rarely occurs on raised and
mulched beds.

It is better to sow tomatoes in two plantings, the second
at the beginning of June. In the fall, when late blight has
passed, these plants yield excellent fruit.

Peppers are much more particular than tomatoes about
warmth and suffer more from spring cold spells. This means
that you should transplant them later. And they need more
nutrients and water—otherwise, they do not grow properly.
Size of fruit is dependent on an abundance of water. Besides
these minor adjustments, however, growing them is similar
to tomatoes. Peppers react well to nipping the growing tips
of transplants, which gives a wide-branching plant. There are
no diseases or pests which threaten them in particular, and
therefore "they react well to mineral top-dressing"—that is,
lush growth is not harmful. In a greenhouse they can be rejuvenated by pruning and will live for 2–3 years. It is better
to cut the fruit with garden clippers since flowering shoots
are easily broken off.

Peppers do have their secrets, though. Alexey Kazarin has
figured out that, in order for plants to grow vigorously and
yield a good harvest, *you must remove one or two of the very
first flowers* formed at the first branching of the plant (Photograph 24). Peppers absolutely adore their young offspring.
After setting their initial fruit, they transfer all their strength
to them and literally stop growing. For the sake of producing
seeds, the pepper plant forgets about any further development! And in our greed we rush to eat those first peppers,
ignoring the needs of the plant itself.

I suspect that "the rule of first flowers" may be equally effective for all fruiting vegetables.

Eggplants, on the other hand, are not so demanding on the soil if there is sufficient water. In the beginning they develop very slowly, but soon transform into veritable trees. They have one issue: Colorados. Sensing eggplants in the vicinity, the beetles will abandon even tender new potatoes! A good line of defense are narrow beds—from the moment of transplanting to the first fruiting keep them completely covered by nonwoven fabric stretched over wire hoops. Bioinsecticides are also good.

Cucumbers

The majority of old varieties are **pollinating** and require their little bee friends to pollinate them. However, most modern greenhouse hybrids are **self-fruiting** (parthenocarpic)—the female flowers set fruit by themselves.

Hence the difference in training plants on a trellis. Self-fruiting varieties are trained to a single stalk, and all side shoots are pinched off above the third or fourth leaf. Secondary branches (offshoots from lateral shoots) are also pinched off.

Pollinating varieties are treated differently. Mostly male (infertile) flowers grow along their main stalk; the female flowers grow primarily on secondary lateral shoots. For this reason, plants are trained to several vines. The main stalk is immediately pinched off above the fourth or fifth leaf, and side stems which soon appear are nipped off above their third leaf. This results in a dense plant consisting of secondary side shoots with a mass of female flowers.

Over the past 15 years, rigorous selection has resolved this issue. Almost all modern hybrids bear fruit without being pinched off—they only have a functionally female type of

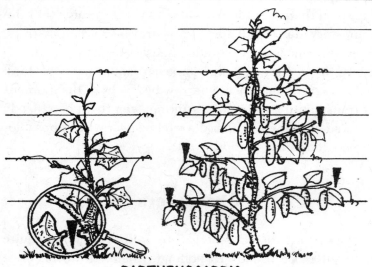

PARTHENOCARPIC

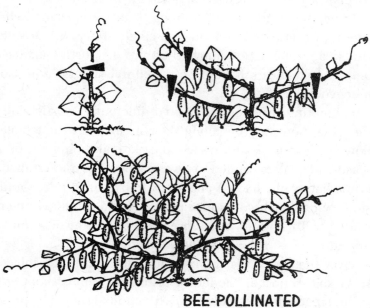

BEE-POLLINATED

flower. There are almost no male flowers—sometimes none at all—and plants often set two to four cucumbers at each node.

Cucumbers are extremely demanding of nutrients and water. They will gobble down nearly raw manure (not pig manure!) and literally devour unfinished compost containing fecal matter. They will also gorge themselves on huge doses of mineral fertilizers. In the process, they bulk up with great satisfaction. However, our joy of watching such vigorous dark-green plants does not last long. These "fatsos" lose their resilience and the first wave of peronospora completely wipes them out. But if we turn to a reference book on chemical protections, we are utterly astounded—the waiting period for fungicides on open ground is 20 days, and in greenhouses—3–5 days. Just think about this: if you do not treat them every week, the plants get burned, but if you do, your cukes will be covered with fungicides, since they should be picked every two days! So much for commercial cucumbers with yields of up to 10 pounds per square foot (50 kg/m^2). They are poisonous, and tasteless to boot. This does not even take into account the nitrates which cucumbers readily accumulate. In short, you must not overdose them with nitrogen! It is better to give them more potassium, phosphorus, and calcium—or, simply put, ashes.

Just like short-season tomatoes, cucumbers can be sown up to the middle of July. We do two plantings, which works well for dealing with peronospora. But there is another way. Cucumbers love partial shading by trees and fences and will climb them with obvious pleasure. Thus sheltered, they are much healthier and bear fruit until frost. Trenches with cucumbers can be complemented by corn or sunflowers staggered 24–32 inches (60–80 cm) apart.

You should water cucumbers only in the morning, because of that same peronospora. If you water in the evening, the damp soil causes dew to form in the early morning hours, and the sodden leaves will exude water droplets, creating ideal conditions for disease!

The most resistant of our varieties are Phoenix and Zhuravlyonok. If there is not too much nitrogen but sufficient potassium, Phoenix endures downy mildew even when growing on bare soil.

In order for plants to grow vigorously and bear fruit over a long season, the principal requirement is *to gather cukes on time*. They swell up in a day or two, and once they are fully swollen, they switch to producing seeds. One overgrown "hippopotamus" causes the whole branch to slow down and lose vigor. Three "horses" will retard and weaken the entire plant! The solution is simple: we immediately gather all except the very smallest fruit. For 3–4 days we can live in peace, and pickles from the smallest cukes become a winter delicacy.

If you coil up old vines and dig them into a shallow trench, leaving the tops exposed, they will form secondary roots and begin to grow as in their youth. This is how plants are rejuvenated in greenhouses. Of course, these plants should be fertilized with an infusion of organic matter.

How can you force cucumbers to bear fruit early and more abundantly? Common varieties should be induced to set female flowers. For this cucumbers must be tormented in various ways. As has already been mentioned, young plants can be dried out a bit—you hold back water until the leaves droop. Before World War II, our greenhouse growers even tried attacking them with blankets of smoke. The effect was the same: plants were frightened and put out masses of female flowers.

Our grandfathers selected cucumber seeds from only quadrangular cucumbers (the "moms") and just from the front end, the nose (so they wouldn't be bitter). Cucumbers become bitter from insufficient water and air in the soil. Fruit will also become crooked or deformed—some cells do not divide due to lack of water and the carbon which comes with it.

Trellises for cucumbers, as for tall tomatoes, are best made permanent, with three horizontal crosspieces and strong vertical wires every 12–16 inches (30–40 cm). Young plants easily wind around them, and it is easy to remove the spent vines in the fall. A canopy on top will also please cucumbers—either a one-sided or two-sided (T-shaped) trellis. They will thank you for the transparent roof with each healthy leaf and additional cucumber!

Nowadays trellis netting is sold everywhere, or you can intelligently work with twine like one of my clients. First, she stretches wire along the top and bottom. Then she takes a spool of twine and winds it between the upper and lower wires along the length of the trellis (see illustration). The plants grow up around the twine.

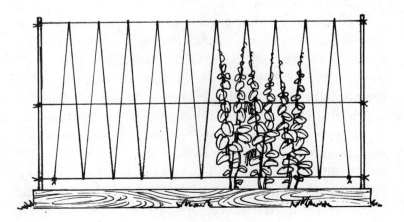

Cucumbers come in many different varieties.

There are **white "Chinese" cucumbers**. These large, pale greenish cukes are quite beautiful as well as productive, thin-skinned, and very tasty—tender and slightly sweet; they are good in salads or pickled. They have just one shortcoming: the plants easily become diseased.

There are "Mexican cucumbers"—**chayote**—which resemble amorphous, light-green "pears." They will keep until May and taste like any cucumber, but coarser and without that delicate cucumber fragrance. Inside the fruit is a huge ingrown "pit." It does not detach and is planted together with the fruit. Chayote is very good in marinades and pickled; when braised or roasted, they remind you of zucchini. The plant is huge—it can cover an entire arbor with a harvest to match. Its main shortcoming is how long it takes to reach maturity. If raised as a transplant in March, it will start bearing fruit in October, and often does not have time to yield any fruit at all, succumbing to the first nippy weather.

There are "bitter," or **Indian cucumbers**—*Momordica*. They are soaked in salted water to remove the bitterness and used for preparing curry, a spicy seasoning. In Russia *Momordica* is an exotic, as is curry.

There are also **"burr cucumbers"** or West Indian gherkins—*Cucumis anguria*. These beautiful, orange-speckled cukes with large pimples are sold in Russian markets as an exotic vegetable. They are eaten in their immature state. And there are other gherkin cultivars as well with tiny tailed fruitlets which have a very mild taste. They are good in marinades.

There are **"red cucumbers"** or Manchu tuber-gourds—*Thladiantha dubia*—which come from the Far East. The small fruit is bright red and very tender with a taste reminiscent of slightly unripe figs, but it is nearly impossible to find them. It is rumored that only female plants were brought to

Russia, so hardly any of the small fruitlets managed to set. On the bright side, the root nodules develop superbly! They form at the end of long, thick roots and are unbelievably tenacious. Watch out! This could be a Guinness Book world record! A more fearsome and ineradicable weed has never been found on the entire planet. If just a couple nodules are left in a flower bed, the following year tuber-gourds will appear along the entire bed and on either side, too—it will keep creeping all summer long despite constant weeding and even Roundup. Probably the best use for this miracle of nature is to allow it to crawl over scarred earth, abandoned ditches, dirt piles, wastelands, and landfills.

There are other varieties of cucumbers whose fruit is inedible. But for diversity of fruit, the real record holders are squash.

Squash

My book *Growing Melons with a Smile* covers squash, melons, and watermelons in great detail. But squash themselves are in their own category. In Russia, they say that watermelons and melons are fruit, but squash are vegetables. And truly, a good table squash concedes nothing to carrots in taste and texture!

In contrast to melons, squash are fearless of weeds and staunchly loyal to summer rains. They love organic matter in the soil, but only in sensible amounts. They swell up with an abundance of water and nitrogen, but the fruit becomes tasteless and does not store well. The smaller, most delicious fruit is obtained on dry, sunny mounds of poor soil. Towards fall, plants start getting burned by powdery mildew, but their fruit is already mature, so there's no harm done.

The most "vegetable" of squash are marrow squash & company.

Marrow squash is a hard-skinned bush squash. At full maturity, the rinds harden and the fruit is inedible, so they are eaten only in the stage of young, unripe fruit—like cucumbers. It is the same with **scallop squash**. They are denser and, in my view, tastier than marrow squash, especially in marinades. **Zucchini**, on the other hand, are more tender, do not harden as readily, and taste better when raw. In view of their close relationship, all of the above intercross magnificently, and if you collect their seeds, they will generously and cheerfully reward you with unpredictable forms of "skallrows," "marrhinis," and "zuccallops."

But those squash which we call **pumpkins**—and Ukrainians "pubkins"—have flattened, often gigantic fruit (up to 200 pounds or 100 kg) which is usually oblate and of varying color and degree of "ribbiness." They are the most delicious and store longer than others. The very biggest, although by no means the tastiest, are the mammoth pumpkins—a true joy for lovers of everything huge! For example, Big Moon, Goliath, and Titan. Recently, I came upon some Titan pumpkins ripening in the field. They were lounging about like reddish-orange, slightly ribbed "blimps" among their huge "elephant-ear leaves." Nearly 20 cubic feet (0.5 m^3) in size, they weigh up to 100–130 pounds (50–60 kg). It takes two people to reach around them. Even the lemon-yellow young fruit, the "babies," weigh in at about 20 pounds (8–10 kg). It is impressive! But these monstrosities are only fit for juice or puree—they contain little sugar. Also, they are very thin-walled and do not have much flesh.

But the tastiest of squash are table varieties. There are very few of them. The flat, often gray, warted fruit rarely reach 22–26 pounds (10–12 kg). But their sugar content is as high as 12%! In comparison, a watermelon has 8–10%. And they contain dry matter of up to 25%, like carrots. Baked and chilled, they are a true delicacy. One of the tastiest squash in the world is Mramornaya, a variety developed by the Krasnodar plant breeder Nikolay Tsybulevsky (Photograph 44). Stuffed with pot roast and garlic and baked in the oven, it is the feast of kings!

Butternut squash is usually cylindrical and brownish. The most common butternut—which we call "Honey Guitars"—has elongated fruit of a pinkish brown color, tapering in the middle. Butternut squash is one of the most unpretentious and productive of squash. Packed with vitamins, it contains twice as much carotene as carrots! It is quite tasty and very useful in the kitchen—its cylindrical shape washes quickly, and the fruit has hardly any seed cavity—just solid flesh.

I should also mention **fig-leaf gourd**. It is truly amazing! It grows thirty or more feet (10 m) long, covering entire fences, and sets new fruit every three days—all the way up until frost. The fruit is green with white speckles, smooth, oval-shaped, and weighs in at 2–4 pounds (1–2 kg) each. The seeds are black, like those of watermelons. You cannot really call it sweet, and by no means should it be considered a "squash watermelon," but rather an ultra-vining, hyperproductive super-marrow-squash. In its unripe form, rolled in flour and fried, it is incomparably more tasty than any other marrow squash. As a lover of deliciousness, I can personally attest to this.

You can eat any squash unripe in the stage of the developing young fruit: calabashes—bottle gourds in the shape of narrow-necked jugs, flasks, or one-and-a-half meter long "snakes" with melon-type leaves, white flowers, and long "horned" seeds; turban (or helmet) squash crowned with a red or yellow "turban"; and even decorative squash with fruit in the shape of small "balls" or "pears." All these are not as flavorful as decorative. I often grow them on a tree or arbor just for their beauty. And the bright fruit in various arrangements is an excellent adornment in the kitchen.

Potatoes

Potatoes are truly our "second bread." Ordinary people in the countryside, who do not know about broccoli or kohlrabi, have never enjoyed the delicate fragrance of butterhead lettuce or chard, and who completely disregard summer squash and green beans, raise at minimum half a ton of potatoes, and often a whole ton, every year—for themselves, their children, and livestock. We despise imported potatoes from supermarkets, which are utterly tasteless, "like soap." We only accept our own potatoes, fragrant and flaky. In the freezing cold Russian winter, this Peruvian guest is our mother's milk! In any case, I could write a whole book about them and, in fact, am doing this right now. But here I will only cover the main points.

In order for potatoes to yield a good harvest, they need three conditions: *cool soil* which is *friable and rich in organic matter*, and *abundant water* at the time of budding and flowering. I will touch on each point separately.

Cool soil is necessary for potatoes due to their heredity— in the Andes they were accustomed to cold. If soil temperature rises above 72°F (22°C), the skins of new tubers become coarse and stop growing—this protects them from an anticipated drought. In northern zones this is not a problem, and potatoes grow without any special strategy. But what are we southerners to do when from the end of May through

August scorcher days hover around 100°F (40°C), often with no rain at all?

We have found a way.

One southern gardener, Ivan Nekrasov, raises potatoes in two plantings. The first is very early—in February—braving the late winter frosts. At a depth of 4 inches (10 cm) even temperatures of 14°F (-10°C) will not bother them. During severe cold spells the shoots will not emerge—they simply wait. Even if young sprouts are damaged by spring frosts, it hardly matters. Just add organic matter and ashes to the bed, and they grow back very quickly. Any loss in yield is insignificant.

In order to beat the heat, you must strive for an early harvest. For this Nekrasov sprouts seed potatoes for several months in warm, light conditions, letting these "light sprouts" elongate as much as possible. I also do this (Photograph 25).

Well-developed eyes are very important.

Evidently, one major cause of meager harvests is poor-quality seed potatoes. Where we live winters are warm, and potatoes sprout early. The shoots elongate like thin threads. What's a seller to do? Break them off! Then break them off again. These are the seed potatoes he takes to the market to sell. It is essential to understand that *normal potatoes can be obtained only from the first sprouts*—and seed tubers can be easily stored right in your apartment.

After digging up summer potatoes and picking out averaged-sized tubers, lay them in shallow wooden crates placed under a window or daylight lamp. The sprouts quickly appear. Once a week sprinkle the tubers with water, sometimes adding a little fertilizer. In this way, sprouts can live for an entire year. Why are they so lanky in the cellar? They are searching for light! But in the light under dry conditions the shoots do not grow lanky; they just sit there and mature in dignity, forming rudimentary leaves and roots. If there is not enough light, some may begin to grow lanky, but you simply pinch off their tops to rein them in.

Over the ensuing months they will have time to wake up and mature every last bud on the tuber, which does not happen with spring sprouting. Two of these mature shoots are enough to obtain a normal yet not overcrowded plant, so they are planted in pieces having two eyes each. The harvest will arrive as much as two weeks early.

Incidentally, cutting tubers is not simply a way of economizing on seed. Not only will a whole potato grow into an overcrowded plant with an excess of tiny tubers, but, even more important, cutting potatoes boosts the immunity and growth of eyes. Test trials by many Russian gardeners have definitely shown that, even under worse conditions and with later plantings, pieces of tubers yield a better harvest and are less diseased than whole potatoes. Cutting is stress which activates the metabolic processes and protective mechanisms of the tuber. Apparently, this results in increased plant vigor.

Mature eyes are ready-made plants in miniature. Surprisingly, they no longer even need the tuber—they have already taken everything they can from it. Planted separately, mature eyes will grow into a normal plant. Musos Guliev, an agronomist in Dagestan (Zone 6), realized this about thirty years ago and came up with his own method for planting eyes. There is nothing complicated about it. The key point is to sprout the eyes in the correct manner. Eyes must be cut off at the optimal time, and plants watered properly. Also, it is important that the soil at the time of planting is not colder than the place where the eyes were sprouted. This preparation requires work, but the results are outstanding:

at a planting density of one plant per square foot (10 per m²), yields can reach 35–40 tons per acre (80–90 t/ha)—almost ten times higher than average in the Dagestan Region. And tubers mature earlier, so you can raise two harvests. A single tuber gives up to 20 eyes which will yield up to 33 pounds (15 kg) of potatoes. As for the leftover "eyeless" seed tubers, they can be fed to livestock.

A second harvest of potatoes is not difficult to obtain in the south using ordinary practices. They are planted around the middle or end of August. It is better to plant old tubers from the previous year. They can easily be stored through the summer in a single layer in low wooden crates set in a cool place.

As freezing weather approaches, the harvest will have time to ripen. These potatoes are more valuable than the summer harvest. Since they were raised in cool weather, they are healthier, not having been ravaged by viruses. The energy for sprouting is greater in fall tubers than summer: Nekrasov considers fall plantings an excellent solution to the degradation of potatoes. Fall potatoes are planted shallowly, at about 2 inches (5 cm), so as not to waste strength on emerging from the soil. If it is dry, you should water. You can gather the summer harvest as soon as plants began to yellow—otherwise, diseases move into the tubers—but the fall harvest should be gathered a week after freezing, allowing tubers to receive maximum nutrients from the plants.

In this way, by planting mature shoots either before or after the hot weather, you can keep potatoes cool. But if you do plant at the normal time, cover the planting with straw, and thickly!

Potatoes under straw have a cool environment, moisture, and plenty of space for filling in tubers. By working a little more during planting time, you free yourself for the rest of the season.

The soil does not have to be dug; you only have to loosen it a little with a hoe. Rows are covered with organic matter, then ashes or superphosphate (two handfuls per running meter), and finally straw is spread out on top in a 5–6-inch (12–15-cm) layer. To plant, just rake out a shallow trench in the straw so that the soil will warm up more quickly and sprouts can emerge into the sunlight. The tubers (or sprouts) are simply pressed down into the loose soil. You do not have to water at all. As soon as the plants emerge, cover the entire plot with more straw. Do not hill up, do not water, do not weed. There will be far fewer beetles, and the harvest— clean, dry tubers—can be collected by hand. If you give a good watering at budding time, the harvest will increase even more.

The **planting pattern** is also important—potatoes will not endure overcrowding which causes them to be small. In our climate it is best to plant in a zigzag pattern of two rows 10–14 inches (25–35 cm) apart with 30–32 inches (75– 80 cm) between double rows. If you treat double rows as a narrow bed, you just stagger tubers between rows checkerboard style. You can use the earth between double rows for hilling up.

Incidentally, about hilling up: why is this even necessary? In Northern and Far Eastern Russia (Zones 3 and 4), where there is an abundance of rain, potatoes are better off planted in elevated ridges, but in the south (Zone 6) hilling up is apparently just a ritual. What do we achieve by planting potatoes shallowly, and then scraping off the space between

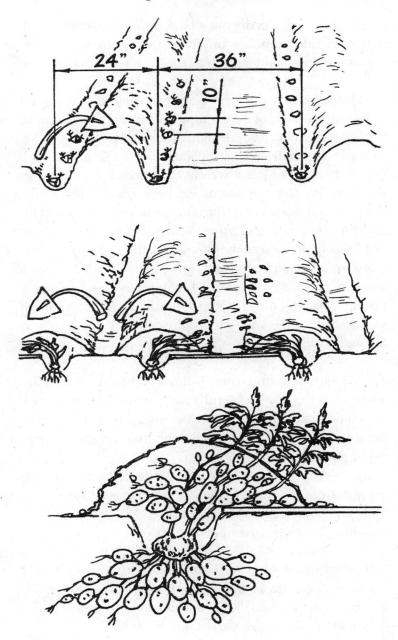

rows so that they can dry out all the more quickly? We would better consider trenches and thick mulch. The fact that potatoes grow well under straw suggests this solution.

Friable soil is the proper physical condition for potatoes. They are not root crops like yams but rather tubers—i.e., swollen lateral stems. To bulk up, they need lots of space. In the friable sandy loams of the Central Russia (Zone 4) with its rainy weather, potatoes produce wonderfully! But the clay loams we have here in the Kuban (Zone 6) are not easy to loosen. Therefore, I dig trenches and fill them with a mixture of rotted manure and straw. The bottom of the trench is loosened and compost or sand added. For mulch I use straw, grass, or even whole bags of spent mushroom compost. I lay down mulch as early as possible, leaving only the tops of growing plants exposed. This allows me to water the potatoes only once or twice throughout the season.

Nutrients and **moisture**. If there is organic matter and some ash, the issue of fertilizing is resolved. Moisture is more important, but this is ensured by the mulch. In our climate (Zone 6) the best results come from raising potatoes under straw.

As for watering, here is the rule of the well-known potato grower Alexander Georgievich Lorkh: *watering before flowering determines the amount of tubers, but watering during and after flowering determines their size.*

The entire world is trying to create a variety which is resistant to potato blight, their principal disease. And not without some success. But how can we speed up the propagation of these valuable varieties of potatoes?

A good answer was found by my colleague from Kazakhstan, Andrey Stepanovich Udovitsky, who is head of the potato breeding program of the Kazakh Scientific Research Institute for Potatoes and Vegetables. For many years now he has been breeding **berry varieties**—those which can propagate by sowing seed from the top berries. Several berry varieties have already been field tested and are now accepted for production. Each seedling yields two-three dozen tiny "seed" potatoes suitable for commercial planting, and each mother plant yields 3,000–4,000 seeds. Consider the savings!

Moreover, Udovitsky created a simple method for obtaining leaf tubers. Before digging up the harvest, while the plants are still green, healthy leaves are cut off and planted in a bed, like transplants. They should be watered immediately. After a month, each leaf will form a micro-tuber (Photograph 26) which will store excellently and, when planted, yield a full-fledged plant.

I am not going to write about the numerous methods of propagation and planting of potato sets—so much has already been written. Better to say a few things about yams.

Yams

My neighbor, Alexey Kochetkov, once brought me some yams. He had selected a cultivar from a collection of Chinese varieties, the most suitable for our climate (Zone 6)—Sweet-100. Since then they have always remained a precious part of our life.

Yams are called sweet, or African, potatoes. Actually, they are not even relatives—yams are tuberiferous bindweed, a type of morning glory. Once I happened to try boiling yams together with potatoes. The yams proved to be much more delicious, richer and sweeter! It's amazing how rich they are—two pieces and you're full! They are very thin-skinned, so there is virtually nothing to peel off. Raw yams taste like corn in its milky stage—sweet and starchy, very pleasant. But when you cook them, they taste somewhere between squash, potatoes, and corn. They are magnificent with garlic and vegetable dressing, and cooled down they are reminiscent of roasted chestnuts.

With all their merits, yams are tropical vegetables—they take six to seven months to mature. Transplanted in the beginning of May, the tubers will not mature until October. But their adaptability is such as to allow you to prepare transplants early without difficulty.

Yam tubers are root crops, set close together in a single family, growing deep into the soil. If you loosen them, they are easily lifted out (Photograph 40).

They can be stored in a box under the bed. In December, they begin to put out sprouts, extending up to a meter long. They are tough and strong. You just take them out into the light, and instantly they green up and sprout leaves. At the end of February, I bury the sprouted tubers halfway into damp sand, so that the tubers can put out roots. From each bud 10–20 shoots emerge, and they grow wildly until May. All the while I propagate the vines by cuttings—they easily take root either in water or in moist sand under plastic. I set out the transplants after all threat of frost has passed.

Yams love organic matter and moisture. They grow vigorously, spreading out four times wider than potatoes. However, beetles and diseases do not bother them. The creeping vines cover the soil superbly, smothering out all weeds. The huge mass of vegetation makes good animal feed. Each bush grown from a couple of sprouts yields 4–9 pounds (2–4 kg) of large, vertically standing root tubers weighing up to 3 pounds (1.5 kg) apiece. In holes filled with organic matter, the roots grow right next to each other, like toy soldiers "standing at attention." This is the point when many creatures begin avidly devouring them—in particular, mole crickets, wireworms, and mice. But there really is enough for everybody! Usually, upon finding the first plant, mice feast for about a month until they have gnawed tubers down to the skin while the remaining plants are completely untouched.

Before the war in the thirties, along the shoreline of the Crimea and in Sochi (Zone 7), yams were widely introduced as a new crop. There were large-scale plantations, experimental stations, and the most up-to-date agricultural technology; they even developed their own varieties. Where all this research has disappeared to, we can only guess!

Radishes

We can all agree that it is impossible to teach worms to speak. And it is just as impossible to grow radishes in the shade! They love sunshine and water. The recommended planting pattern—2 x 2 inches (5 x 5 cm)—does not work for me; it's too cramped. Perhaps I use varieties which are too leafy. So I plant every 2 inches (5 cm) in the row with 3–4 inches (8–10 cm) between rows.

If the soil is sufficiently clear of weeds, it is best to broadcast radishes. After raking the bed level, I simply scatter out seeds by the handful, trying to maintain an approximate density of one seed every 2 inches (5 cm). Scatter, rake, water. Later, I thin out excess plants while weeding.

They say that ideally you can obtain up to 2 pounds of radishes per square foot (10 kg/m²). Does anyone really know how to do this? I don't.

Radishes are not heavy feeders. In fact, the reverse is true: on fertile, organic soil they "grow elephant ears," putting out leaves to the detriment of developing roots. They grow well on both clay and sandy soil and appreciate a thin mulch of compost.

Radishes are water-lovers and are very demanding of it! This is one vegetable which does not mind being watered with a hose. The reason for this is the "wateriness," or tenderness of the radish root. Let them imbibe freely on the surface! They will be harvested quickly, so do not need to develop deep roots.

The most important thing is to harvest radishes at the proper time—a couple days late and they become coarse, losing their charm. Moreover, they suffocate their neighbors.

There are radish varieties which even have edible leaves— for example, Mokhovsky—although, honestly speaking, mustard greens and cress are incomparably tastier than radish leaves.

Radishes are divided into **spring** and **winter** varieties. We are accustomed to the spring ones—these small, round or oblong, scarlet roots mature in less than a month. Southerners have to sow them under plastic as early as February and March, because by the middle of May they may bolt from the heat. From the beginning of April to the beginning of May, you can sow them in outdoor beds. Radishes can again be sown at the beginning of September, and you will still have time to eat 2–3 harvests before the cold weather sets in.

Spring excites the blood and inspires enthusiasm. After preparing an early bed, it is tempting to immediately sow several packets of radishes! This is the most foolish work which I have ever done. In just three weeks all the radishes were maturing, and there was no way we could possibly eat them all. They were over-ripening—you could see them everywhere. Restrain yourself! Don't repeat my mistake. Each week sow a small, 10-square-foot (1-m^2) bed, and you will enjoy a continual fresh harvest.

Winter radishes are a true adornment to the vegetable garden. Generally, the roots are elongated like carrots, and their color ranges from dark lilac to greenish to white. They can weigh up to half a kilogram, store well, and maintain their tenderness until spring. Plantings are done in a pattern of 6 x 6 inches (15 x 15 cm), and the soil beneath them should be loosened as deeply as possible. Unfortunately, in Russia these varieties are still little known.

Turnips are best sown as early as possible; otherwise, cruciferous flea beetles riddle the young leaves with holes. In the south, it is too hot for them. I have not encountered a "heat-tolerant" variety where we live (Zone 6). **Black radishes**, on the other hand, are sown in July-August for eating during winter, although I cannot say that they are a particularly popular crop here.

Carrots and parsnips

The main issues with carrots in the south (Zone 6) are dense soils and drought.

In order to obtain large, high-quality roots, you have to prepare the bed specially—this has been proven through experience more than once. The simplest method is to dig a narrow trench one shovel deep and fill it with sand and rotted manure.

To achieve award-winning roots, you can even use a garden drill: deep, individual holes are drilled for each plant and filled with sand. Moisture must be provided from below, and the more supplied, the larger and juicier the carrots. Therefore, both water and mulch are important.

Organic matter is suitable only if it is very well decayed. If there is a surplus of nitrogen—as in manure or nutrient-rich compost—roots become forked and very bitter.

Carrot plantings are done slightly denser than bulb onions—2–3 inches (6–7 cm) in the row with 8 inches (20 cm) between rows. It is even better to use wide or double rows with the plants staggered between rows. Carrots can be planted from the end of March until the beginning of July, yielding two or three harvests. They may be left in the ground for winter, but mice will sometimes find them.

Parsnips are an undeservedly forgotten wonder. The flavor of these roots when boiled is outstanding—like huge, tender, sweet "parsley roots." Russians call them "northern bananas."

They are exceptionally hardy and resilient—fearing neither cold, nor drought, nor disease, nor pests. They respond to watering and careful tending with roots weighing up to 2 pounds (1 kg). The plants are vigorous and best planted in double rows in a zigzag pattern with 6–8 inches (15–20 cm) between plants.

Parsnips keep better than carrots. Varieties can have round or elongated roots. The latter are better grown in sandy trenches—you can work up quite a sweat digging them out of clay!

Parsnips do have one negative feature: their seeds lose viability after just one year! And they sprout very slowly. One solution is to gather your own seeds. This is easy. You just leave a couple roots in the ground until the seeds mature.

Before sowing seeds you should test them "for floating," and then rinse them several times with hot water over 24 hours to remove growth inhibitors (see Chapter 11). You can sow them very early in the spring.

Onions

Bulb onions are either **hot** (store well) or **sweet** (store for only a short time). Most of our varieties in Russia are hot or semi-hot. I have eaten genuine sweet onions only in the Crimea (Zone 7). This was the heirloom variety Yaltinsky. You see the beautiful crimson "braids" of onions for sale at road stands. The flat—sometimes even indented—crimson-purple bulbs are not hot in the least! Other "sweet" varieties are actually much hotter.

Usually, onions are planted as very small bulbs called sets. They should not be planted too early; during short days onions "bolt," producing flower stalks. We plant them at the beginning of May. It is best to plant only the smallest bulbs, no bigger than a filbert. Large sets usually bolt, even more so when it is cool in the beginning of summer. The stalks can be broken off in bud, but such bulbs have to be eaten right away and not "shelved away" for later.

In practice, any bulb onion in the south (Zone 6) can be sown as seeds (blackies) at the beginning of September. The shoots overwinter, and towards the end of June yield marketable onions of average size. Especially good in this regard is the early variety Elan developed in Russia. If they are sown in September, you will get large bulbs as soon as the end of May. Elan onion plants overwinter very consistently, but not all varieties do, and it is best to cover beds with straw during winter.

Onions do not tolerate any neighbors or shading at all. It is best to plant them in double rows: every 3 inches (7–8 cm) in a zigzag pattern with 8 inches (20 cm) between double rows. The only good companions for onions are carrots. Plant them at the same time, alternating carrot and onion rows. When the onions have grown to their full height, the carrots are just sprouting and do not bother them. Onions gradually leave for the table, and the carrots take their place.

Planting blackies all at once in a set pattern can be difficult to maintain: the sprouts are hardly visible and weeding is extremely painstaking. Therefore, beds for planting should be completely free of weeds. It is easier to sow seeds in a crack between boards.

Onions do not require loose soil full of organic matter. An overabundance of nutrients makes them too watery, causing them to store poorly. Watering and fertilizing should be done only in the first month and a half when leaves are shooting up wildly. After this, they must be compelled to ripen their bulbs. Very specific conditions are required for this. First, the soil surface has to be dry with good capillary flow of water from below. This forces the onions to put out deep and powerful roots. Next, as soon as the leaves stop growing, the onions should be raked out to expose almost the entire bulb. Light and warmth signal them to store up reserves! A couple weeks later you can stop watering—it is time for the bulbs to "pupate" and mature. If it rains during this time, the onions may start growing again, and they will not keep well. At that point, they should be slowed down. Russian gardeners knock down or trample the leaves—"training the onions"—after which the bulbs can lie back and mature in peace.

In Russia, **shallots** or bunching onions are very popular. Instead of a single bulb, they form a cluster made up of long individual onions. There are two types of shallots: "forty-toothed" scallions and a large, light-colored variety we call "goat tits." They really do remind you of a goat udder. These onions are sweet and store well; we love them. Once I saw a completely white-skinned "tit"—it was marvelous—but since then I have not been able to find anything like it.

Leeks are an amazingly delicious onion for garnishes or pies. They put out a tall, thick pseudo-stalk—an elongated base of leaves growing tightly together. You can raise them as transplants or direct seed them in the fall—they mature in six months. The full-grown leeks will keep in beds to be harvested for the table throughout the winter. Like cucumbers, they are very demanding on the soil; without sufficient nutrients, they turn out scrawny, and there is no sense in growing them.

We love perennial onions very much.

The most fragrant of them are **chives**, or "wild onions." Chive plants consist of a sheaf of tubular leaves which have a delicate, spicy aroma. **Nodding onions** (*Allium nutans*) are very beautiful; the leaves are flat and rounded at the end. Their flavor is mild, and they have a "slipperiness" which is tantalizing in salads. **Scallions** (*A. fistulosum*) arrive in the early spring. They have vigorous, tubular leaves which are quite pungent. **Chinese chives** (*A. odorum*) have a dense clump of small, tender leaves with a fragrance like green garlic—more exactly like wild leeks. **Altai onions** (*A. altaicum*) are extremely early, tender, and pungent. They are similar to scallions but even more vigorous. The very largest of the perennial onions are **giant onions** (*A. giganteum*). Their leaves are almost as wide as your hand, and the flower head nearly as tall as a person. In early spring, its greens are the first onto the table.

In Russia, other onions are raised as well: **tree onions** (*A. proliferum*), **broadleaf wild leeks** (*A. ampeloprasum*), and various other wild types: **Ivory Queen** (*A. karataviense*), **Pskem onions** (*A. pskemense*), **flowering onions** (*A. aflatunense*), and **lily leeks** (*A. moly*). They all multiply by dividing, yield bulblets, and some, like garlic, form micro-bulblets (bulbils) on the flower heads.

Lettuce

Most Russian country people consider any green vegetable without fragrance to be "lettuce." These include various types of leafy, semi-heading, and heading lettuces, romaine lettuce (with long, narrow heads—my favorite), endive, garden dandelions and orach, all kinds of salad cabbages (napa cabbage, pak choi, etc.), mustard greens and cress, garden chicory, and other leafy herbs: arugula, lamb's lettuce (*Valerianella olitora*), and so on. But for me lettuce means a specific, much-loved family.

Most green vegetables are a lot like radishes—they mature very quickly and love water and nutrients. They grow excellently in organic matter. You can sow them 2–3 times in the spring, and in the fall as well. When still young, they will overwinter in beds and, when spring comes, will rapidly grow to marketable maturity as if nothing happened.

Lettuce can be crowded among other plants for a long time—they wait patiently for freedom, and then quickly expand and fill out. When harvesting, you do not necessarily have to pull up the plants by the roots. If it is still not too hot, simply remove the heads, leaving the lower leaves, and the plant will put out several more smaller heads.

At the beginning of summer, lettuce becomes coarse and bitter from the heat and sends up flower stalks. But in April-May, when plants are spaced every 6–8 inches (15–20 cm) and have grown to their full size, they are still delicious. If you are a connoisseur, I would recommend that you blanch lettuce. In the final week of growth, gather the plant "into a bundle," bind with a rubber band, and cover with an empty flower pot or box to exclude light. Wait for about ten days. The taste is exquisite!

True love of lettuce comes about through its proper consumption—an especially subtle pleasure. First, you create a beautiful still-life (Photograph 41). Then you prepare a delicious dressing by mixing together vegetable oil, salt, sugar, vinegar, and pressed garlic. You can also add pepper, spices, and sour cream according to your personal taste. Beat to a uniform consistency.

In your right hand, take a head of romaine or several leaves of leaf lettuce rolled together. It only stands to reason that a shot glass filled with some basil liqueur would be in your left hand. This can be awkward, so I often dispense with the glass. What you do is dip the head in the dressing and bite off as much as you can, opening your mouth wide. Chew carefully, savoring all the subtleties of taste and noting how the dressing might be improved. This becomes clear towards the end of the head. The most delicious part of lettuce is the heart with its tender, delicate leaves.

With sufficient practice, you can start wrapping other greens into the lettuce as well: chives, dill, cilantro, or garlic greens. And once you have mastered this, you may want to add pieces of meat, cheese, egg, and other delights, too. This is such a taste treat that there is no reason to even mention its health benefits!

Of course, I am not talking about the paltry lettuce which they sell at the market. A good lettuce plant is the size of a soccer ball and weighs about a pound (0.5 kg). This is what grows in my garden on organic matter with sufficient space and an abundance of water (Photograph 42).

The most ephemeral type of lettuce is **cress**, which can be eaten every couple weeks after planting. Traditionally, it was sown on cotton batting or cloth to decorate Easter treats with its tender leaves. It is important to eat only young plants. Once flower stalks begin to appear, it's over—the greens coarsen and lose their flavor. I would also highly recommend that mustard greens be eaten only when young while the leaves are still tender.

Garden chicory is a special case. It should be sown in the summer, so that by winter it forms a large, powerful root. If during the winter you place it in a warm box with earth and keep it in the dark, it will put out a small head of sweetish, fragrant, amazingly tender and tasty leaves. A true delicacy!

Black salsify

Black salsify is similar to common salsify or thistle—they are close relatives—but its root is the most refined and highest quality of all our root crops. The flavor of the tender and fragile raw roots is reminiscent of ripened filberts. It is covered with a black skin, for which reason it is also known as "black root." Black salsify acquires its special taste, as well as its proper size, after two years of growth.

The main condition for a good harvest is very loose sandy soil rich in organic matter. If you have clay, it's worth the extra effort to construct a raised sandy bed. The edible roots are very thin and extremely brittle. They grow deep into the earth, so digging them out of an ordinary bed can be like hand-digging a foundation!

As a rule, black salsify is sown in the spring. It loves water and fertilizer. The roots can be eaten that first autumn, but it is better to leave them until the following fall—they become twice as thick and much tastier. It is even better to leave them until the third spring. Blanched black salsify leaves are also edible, but while the plants are maturing it is sacrilegious to touch them at all. However, in the spring, before digging them up, it is a holy undertaking. Cover the plants with a 6–8-inch (15–20-cm) pile of hulls or sawdust. When the tips of the leaves appear, you can eat both the tops and the roots.

Beans and asparagus beans

I just recently discovered the charm of these "vertical" crops. Now I plant them wherever I can. In summertime they are my favorite food.

Pole beans usually grow on stakes or twine. In the fall, stakes are easy to clear of dried vines. Sow 4–5 seeds under each stake or piece of twine. Boiled or braised, green snap beans are especially delicious—and they are stringless.

Many of our varieties take a long time to mature—you must wait until September for the harvest—but all the same do not sow them too early. Beans love the heat. In cold weather, the young sprouts just sit there hardly growing, waiting for warmer times. Meanwhile, they may succumb to rot. So they should be sown in the middle of May; in warm conditions beans will grow quickly and vigorously. They particularly enjoy growing along a southern wall. They respond well to watering and fertilizing with a noticeable increase in their harvest.

Dry bean varieties have fibrous pods which quickly become coarse, but I have boiled up even these when still immature; they are quite delicious. Recently, I discovered a new "dish": I cook the yellowing pods of dry beans in salted water, cool them off, and squeeze out the young beans to eat with butter. Truly marvelous!

Bush green beans are wonderful for intercropping with trellised vegetables—they tolerate semi-shade and can be planted densely. The pods are completely stringless, and their flesh is delicious. If you pick the entire harvest at once, you will get three flushes of beans. Be aware that, when beans are filling out, they love lots of water.

However, the most exquisite dishes are made from young asparagus beans.

Asparagus beans (cowpeas) have dark, triangular leaves and snake-like pods which can grow over 2 feet (0.5 m) long (Photograph 43). These beans retain their tenderness all the way up to yellowing, although they do acquire tiny, longitudinal fibers. Boiled or lightly braised asparagus bean "snakes" are truly the "caviar of vegetables"!

One characteristic of asparagus beans—as well as many other beans—is that at the base of the flower stalks are the buds from which new flowers can grow. If beans are picked young, the bud vigor has not been fully expended on seeds— and it will reawaken to life. By all means, do not break off this bud! I always cut the harvest, leaving a piece of bean— the "butt"—on the bush. In response, the cut-off part produces growth regulators, and a store of nutrients remains in the "butt." This allows a new flower to emerge, followed by a bean very shortly afterwards. In this way, you can gather nearly three full-fledged harvests in a season.

Corn

As has already been mentioned, corn is a wonderful crop to plant in wide belts—both as a defense against heat and for the delicious ears of corn.

There is no need to sow corn early—it loves hot weather just like beans. The sprouts require sun and lots of space. Squeezed in among other plants, corn stops growing and will not mature properly. I have not yet discovered any particular subtleties for raising corn.

The entire world uses **sweet corn** as a vegetable. It does not grow as tall, and the ears are not as large, but its kernels essentially will not harden. If you boil them for about a quarter hour, the ears are sweet and tender; you barely have to chew them. We here in Kuban are not great fans of sweet corn—the flavor is not quite the same, lacking that special corn fragrance!

Common grain corn is half again taller and its ears are twice as large. The kernels harden quickly, but in middle dough stage they are amazingly tasty—especially with butter and salt. They are not as tender as sweet corn, but the flavor is fuller-bodied, the aroma fills the entire home, and "the mouth is glad for such large ears"!

We sometimes also raise popcorn. Throw a handful of kernels into a sizzling-hot frying pan and immediately cover with a lid. When the popping begins, it sounds like a battlefield. We eat the popped corn slightly salted. I never buy bags of popcorn at fast food joints—they likely couldn't even fry potatoes without adding chemicals.

Key points about culinary herbs

When we were living the good life on the Black Earth soils of the Volga (Zone 4), we raised nearly thirty different kinds of cooking herbs on our 3,000-square-foot (300-m^2) plot. Now we do not grow so many. I have come to realize that it is easier to allot space for them in permanent beds. In fact, many will successfully go to seed and sprout up in the spring as volunteers. All you have to do is thin out the excess. And they need very little care—just water when necessary and harvest in June and in the fall.

Unfortunately, I have never been accustomed to using culinary herbs. In practice, it is easier for me to grow them than to cook with them. But I love the various aromas and am enjoying learning to utilize them in the kitchen. Moreover, fragrant herbs create an aromatic garden. This inspires me to view them with twice the interest.

PERENNIAL HERBS are especially easy to grow in the garden. I have never known them to be attacked by pests or to require any special care. In June, you simply cut off the plants "at the knees," and in August you get a second harvest. We maintain a special bed for them.

Tarragon (in the Caucasus—*tarkhun*) is a kind of wormwood. It is wonderful in salted cucumbers and other marinades, and is delicately fragrant in salads. It is outstanding in a bottle of vodka as well as in tea and hot fruit drinks. Atlantic mackerel, stuffed with green tarragon and a lemon wedge, lightly sprinkled with salt and pepper, and grilled on a barbeque is a wonder beyond belief. It is called mackerel a la flamande.

Hyssop behaves in our garden like a perennial—it overwinters well. The fragrance is close to lavender but goes very well with food. It is suitable both in meat dishes and as an additive to tea. A very universal spice!

Lovage (on the Volga—*zorya*) is a relative of celery with a similar fragrance but even more aromatic. Dried greens impart an amazing quality to soups and meat dishes. Fresh greens liven up salads and appetizers. The main thing is to not use too much—it is very pungent.

Thyme (creeping thyme) forms beautiful cushions on my alpine rock garden. There are many varieties, and fragrances are quite diverse. It is very good in tea, and a nice flavoring in preserves. It imparts a subtle flavor to meat and fish.

Lavender is useful as a household fragrance—for example, for scenting linen. The same for its relative—**rosemary**. Pruned short and covered with mulch, they overwinter fairly well in our climate.

Garden **balsam** is in the composite family and has undivided, oblong, blue-gray leaves and a distinct sage-mint fragrance. It is good in tea and for flavoring fruit dishes and pastries. It also imparts a special charm to fish.

Lemon balm includes both garden and wild varieties. The garden variety is large (up to 3 feet or 1 m high) and bushy with fuzzy leaves. I prefer the wild variety—its fragrance is much purer. In humid air the dried leaves of both kinds acquire an unpleasant "catty" smell. For this reason we prefer to sow lemon grass—**citronella**. Its fragrance is clean and long-lasting, and it is much easier to dry.

We have dozens of various species of **mint**. The most "refined" and confectionary is Egyptian mint while the most fragrant is peppermint. The aroma of spearmint is best suited to meat and vegetables. There are also wild meadow mints with complex aromas. It is better to plant mint at a distance or in a box—they are extremely active rhizomatous weeds. In our home we are not used to drinking mint tea. Instead, anise hyssop immediately became our favorite.

Anise hyssop (*Agastache foeniculum*) is a spice with white flowers, a relative of mint. It is often confused with **Korean mint** (*Agastache rugosa*), a spicy and medicinal variety with pink flowers. Incidentally, their fragrance is identical, and under cultivation they often intercross. An inimitable bouquet of anise hyssop subtly combines the fragrances of anise, fennel, thyme, and garden savory. It imparts its own tone to any dish: tea and sweets are intensified, lending them the bold yet reserved flavor of the North; on the other hand, it imparts a Southern lightness and nonchalance to fish and meat dishes. Unfortunately, where we live (Zone 6) it is difficult to overwinter anise hyssop, so it has to be reseeded each year.

We raise various types of **sage** as a decorative plant. The fragrance of sage does not strike us as culinary.

ANNUAL CULINARY HERBS, as a rule, reseed themselves fairly well, yet we still sow them in pots since they are more reliable that way.

There are various types of **basil** (in the Caucasus—*regan*): lemon, cinnamon, clove, and common. It is marvelous for flavoring canned vegetables and pickles, and excellent in salads and infusions. Mix together sugar, lemon, a clump of basil, and boiling water, and let steep and cool—this makes a first-rate, refreshing drink. Cut as flowering begins, basil will yield a vigorous second harvest. Ants love to pilfer the seeds, so it is better to plant it in a box.

Catnip is a relative of mint with a complex but very pleasant lemon-mint aroma. It is exceptionally good in tea.

Savory possesses a unique, sugary flavor. It is only good dried—the fresh leaves smell almost like "kerosene," as do many highland wild thymes. We use it for tea, and sometimes for fish and soups. It reseeds itself well.

Garden **marjoram** is the herb with the most striking smell. It is the familiar fragrance of "bergamot tea." Cultivated varieties of marjoram are distant relatives of mint. It is difficult to grow—the seeds germinate poorly, and the plants are rather weak—so it is better to raise transplants. Be sure to fertilize and water well. You should always plant a little extra—you can never have too much!

Celery—both root and stalks—is a multi-purpose vegetable. Dried greens are wonderful, a distinctive component of first and second-course dishes. The fresh leaves enliven any salad. "A celery repast will help you run fast!" my horticulture professor, G. I. Tarakanov, used to say. Our favorite "invigorating" salad is finely grated celery root, mayonnaise, and a crushed clove of garlic. On a different note, celery is very soothing when used in sauces and vegetable stews.

Coriander (in the Caucasus—*kinza*) is the source of two completely different fragrances. The fresh greens—with their striking "bug smell"—at first repelled us. But after becoming acquainted with Caucasian cuisine, we would never set a traditional table of shish kabobs, lula kebabs, lobio, and other dishes without it. Dry coriander seeds are a well-known spice throughout the world. They can be added to bread, meat dishes, and soups. Of course, Caucasian cooking is unthinkable without them.

Dill and **parsley**. Does anything really need be said about them?

I can say two things about herbs with confidence: first, all herbs cut in the middle of summer will yield a vigorous second harvest towards fall. This is good! And second, you must dry herbs quickly in warm shade. A very good place is a hot attic, even better in an electric dryer. If damp weather occurs while drying herbs, the harvest could be lost. The herbs, of course, will eventually dry out but may lose their fragrance, or acquire the long-lasting and unsavory odor of rotten hay.

* * *

This is far from everything that I could say about gardens and vegetables, but is certainly sufficient for a general book about vegetable gardening. If I have omitted anything—well, you can't embrace infinity. More details are in my other books. In the end, I hope and trust that your own experiences will become an invaluable sequel to this book!

May God help you, and you—Him!

Glossary

Aerobic bacteria are those breathing oxygen in the air.

Aikido is a Japanese school of philosophy and martial arts based on love for everything living, including the attacking enemy. The essence of this technique is to be absolutely invulnerable, not attacking and not inflicting blows. You are completely relaxed, and your enemy's own strength is used against him.

Akvarin—a compound fertilizer with trace minerals, common on the Russian market.

Ammonia—a compound of hydrogen and nitrogen.

Anaerobic organisms are those which live in an airless environment.

Asparagus beans (*Vigna unguiculata* subsp. *sesquipedalis*)—"Chinese long beans" or "cowpeas" are a bean variety with long (up to 2 feet), slender pods. They are described in the section "Beans."

Bioactivators—bacterial preparations which speed up decomposition of organic matter in biotoilets and compost piles—for example, preparations of the Belgian company Agrostar. They contain living microbes and a range of enzymes.

Biohumus—compost obtained utilizing earthworms. It is very rich in composition and highly fortified with microbes.

Bulbils—mini-bulblets which garlic develops instead of seeds in their flower head. In the first summer after planting, each bulbil will grow into a single small bulb. In the second year, this bulb becomes a normal garlic head divided into cloves.

Capillarity (from the Latin word *capillus*, "hair")—the presence in soils of tiny fissures and channels, along which water can percolate down or even rise up, since the forces of adhesion of water to the walls (wetting) are much greater than the weight of the water itself. This is how water moves up along a wick.

411

Chaff—the outer hulls, shells, or seed husks which are removed in the process of threshing grain.

Compost is a partially decomposed mix of various organic materials. *Humus* is the stable, fully decomposed outcome of the composting process.

Dacha—a summer cottage with a garden common in Russia.

Dolomite powder is ground up dolomite, a mineral which contains calcium carbonate (limestone) and magnesium carbonate. Ground limestone is ordinary chalk.

EM, or **Effective Microorganisms**—various microbial preparations for accelerating decomposition of organic matter; also, for treatment of water, municipal effluent, cesspools, and landfills. They were invented in Japan where they are still produced.

Erosion—loss of soil exposed by plowing and subsequently washed away by rain or blown off by wind.

Fertigation—watering with supplemental fertilization through an irrigation system.

Fiber, or **cellulose**—a polysaccharide, or "starch which has been stitched tightly together," found in the cell walls of plants. It imparts rigidity and helps create structure. Woody tissue is cellulose "stitched" by a similar polymer—lignin.

Fokin hoe—a multi-purpose hoe designed by Vladimir Fokin. It is one of the most popular gardening tools in Russia.

Germination energy—simultaneous and vigorous seed germination.

Gley—a layer of sticky, muddy clay containing very little air. It is formed by chronic waterlogging and is typically a blackish-blue color.

Grass rotation system of farming—a complex agronomy which brings together four basic farming practices: wind protection and snow retention utilizing hedgerows; grass rotations (the field is left under perennial grasses for three out of eight years); wise cultivation of the soil; and rational fertilization of plants.

Green manure—plants grown to improve the soil. Their main purpose is to provide soils with fresh organic matter. As in nature, green manures are most effective on the surface as a mulch.

Greenhouse effect—radiant sunlight passes through clear plastic (or glass) and heats up the soil. The warm soil then begins to radiate heat—infrared rays—which are reflected back by the clear plastic. The plastic becomes a "trap" for these infrared rays. The air is heated by the soil, and this warm air cannot escape to the outside, causing overheating. The smaller the volume and better sealed the greenhouse, the greater the greenhouse effect.

Humates--fundamental substances in humus, humic acid salts. They have a stimulatory effect. Many fertilizers based on humates are currently on the market.

Humus—"dregs and scraps"—more exactly, "leftovers from the feast" after microbes and fungi have decomposed the organic matter of plant residues which accumulate in the soil. The final product of microbial decomposition, which contains very little energy or available organic substances.

Hydrogen sulfide—hydrogen combined with sulphur, a flammable gas which smells like rotten eggs.

Infertile flowers—the male flowers of cucumbers and other members of the squash family. They give only pollen without setting any fruit.

Know-how—literally: I know how to repeat a good result, and I can even improve on it.

Kristalon—a compound fertilizer with trace minerals, common on the Russian market.

Late blight (*Phytophthora infestans*)—fungal disease of the nightshade family (Solanaceae)—see chapter "Meeting pests with a smile."

Lux—a unit of measurement of surface illumination. Difference in illumination is easy to see by putting the same surface in various places and observing it through a camera at the same distance.

Magnesium—an essential nutrient found in chlorophyll, the basis for photosynthesis.

Methane—a basic hydrocarbon, a flammable gas.

Mineralization—the decay of soil organic matter into simple compounds; the disintegration and dissolution of minerals.

Monoculture—when a single crop is grown over a large area.

Mulch—everything which covers the surface of the soil, as in nature.

Mycorrhiza—literally "fungus root"—is a symbiosis between fungi and roots. The mycelia of many kinds of fungi penetrate small rootlets. In exchange for sugars from roots, fungi supply roots with water and minerals. It has been suggested that it is fungi which provide soil cohesion and information exchange between all the plants of an ecosystem.

Nitrates—nitric acid salts, a form of available nitrogen.

Nitrification—the conversion of the nitrogen in organic matter into simple nitrates easily absorbed by roots. In the soil this is performed by nitrobacteria.

Nitrogen—an essential nutrient found in all proteins. A surplus of nitrogen causes "obesity"—excessive growth of plant mass, bloatedness, and weakness of tissues with a decrease in resistance to disease and cold. It is such rank, swollen vegetables which are so appealing to the eyes of modern-day farmers.

Parasitic worms—parasitic intestinal worms. Generally, they pass through their various phases of metamorphosis in diverse habitats.

Pathogens—organisms which cause diseases.

Perlite—a mineral, white when milled, elastic, and light-weight; it absorbs water at thirty times its own weight. Good for rooting cuttings and for loosening soil.

Permanent—endless, continuing in perpetuity, ever evolving.

Peronospora—fungal disease, false powdery mildew—see chapter "Meeting pests with a smile."

Phacelias—early, cold-resistant plants, excellent green manures and very strong nectar bearers.

Phosphorus—an essential nutrient which influences flowering and fruiting.

Phytoncides—various bacteria-killing substances synthesized by plants.

Pleasure—enjoyment. The emotional experience of success—the reward for victory, achievement, and a successful life. It is extremely beneficial and vital for your health. To live devoid of pleasure is mortally dangerous, and therefore disrespectful to family and friends. For a sensible person, life as a whole is pleasure.

Polyphagous insects feed on many different types of food.

Population—representatives of a single species which reside in a specific place under specific conditions and selective factors.

Potassium—an essential nutrient responsible for general regulation of life processes, development of fruit-bearing organs, immunity, and tolerance to adverse conditions in the outer environment.

Pricking out—transplanting very young seedlings (at the time of their first true leaves) from flats into pots. In the process the tap root is shortened "in an effort to develop lateral roots."

Rastvorin—a compound fertilizer with trace minerals, common on the Russian market.

Result—here: that which you want to obtain, the goal of intelligent action and its immediate outcome; also, that which is suitable for marketing, what people will pay for. A result either exists or does not exist. A "bad result" is really just the lack of a result.

Saltpeter—industrial name for any salt of nitric acid (i.e., nitrate).

Saprophytes—organisms which feed on dead organic matter. All microbes and fungi which decompose plant residues are saprophytic.

Side grafting—strips of the outer cortex up to 4–6 inches (10–15 cm) long are cut off from two young seedlings, and the exposed portions are pressed tightly against each other and wrapped. After two weeks, when the plants have fused together, begin pinching off one of the seedlings, limiting the nutrients flowing to it. After a month, remove it completely. The remaining plant is left with two root systems.

Stability—when nothing is changing. Actually, a state of suspended growth which indicates that decline is about to set in. Only when stability halts decline can it be considered a good thing, but if growth does not subsequently follow, then decline will again ensue.

Structure—not simply the physical condition, but a natural, optimal, and long-term (permanent) soil formation which provides for the life of plants, animals, and microbes, ensuring self-regeneration of fertility. In other words, the normal condition of natural soils.

Struggle—a type of misguided activity: the attempt to eliminate an effect while ignoring that this only strengthens and increases its underlying cause.

Success is a conscious and reproducible outcome which improves the life of a person, his partner, colleagues, and the people and natural environment around him. The ability to achieve success is, in fact, what constitutes intelligence.

Sympathy—a low-level response to others' misfortunes when, instead of helping and improving life, you become sad, upset, and inactive. For people who are not particularly strong spiritually, sympathy is an asset. The majority of chronic illnesses and many childhood traumas are induced by a subconscious desire to receive sympathy.

Terawet—an efficient acrylic polymer which is very water absorbent. It swells up to 400 parts of water that resists evaporation but readily releases moisture to roots. It creates a reliable water reservoir in the soil. Innocuous and inert, it works in the soil for up to ten years.

Trellis—a structure to support climbing plants or to train trees on.

Unoxidized state—not combined with oxygen—that is, in a reduced form. Conversely, oxygen compounds are **oxidized** states of substances. It is these forms which are assimilated by plants. Combustion is the oxidation of organic matter accompanied by the generation of energy. We breathe in order to oxidize what we eat—i.e., to "combust"—and to utilize the energy produced by this process to live.

Urea, or carbamide—the most concentrated of nitrogen fertilizers, containing 46% nitrogen. In a dilute solution, it is easily assimilated by plants.

Windbreak—a row or strip of several rows of tall plants sown to protect primary crops from sun and wind. In Russia, windbreak plantings of grains together with corn have been tested under various conditions. Harvests were nearly doubled. Windbreaks did not catch on, however, since "it is not as easy to harvest the field."

Worm casts—bits of worm excrement. They have a special name because of their unique qualities and special role in soil formation.

Index

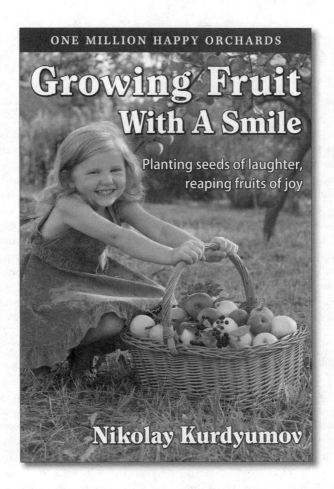

ONE MILLION HAPPY ORCHARDS

Growing Fruit
With A Smile

Planting seeds of laughter,
reaping fruits of joy

Nikolay Kurdyumov

Gardening With a Smile Series Is Taking You to New Heights

In his hilarious sequel *Growing Fruit with a Smile* Kurdyumov uncovers unorthodox approaches to insightful, laid-back cohabitation with your orchard—all delivered with his hallmark humor and in-depth understanding. A jaw-dropping read for both experienced fruit growers and backyard gardeners planting their first tree. Richly illustrated and packed with over 500 pages of *amazing* information not found anywhere else, it is so much *fun* to read! You were *never* so close to transforming your gardening experience into a bliss. Literally. Please find out more at

www.DeepSnowPress.com

Discover More Amazing Titles From Deep Snow Press

The Art of Soaring by Dolokhov & Gurangov
ISBN: 978-0-9842873-1-4. Deep Snow Press, 2010. 239 pp.
When first published, *The Art of Soaring* stayed at the top of Russian bestseller lists for a whole *year*. Revealing potent ancient techniques for manifesting your reality through humor, the book became an instant favorite with over *one million* readers from all walks of life. Changing your life *on the spot* has never been so much *fun*! The theory section is followed by *dozens of* tantalizing real-life stories of healed personal relationships, financial success, miracle cures, and more. Simple and irresistibly positive, *The Art of Soaring* will make you feel *lighter*, and as you start applying these amazing techniques, get ready for miracles and laughter to enter your everyday life. Visit www.DeepSnowPress.com to find out more, and prepare for takeoff!

The Power of Luck: A User's Manual by Dolokhov & Gurangov
ISBN: 978-0-9842873-2-1. Deep Snow Press, 2011. 272 pp.
Building up the runaway success of their bestseller *The Art of Soaring*, the authors propel you into the stratosphere of light and laughter. With its hilarious real-life stories and a veritable avalanche of everyday magic, *The Power of Luck* unveils an ancient tradition of dissolving any problems in humor. It offers a path to laughter, freedom, and power. Put luck to work and let *your* results speak for themselves! Things you *never* believed possible are now within your reach. Have noisy neighbors? Use the mute button on your remote control to calm them down! Tomatoes not ripening on time? Walk your garden in a swimsuit, and they'll blush red! This book's mind-bending and efficient techniques expand our vision of what can be achieved in this life—and *how*.

DEEP SNOW PRESS
www.DeepSnowPress.com